Creeping Karma:

A bitch in a skirt

Creeping Karma: A bitch in a skirt

Zaneta Cannon Robinson

Library of Congress Control Number: 2022912557

PAPERBACK: 978-1-957575-90-2
EBOOK: 978-1-957575-91-9

Ordering Information:

For orders and inquiries, please contact:
1-888-404-1388
www.goldtouchpress.com
book.orders@goldtouchpress.com

Printed in the United States of America

Contents

ALL CHARACTERS AND SCENARIOS IN THIS BOOK, EVEN THOSE BASED ON REAL PEOPLE ARE

ENTIRELY FICTIONAL. ANY RESEMBLANCE TO ACTUAL PERSONS LIVING OR DEAD IS PURELY

COINCIDENTAL. THE STORY AND CHARACTERS WERE CREATED FROM THE AUTHORS IMAGINATION.

CREEPING KARMA: A BITCH IN A SKIRT

CHAPTER 1
THE CRUELTY BEGINS

Karmell Boston grew up in Columbia, South Carolina. She was from the northeast side of town where the rich black folks stayed. Karmell was an only child with two well off parents. Karmell had everything she could ever want or need, except love and attention. Karmell's mom, Molly Boston, was the head nurse at the county hospital and her dad, Karmelo Boston, was one of the top real estate agents in the southeast region. Karmelo was always out of town for some sort of business that never included Karmell or the family.   The Boston's were simply too busy and selfish to be bothered with parenthood. Both parents traveled separately and worked long hours. Karmelo conducted in weird activities that Molly turned a blind eye to because for them it was all about the money and power. A daughter interfered with their plans and mischievous acts. To make matters worse Karmell had buck teeth and was often teased about her nappy hair. You would think that her mom would take her to a salon to make her presentable but that would be too much, like motherhood, for Molly to do. Sadly, Karmell practically raised herself. Watching the discovery channel and reading books gave her knowledge and experiences with the outside world. Most of her essential things came from her best friend and next-door neighbor, Yahtia Beeks. Yahtia and her brother, Craig, kept Karmell knowledgeable about all the teenage things she needed to know.

The Beeks' family was Karmell's safe haven. Naturally, she spent as much time with them as she possibly could. Karmell prayed every night that she could one day be a part of a family such as theirs. They treated Karmell like she was a human being and made her feel safe and wanted. Ms. Toyah Beeks heart broke every time she saw Karmell because as a mother she could not stand to see the way Karmell was treated. Toyah never said anything about Karmell always being at her house. Toyah would encourage Karmell to stay most times. As far as Toyah was concerned, she had two daughters. Not giving birth to Karmell did not mean anything to Toyah. A connection has always been there as if she did birth her. When Toyah gave Yahtia "the talk", she gave it to both girls, knowing that Karmell would not be taught no other way. Toyah's husband, Juan, felt the same way. Juan included Karmell in everything he did at home with his kids as he supported his wife's decisions in Karmell's situation. Juan wanted to kick Karmelo's ass so many times for the treatment he and his wife was giving Karmell. Juan once confronted Karmelo about his own daughter Yahtia. Juan thought he seen Karmelo jack his dick on the side of the house while Yahtia and Karmell were jumping rope.

Yahtia had an older brother Craig, who deemed himself the protector of the girls. Craig was a proud big brother and dared anyone to mess with Yahtia or Karmell. His best friend who he claimed as his brother, Ozias King, made sure to reinforce the idea to protect the girls. The boys knew about the bullying and the abuse Karmell was going through, and they made it their business to see about each one of the bullies. Ozias fought damn near every kid in the neighborhood and school defending Karmell's honor. Ozias and Craig was sent to Juvie for a few months for their violence and lack of remorse towards the bullies but that did not faze Ozias. When Ozias got out, he personally went to see about a few teachers that had been messing with Karmell. One lady, an old racist English teacher named Ms. Hawthorne, had allowed another kid to put gum in Karmell's hair. The kid was allowed to slap her causing her nose to bleed. Ms. Hawthorne wrote Karmell up for disrupting class, resulting in a suspension for Karmell. Ozias saved his gum for a week and held the lady down stuffing parts of the wet gum up her nose and ears. Just when Ms. Hawthorne thought it was over, Ozias put the gum throughout her hair. Ozias King did not play about Karmell Boston, she was his to protect because he knew he would always be in her life. It was ridiculous how people mistreated Karmell. It was even worse because her own parents would never come to her rescue. Karmell tried going to her parents about the bullying, but they ignored her. Molly raggedy ass even yelled at Karmell telling her to stop being a whinny brat. Molly then stated, "Snitches get stiches like bitches." Ozias even offered to do something to them for Karmell, but she told him no. Things never got better for Karmell, in fact, they got worse.

By the time middle school came around things had escalated from bullying to abuse. Kids would throw books and rocks at her. Karmell started bringing extra clothes in her backpack, because the kids enjoyed torturing her with everything from old food to water balloons was thrown at her, especially at the bus stop. One day she got jumped in the girl's locker room after PE class. The girls beat her, held her down, and put perm in her hair. The mean girls threw her in the showers and left her there. This caused her hair to fall out and Karmell had chemical burns on her scalp. The school resource officer called all the parents to the school to figure out what was going on, but the girls lied saying that Karmell started it. Their parents backed them. Since Karmell's mom did not even bother to show up on her behalf, Karmell was suspended with everyone else because they claimed she started the fight. Molly and Karmelo grounded Karmell for being suspended. They said that she was acting out for attention. Karmell was so numb to the neglect from her parents that she just shrugged it off. What could she do? Karmell had no clue how to make her parents want her, so she stopped trying.

Toyah was not hearing that. She had had enough of Molly's inconsiderate and intolerable acts towards Karmell. Enough was enough, so Toyah went next door to address the situation. Juan was always supportive of his wife and kids because that is what Karmell was to him, his daughter. Juan was right by Toyah's side. They were both genuinely concerned and hoped that hearing about the maltreatment from the adults would light a fire under Molly and cause her to do something. WRONG!!! Karmelo opened the door for the Beeks' as he was on his way out. Karmelo barely acknowledged them. Molly greeted them with attitude and immediately gave them hostility and negativity. Things got heated quickly when Toyah asked, "Molly, why don't you like your daughter?" This prompted Molly to put them out of her house. "Get the fuck out. You do not know me or my life. Deal with your bad ass kids and I'll deal with mine." Molly interrupted, "Bitch. I will continue to love and care for all my kids Karmell included. Since you can't balance your schedule to be a mother. I got her believe that bitch." No goodbyes were uttered as Molly slammed the door as soon as the couple stepped through.

A very pissed off Toyah stomped all the way to her house. "I can't believe that raggedy bitch." Toyah screamed with tears in her eyes. She was heartbroken for Karmell. Toyah just could not accept that someone would purposely abandon their child especially one as sweet as Karmell. "Mama T", Karmell called to Toyah, using the nickname she came up with, "What's wrong?" Toyah straightened up her clothes and wiped the tears from her face. Before Juan left the room, he patted Karmell on the back, "Hey sweetie" while Toyah was holding out her hands for a hug, which Karmell took. After a few minutes Toyah said, "I am so sorry your mother won't be there for you." "It's ok Mama T, I'm used to Molly not caring about what happens to me." Karmell shrugged but continued to hold on to Toyah for dear life. Karmell's shoulders shook, as she began to cry hard into Toyah's embrace. A mother's hug is something she never had, and it felt good to her soul to get one. The two moved to the couch to sit, never breaking the hold. Toyah whispered to Karmell. "I got you baby. You are my bonus daughter." This made Karmell cry even harder to hear that she was being accepted into a family. Karmell felt the sincerity in Toyah's words that just did something to her. "Why doesn't anyone like me? What did I ever do?" Karmell asked. The hurt in Karmell's voice when Karmell asked the question made Toyah cry.

Juan had been listening from the hallway and that was his breaking point. He let his wife soothe Karmell, but he was determined to give her a family with the security she deserved. Juan went to the back room for Craig and Ozias to help him move the extra bunk bed from the shed into Yahtia's room. Quickly and quietly, Juan told them. "What's going on pops?" Craig asked being concerned. Juan briefly explained. They all scrambled to set up the room so that it would accommodate both girls.

Juan walked back into the living room with all the kids. "Karmell, Fuck your parents". This caused everyone to laugh with a smile, "No disrespect baby girl but they are crazy for not wanting to be a part of your life. That is their loss. You are a part of our family, and that's final. We will take care of you and love you the same as Craig and Tia." Juan added, to Karmell, with much aggression as he almost started crying. "Now we can be sisters for real, you even have a bed. You got to bring all your stuff here, don't ever go back to them people. Especially your dad he's the devil." Yahtia said sounding sad "What has he said to you Tia?" Juan spoke up loudly being a dad. "Oh, nothing pops." Confusion written all over Karmell's face, she looked from Yahtia to the others. Realization set in and Karmell ran to the room that was now hers as well. Karmell was now all smiles. "Thank you" was all she could say. "Like pops said, we family now sis." Craig said. That night Karmell went next door and gathered as many things as she could carry. Vowing to herself that she would only go to the Boston's residence when necessary.

Craig and Ozias doubled down on their efforts to protect Karmell after that night. They put the word out that anyone who messed with Karmell they would get fucked up. For the most part, the kids listened. If they didn't, they made sure Craig and Ozias did not hear about it. Dax Riley was the only person who went against the grain. Dax thought he was above the law, not caring about shit or no one else. Dax was a sociopath that got off by hurting others. So, the hood warning was what he needed to purposely fuck with Karmell. Dax plotted on her so one morning at the bus stop he pulled a five-pound weight from his backpack. Dax took that weight and swung it, hitting Karmell in her head. Karmell was out instantly. Dax started taunting her about being weak and ugly. The way her body crumbled to the ground, Karmell was hurt. Once Dax saw the blood pouring from her head, he laughed loudly and began kicking her unconscious body. To add insult to injury, he pissed on her bloody body soaking her with his urine. Dax then spat at her and walked off like nothing ever happened. The other kids were traumatized and would not dare say anything to Dax in fear of getting similar treatment. When they were certain Dax had left, several kids called 911 for an ambulance. Thank God, another child had the kindness to cover Karmell with a sweatshirt and call Yahtia. Karmell was taken to the county hospital where she had to be placed in a medically induced coma just to stop the seizures and ease the pain.

The authorities notified her parents (after several attempts) about Karmell's situation. Her father finally answered the phone. "Well, I'm out of town right now so call her mother was the only response Karmelo gave before hanging up. Molly was at the hospital working her shift, that made it easier to reach her. When Molly received the news about her daughter, Molly seemed aggravated. "Damn that girl always doing something." Molly rolled her eyes sighing and breathing hard. "I'll be there when I can." Molly said as she walked away to take care of other patients. The officers just shook their heads. The entire nurses' staff were in disbelief. It took two more phone calls and another visit from the police for Molly to finally to make it to the ICU. Molly had a full attitude when she arrived. "This shit is interfering with my workday." Molly said as if Karmell was not her child. The charge nurse handed her the paperwork and as soon as she was done consenting to treatment Molly went about her day. "Mrs. Boston, would you like to see Karmell?" the nurse asked before Molly could leave. "NO! I have patients that need me. I signed the damn papers, do whatever you think needs to be done." Molly said, with a frown on her face, then walked quickly back to her floor. Toyah was walking up to the nurse's station as Molly was leaving. Toyah overheard what was said and she was so mad she started to shake. The head nurse said, "How can you treat your daughter like a stray dog? Not even with the kindness she gives her patients upstairs." Toyah responded, "I have been watching this dog face bitch mistreat this girl her whole life and I'm sick of it!" Juan had walked up behind Toyah and began rubbing her arms. "I know baby." The couple began asking questions about treatment and the status of Karmell. Per hospital policy, the couple were not given any information. Toyah was screaming at the staff. "I've taken care of that girl for most of her life, and you see the bitch that pushed her out don't give a fuck. Let me take care of her." The nurses were crying but stood firm. "We wish we could." Toyah walked off headed to the stairs. Toyah had made up her mind, she was about to make Molly regret her actions.

Toyah got to the floor and asked for directions to Molly Boston's unit. After finding it, Toyah turned on her inner ghetto. It had been years since she had to act out. Toyah was ready to die behind the little girl she considered her own. "Did y'all know that Molly Boston neglects her daughter?" Toyah yelled out in the middle of the floor. Toyah proceeded to tell anyone nearby about the way Karmell was being mistreated. Molly rounded the corner and damn near sprinted grabbing Toyah's arm and pushing her into an office. "Bitch get off me." Toyah snatched her arm away. "What the fuck are you doing? This is my place of work." Molly stated. Toyah fuming, "This the only place you seem to care about, and your daughter is downstairs fighting for her life. You would rather do anything else to keep from loving her." Molly responded, "If you feel like you can do better, then do it. I have a career and I do not need you or Karmell bothering me with her issues. Y'all getting on my damn nerves. Now if you will see yourself out. I have patients to tend to." Molly opened the door with a mug of disgust on her face. "Toyah if you pull this shit again, I will have you arrested." "Fuck you!" Toyah responded as she shot her a middle finger on her way out the door. "You will need your daughter one day, you miserable hard face bitch.", Toyah screamed out.

Juan met Toyah at the elevator shaking his head. "Wild animals take better care of their young." Toyah said reaching for her husband. "I just can't believe how she treats that girl." The nurse from earlier called out to Toyah. "Ma'am" Toyah got nervous. "This bitch done called the damn police. I'm going to jail." Toyah said nervously. "Oh, no ma'am", the nurse said with a smile. "Can you follow me out please?" The nurse turned trusting Toyah to follow. When they got outside the nurse lit a cigarette and handed Toyah a piece of paper while giving her a hug. "I'm not supposed to give you any information, so let's keep this on the hush. I am a mother at the end of the day, and I feel your pain. Take that bitch down." Toyah opened the note and broke down. It had all the information regarding Karmell's treatment and the number to a social worker. Beside the number was a note. "This is my sister's number. She is expecting a call from you. Please get this little girl and love her."

While in the ICU, Karmell's head was swollen, and she was unrecognizable. Yahtia cried her eyes out while Craig and Ozias were out for blood. Even though Craig told his mom they would not retaliate, Craig could not let it slide. "That's my sister man." Craig said to Ozias. Understanding and feeling the same way, the two boys agreed to make Dax pay for this. Most of the kids hung out at the arcade room on the westside and Craig knew he would find Dax there doing his bully thing. Soon as Craig and Ozias walked up, Dax was taking one of the younger kids' money out of his pocket. Stacey Hill, a girl who liked Craig although Dax was crazy about her, was used to lure Dax to the back of the arcade building. Dax walked to the back with a Christmas smile on his face thinking Stacey wanted to hunch his dirty ass. Ozias kicked it off by slamming the tin trash can over his head. Dax received a beat down to the highest power by the friend duo. Dax left the back of the arcade with fractured ribs and two broken arms. "You wanna hit girls with weights huh? You pussy ass nigga. How does this feel?" Ozias kept asking over and over while he lay the smack down on Dax. Dax could not use or feel his arms, he was completely helpless. That did not stop Craig or Ozias from kicking his ass and doing him dirty. The owner heard the commotion and called the police. When the police arrived the kids inside the arcade had already told them who Dax was and Dax was placed under arrest for the assault on Karmell. Dax left by ambulance, fucked up the same way he did Karmell.

Karmell had a long recovery process; she was visited by Yahtia and her family daily. Ozias was by her side 24-7. He had taken a liking to Karmell and was overprotective of her. Ozias had a scenario in his head of Karmell being his girlfriend someday. Ozias had beaten so many kids up for talking down on Karmell, he made himself a promise that no one else would harm her again. Karmell was treated like a runaway slave from some of the kids. She would get beaten, spat on, hair pulled and some of the older kids would throw soda pop cans at her causing her to have cuts and bruises throughout her legs and arms. Molly did not visit or check on

Karmell once even though she was only one floor down. Toyah went to talk with her and demanded Molly to give up her rights since she had no time for Karmell and clearly was too busy to see about her health. "Bitch I know you not coming at me again on my job about my child. Karmell is ok she's in the best place ever, can't nothing happen to her in the hospital." Molly said. "How would you know, you haven't been to see her, and she's been in a coma for two weeks." Toyah responded angrily. "Yes, a coma, so what the fuck can I do? She's sleep bitch. I got to continue making money, if I run every time Karmell has a problem I'll be jobless, Molly stated without an ounce of care." "This is not the time or the place but just to let your trifling ass know your daughter will be at my house staying with my family and I. Karma is a bitch. I hope your raggedy ass bleed to death. Your priorities are all fucked up and twisted." Toyah spoke with much anger before she walked off. During the time Karmell was recovering, Toyah and Juan adjusted their home even more. Karmell would continue to live with the couple, Yahtia, and Craig as a family. Two months had past and Karmell was good as new. Karmell did not know how to accept having a real family and parents that cared about her. Karmell finally felt like she had a purpose, she felt loved and enjoyed getting the attention she had longed for.

CHAPTER 2
BEING BULLIED

Summer had passed by, and it was time for high school. Karmell and Yahtia were starting the 9th grade and Craig and Ozias were starting the 11th grade. "I'm so happy were out of middle school, we have been waiting on this day to start high school." Yahtia was ranting with excitement. "You been waiting on this day not me." said Karmell. Yahtia looking confused. "What's wrong sis?" "You know these fuck ass kids going to start with the harassment and fighting me. I'm so tired of getting abused by these kids." said Karmell. "Nobody is going to fuck with you sis; I promise we are going down together like Martin and Will on bad boys." Yahtia responded gleefully.

On the way to school, Dax older cousin, Tina, spotted the girls walking and decided to pop her truck and pour motor oil all over Karmell's new clothes. Yahtia started to beat Tina with her backpack but within seconds Tina was back in her car. Dax had received six years in juvie for what he did to Karmell, and Dax family and lots of kids blamed her for his wrongdoing. Karmell started home, mad as hell but she could not even cry anymore, because she was so accustomed to the mistreatment. Karmell forced Yahtia to go to school instead staying behind with her. Karma convinced Yahtia she would be ok.

When Karmell reached the house, Toyah was leaving out for work. Toyah noticed Karmell's clothes covered in oil. "OMG sweetie what happen?" "The usual fuckery somebody just wanted to ruin my day." "Well, we not going to let them," said Toyah. "Let's get you cleaned up and I'll take you to school." "I don't know about that Mama T somebody else is waiting to do something else to me; it's never going to stop. Nobody likes me." "I think it's time for you to fight back. Stop excepting what these evil kids are doing to you. You must stand up for yourself. Stay on guard and catch them before they do anything to you. You can't keep being a punching bag and made fun of." Toyah talked with Karmell the whole time she was getting ready. Karmell felt much better and was ready to start her first day of High school. Toyah dropped her off and Karmell made it just in time for homeroom. Schedules were passed out and the bell ranged, it was time to switch classes. In the hallway, Karmell finds Yahtia. Yahtia screams, "You came back sis yaaay." They matched up their schedules and noticed they had three classes together, and off they went happy as can be. Tonjaya Riley, known as TJ, was the neighborhood thot. She had been fucking since K-5 and TJ also had been bulling Karmell since the fourth grade. TJ was also the first cousin to Dax.

While sitting in first period waiting on the teacher to come to get class started, TJ was about to put on a show and come for Karmell, but Karmell was on guard remembering what Toyah had told her earlier. TJ raised up her cup and attempted to pour her drink on Karmell. Karmell flipped her hand up extra quick and counter acted TJ's move. That caused the drink to spill all on TJ. The class went berserk in laughter. Karmell then mushed her and grabbed the side of her forehead, "I had to change clothes once I'm not about to do it again. So, take your thot ass back under the gym bleachers and get finger fucked and sandwiched by the football team like you been doing."

From that day on Karmell Boston was reformed and started fighting back. Day after day different people would try her and Karmell quickly became the kick ass queen. With the right help and push, Karmell would be a beast against the enemy. Karmell stayed in defense mode and began to have all the fun with the bullies, because she was no longer afraid to attack back. The bullies could not get a laugh or intimidate her anymore, so they all began to team up and plot on Karmell. Karmell was a natural born track star, and she began to win several gold medals from track and field events. Karmell had become the Jackie O of the hurdles. Karmell constantly did intense work outs and by the time she was a junior she was compared to Forrest Gump because all she did was run. Karmell was offered multiple scholarships for track and field. Karmell knew she had to put her legs to use and flea from Urban Watts. His nasty ass wanted to violate her in the worst way and had been contemplating for a while. Urban was a twenty-two-year-old senior that came to school just for lunch which was the only thing he could pass. Urban stayed looking for a vulnerable girl to fuck and suck on his diseased dick. Urban was like an animal hunting for prey the way he was focused on Karmell. Urban tried so hard to catch her alone but felt defeated because all the other girls he targeted he was successful.

Karmell had a track meet coming up that she trained long hours to prepare for. Her team was depending on her to take them to the national championship. The coaches were all excited because they knew with Karmell running they had this in the bag. Karmell started her day getting her gym bag ready, she ate a light breakfast and was filled with much excitement that she shared with Yahtia and her parents. Karmell left the house early. The bus was scheduled to leave from the school in two hours. Karmell wanted to get her last run in before the track meet. Toyah offered to drive her, but Karmell said she would be fine. Karmell wanted to run off her nervous energy. Karmell placed her ear buds in, and she begins jogging lightly. On her route to the school Urban Watts. along with his delinquent friends, spotted her jogging. They huddled up like a football team coming up with a play. Urban was determined not to let her slip away this time. The crew spreded out and were determined to catch her, they knew she had the speed of a Cheetah. They covered all possible corners trying to trap her and keep her from getting away. Urban approached her first running up fast beside her. Karmell did not hesitate to take a sharp left and started to put some fire underneath her ass and increased her speed. Deno and Suber, two of Urban's accomplices, were waiting for Karmell when she made a turn. Karmell shook them off, as she gained even more speed and determination to get away. Just when she was in the clear, Tommy another accomplice, pulls in front of her with a mo-pad. Tommy had just stolen it from a kid a block over. Karmell smashes right into the mo-pad flipping over scrapping her knees and elbows. Karmell jumps up quick and proceeded to run. Karmell was grabbed forcefully and pulled behind the liquor store. Urban licked her face and forced kissed her mouth. Urban's dick begins to rise. "You can't run forever bitch; I got your ass now." Urban said while breathing heavy on her neck. "What I ever do to you, let me go." Karmell begins to fight, smacking the fuck out of Urban and one of the other guys. Urban snatched her gym bag from around her shoulder and starts to rip her clothing off. "Don't act brand new to this, you know we use to playhouse together". Urban continue to lick her face. The other guys joined in. Once Karmell was naked, they grabbed her head and tried to force her to suck Urban's dick. Karmell kept refusing and held her mouth closed tight like glue. They punched her repeatedly in the face and groped her vagina aggressively. The men fondled her breast and violated her body in the worst way. The guys could not get her to open her mouth. Just when they were about to rape her, an elderly couple walks up and screams out. "STOP! LEAVE THAT WOMAN ALONE WE'RE CALLING THE POLICE." The guys took off running as the elderly couple assisted Karmell with her clothes then took her to the county hospital.

Karmell did not call Yahtia, Toyah nor Juan. Karmell wanted to be alone. The ER charge nurse Pricilla knew Karmell was Molly's daughter and immediately contacted Molly on her floor. Pricilla informed Molly about her daughter being treated for facial injuries in the ER. Karmell act as if she did not even hear Pricilla call her mom. Karmell already knew the outcome. At this point all Karmell wanted to do was rest. Karmell was feeling so disappointed about the track meet. Toyah and the family were so worried after Karmell was a no show for the track meet. The coaches, teammates, and everyone was in a panic. Toyah and Juan called the police station and hospital. The hospital was indeed where Karmell was at, and Juan was on two wheels making it over to the county hospital. They arrived and were escorted to her area where they all bombarded her with questions, but Karmell continued to be mute. Karmell was numb from what she had been through. Running track was the one thing that made her feel important and gave her therapy, but it was sabotaged by a group of coward thugs.

CHAPTER 3
GIVING MOTIVATION

Three weeks had gone by and Karmell had stopped going to school. Karmell was fed up with the bulling and fighting. Toyah had reached out to the high school counselor, Ivy Jacobs, who was also a youth life coach. Toyah explained Karmell's entire life story to her. Ivy immediately scheduled a home visit to further evaluate Karmell's issues and Toyah's concerns. Ivy has outstanding success stories with helping the youth. Ivy targets building confidence and facing fears. Ivy always starts out soft, but also is known for packing a mighty punch when trying to get her point across. Ivy was strategizing her plan on how to help Karmell, she was not about to let Karmell ruin her life nor drown in misery. When the day came for the visit, Ivy had a complete notebook full of ideas to flip Karmell's life around and make it normal as possible. Karmell was on the couch eating a bowl of cereal when Toyah walked in with Ivy in tow. "Karmell this is Ms. Ivy Jacobs the school's youth counselor." Toyah stated. Karmell stood up and wiped her hands on her shorts then reached out for a handshake from Ivy. "Nice to meet you." Karmell said softly. "I'm leaving out for work Karmell, I'll see you later on." said Toyah. "You can finish your breakfast Karmell then we can have a chat if you don't mind." said Ivy. "I'm all done. You're here to tell me to go back to school huh?" "Yes, I am, along with some other things." Ivy replied. "First I want to let you know how smart and intelligent and beautiful you are." "You must get paid to say that because I'm not beautiful, look at my teeth." said Karmell. "Just because you have buck teeth don't make you ugly, we can easily fix that problem if you like. Would you like for me to help you fix your buck teeth Karmell?" "Yes, ma'am I would like that." "Is there anything else I can help you with Ivy asked." The two began talking and covered so much ground, Ivy noticed Karmells smile. Ivy had a clear understanding about Karmell and felt like she had been knowing her for years. Karmell broke her silence and shared so much with Ivy and got all that built up frustration and anger off her chest by doing so. Karmell felt like a new woman with lots of overdue confidence. Ivy had given her some great advice and Karmell had taken a deep liking to Ivy, no one has ever checked her and made her feel special like Ivy. Karmell intercepted all the motivation and words of wisdom Ivy had to offer.

Later that day, Karmell was at the dentist office getting her gums clipped from the root of her mouth. The dentist gave her a purple set of braces on her teeth and Ivy gave her three days to heal; told her she must return to school after that. Karmell had not been to her parents' house in months, but she had to go over to find her social security card because she was about to apply for a job. As Karmell walks in, she notices the house was in a total wreck. Apparently, no one had been staying in the house. It appeared that her parents had moved out. Karmell could not be sad, because they were never parents to her anyways. They only gave her life. Karmell went to the hidden cash spot that her parents always kept substantial amounts of cash stored away for her to buy things for school and pay the bills. Karmell pulled out two envelopes one from her father with a letter for her mom along with 5,000 dollars in cash. The second envelope was a letter from her mom to her father with 10,000 dollars in cash. Both letters consist of the same words, they were leaving each other. They specified the money was to take care of Karmell and help with the house. Karmell was seventeen, so no need for CPS to get involved. Toyah and her family stepped in as usual and helped her clean out the house. Karmell bought all new furniture; Karmell and Yahtia had fun decorating. They created a women's pad for themselves. Karma changed the locks on the doors and upgraded to a high-tech security company, Secure Us. Juan contacted a friend, Dyson Yeargin, that worked at the probate court. Dyson legally placed the house in Karmell's name. The proper paperwork was completed, and the courts had clarification that both parents abandoned the home along with Karmell. Those actions left Karmell with full ownership. Under no circumstances will the Boston's be allowed back in the house without the approval of Karmell. Karmell felt joy that she had her own house at seventeen especially after all the hardship she endured from her parents; Karmell should be entitled to so much more. Ivy seemed to be having a breakthrough with Karmell. Karmell was full of excitement, she finally had the confidence she needed. Karmell had begun to keep a journal that she loved to write in because it was her favorite color, purple. Karmell had notes and stories of all the heinous and malicious acts people had done to her over the years.

Karmell has been carrying a secret around about a vile act that that she experienced at school just a year ago. A classmate of hers, Rhonda Humphrey, known to everyone as Hershey is a fat sloppy stud that loves pussy. Hershey gets a kick out of taking pussy and loves to have an audience while doing so. Something about a girl screaming "NO!" gets Hershey off sexually. Hershey and a few of her other stud friends caught Karmell off guard on her way to lunch. Karmell was listening to music from her ear pods not paying attention to what was coming from behind her. As she walked closer to the janitor's supply closet, she was pushed inside. One of the studs covered her mouth and the others stripped her bottom clothing off. Hershey spreded her legs and began to mouth-rape her. Hershey was devouring her pussy aggressively and took the rape a step further by assembling the strap-on onto her body and inserting it into Karmell sexually. Hershey gyrated until she was satisfied with pleasure while the other studs were wishing for a turn as they held her arms and legs. When they were done, they dropped her on the floor an exited the closet like nothing ever happened. Karmell had been carrying that secret around feeling shameful and violated to the max. Karmell stayed clear of Hershey and her dike friends and kept her thoughts written in her journal of how she wanted revenge on all the people that wronged her. Karmell was one tough cookie because she had been mistreated the most from random people, for no reason at all. Majority of the abuse was horrific and insane; you would not think humans would be so evil. Karmell bended a few times but she never broke and was determined to turn things around and become a boss bitch. Karmell was not excepting any more harm from anyone but God. Karmell started dating Ozias King, he finally got up the nerve to ask her out. Ozias showered her with flowers and candy and all the things young girls like, he even bought her a necklace with a K charm attached. Ozias had an open nose for Karmell, he could not understand why people did not like her. Ozias adored her and loved being in her company. Ozias had in his mind he was going to make Karmell his wife and make her shine on all her haters like wet paint.

During Karmell's senior year, she and Yahtia was working part time at Foot Locker in the mall. They were having a talk about college, and both decided to attend an HBCU in Columbia, South Carolina called Grady University. Karmell received a track and field scholarship and Yahtia received an academic scholarship. "Sis I think we should change the game up and dress conservative this upcoming school year." Yahtia spoke. "What are you thinking?" Karmell responded. "Let's give them the bougee sophisticated look. "What about dresses and brief cases no back packs?" said Yahtia. "Nah we got to keep it classy and rock skirts, tailor made shit." "My cousins' mom, Kanowi, is a beast tailor, her designs are on point." Karmell said to Yahtia. "Definitely the brief cases I like that sis." Yahtia said smiling at Karmell. From then on out the two only finessed skirts. They had all distinctive styles, colors, and lengths. Kanowi completed most of their attire with half shirt's, bra tops and some blouses. Their shoe game was either sneakers or heels. Between Karmell's therapy with Ivy and Ozias making her cold hearted, Karmell was smacking any bitch that moved funny. Karmell had begun her first stage as a bad bitch and Transformation 101 has been completed. Ozias nor Ivy took their foot off Karmell's neck; they were determined to make her a kick ass bitch and know her worth.

CHAPTER 4
THE TRANSFORMATION

Karmell and Yahtia graduated high school and along the way they had to keep hating ass people away from Karmell. Shit had slowed down because Ozias was very heavy in Karmell's life. Ozias and his friend Craig, Yahtia's brother always protected them. A few mutha fuckas tried some slick shit, but the shit backfired. Ozias and Craig beat each party to sleep and made them author a report on how not to bully people. The parties involved had to pass out written reports to teachers and students. The bullies were also made to place themselves on after school detention plus volunteer at local shelters and community centers. Karmell was being looked at in a unique way. Instead of girls trying to bully her they begin to copy her style. Karmell and Yahtia were the best dressed, their wig install game was on fleek. Their nails were dripping a fresh coat every other day; you would think they were selling dope or pussy. Karmell went from nappy hair and buck teeth to an all-out diva. Karmell even had niggas asking her out and following her around like a lost puppy. That is until Ozias popped up and let it be known that Karmell was his girl. The girls set up a graduation party at the Jackson community center. High school kids from all alma maters were there and the party was lit for the youngsters. Karmell and Yahtia notice that all the females were dressed like them in skirts and half tops and jackets. Most of them even had frontal wigs identical to theirs. "What the fuck are these half dead ass bitches trying to prove?" said Yahtia. "I don't know sis but none of these clowns could even come close to us on their best day. We are a hot commodity in these streets sis, these hoes been studying us like a final exam." Karmell said with a smile. The party stayed in cruise control the entire night and a lot of the old heads were in attendance reminiscing about their high school days at Robinson High. Craig surprised Karmell and Yahtia with tickets to the Lovers and Friends concert tour in Atlanta featuring all the heavy hittas in the hip hop industry. The concert would take place the week before they head out to college. The girls jumped for joy giving Craig tight hugs showing much apperception. "Who's the best brother?" Craig asked aloud. The girls gave an immediate reaction and they both screamed, "YOU ARE." The girls headed back towards their guests to brag to some of their haters about their tickets. Ozias was side eying Craig with a mean mug plastered to his face. "Nigga you know I don't want my girl in no damn Atlanta alone with all the bull-shit she has been through." Ozias stated. "Get your nuts out your ass, you worry to damn much." Craig responded. Craig then held up two more tickets showing that he was on the same page. They were secretly going to the concert to keep a close eye on the girls. "That's why you, my nigga." Ozias said with the cutest smile, which always made the ladies panties wet. The rest of the night went by with almost no incidents. Karmell and Yahtia were in the middle of a conversation when a girl, Kenyatta Michaels, approached them. Kenyatta had a thing for Ozias, she crushed hard over him. Kenyatta let him smash a few years ago and was going around telling people she was his girlfriend, but he quickly shut that shit down, leaving her sad and embarrassed. Kenyatta still could not let that go, she had trouble understanding how or why Ozias picked Karmell. Kenyatta was determined to breakup their happiness and approached the girls with a fake ass smile. "Hey y'all!" said Kenyatta. Yahtia spoke back but Karmell just looked. Karmell could smell the treachery on this hoe a mile away. "Damn girl, don't look so mean." Kenyatta joked with Karmell. "I Just wanted to let y'all know this party is dope as fuck." Still not buying it but deciding to play along Karmell answered, "Glad you are enjoying yourself. Did you need something?" Kenyatta was pissed at the way she was being chumped off. Rolling her eyes and placing her hand on her hip Kenyatta says, "As a matter of fact I do, I want my nigga back bitch. You're on notice hoe. You think because you put on some nice clothes and got them damn teeth fixed that you the shit. News flash, you still busted.", as if she was checking Karmell. It could have been the alcohol or the weed, but Karmell just smiled. Something inside of Karmell just clicked, she heard the words of Ivy in her head, "Stop letting people get away with talking to you crazy." Yahtia was going off on Kenyatta cursing her out. Karmell simply pulled her hair up in a bun and grabbed her keys placing them in between her fingers. Taking everyone by surprise, Karmell reached up and grabbed Kenyatta by her weave. "BITCH!" was all you heard before a crunch sound. Karmell rammed her knee into the poor girl's nose, breaking it instantly. Trying to at least get a lick in, Kenyatta started swinging but she was blinded by the blood that was in her eyes, so nothing was landing. The entire gym had moved out the way to watch the fight. Yahtia ran to get Ozias, she knew they were going to have to leave before the police showed up. Karmell took no mercy on Kenyatta. Karmell beat her ass for everything old and new and was so amped, she could have gone a few more rounds thrashing across Kenyatta's face. By the time Ozias and Craig pushed their way to the front of the circle, they realized Kenyatta was out cold. Kenyatta was only standing because Karmell was holding her up with one hand while delivering blows with the other. Ozias grabbed Karmell and threw her over his shoulder and carried her like that all the way back to the car. Craig and Yahtia jumped in the front seat while Ozias dove into the back after tossing Karmell in. They pulled away quickly, nearly getting hit by the ambulance. Once on the other side of town, they calmed down and decided to stop at a QT. They got to the gas pump and all three looked at Karmell who seemed to be in a daze. When she realized they were staring at her, she gave them a side eye. "What y'all looking at?" Craig went into defense mode, holding his hands up, "Calm down Rhonda Rousey, I don't want NO problems." They all shared a laugh while Karmell playfully hit him. Yahtia went inside the store to get some snacks because she had the munchies from that good green they were smoking. Ozias took this time to inspect his woman. "You good baby?" Ozias gently asked. "I mean I know the bitch ain't touch you, but are you ok though. What made you snap?" Karmell became embarrassed for the first time. Karmell realized she did all of that because a bitch was coming for her man. Blushing hard, Karmell responded, "You." A smile playing on his lip. "Say that shit again bae." Rolling her eyes playfully. "Nigga you. The bitch said she wanted her man back and she was putting me on notice. I snapped." The others had gotten back in the car and heard the conversation. Yahtia told them everything Kenyatta had said. Shrugging her shoulders while looking at her nails Karmell smacked her lips and rolled her neck, then sarcastically said, "what can I say, some shit I just don't play about." Ozias shook his head. His dick begins to get hard, and he was turned on by Karmell's actions. Ozias could not say anything, he only gave a flirtatious smile. "Ok BONE CRUSHER let's talk about this trip to Atlanta." Yahtia said wagging her eyebrows. They talked and laughed and vibed for the rest of the night. Yahtia whispered in Karmell's ear, "Bitch Ozias must be a painter cause clearly, he's deep stroking the hell out of them walls. Nobody throws hands like that unless they getting that good joog." "He got that big dick energy, straight butter Karmell responded." They gave each other a high five then bust out laughing. They ended the night in the living room after telling Toyah about how Karmell beat up Kenyatta. Toyah tried to play mad about the fight but was just as happy that Karmell had taken up for herself. Toyah rushed up stairs to tell her husband about the fight. Juan jumped up from playing the video game and screamed, "Yes! I hope she beat that ass!"

The girls had three weeks till college day where they would receive their classes and have one last tour of the school. During the tour they would find out their assigned roommates for their dorm room. Karmell and Yahtia finished their last week at Foot Locker, and both had Kanowi busy making them new designer skirts. They had over one hundred lace frontal wigs packed up like they were top models, the ladies were excited to begin their new journey.

CHAPTER 5
CREATING A MONSTER

It was the night before college day and the girls were so excited, it was like the first day of school times ten. Their outfits were laid out, complete with accessories and shoes. Karmell and Yahtia had gotten their hair stylist to give them an epic slay. Their nails were designed with diamond stones with the wet paint polish. They both had become fashion icons. After talking and wondering what the next day would bring, the girls drifted off to sleep. They both were up before the alarm clock went off, they both had the bubble guts. Not letting that stop them they both proceeded with their day, they were determined to make this the best adventure yet. After getting dressed and taking the mandatory pictures for social media, they both grabbed a quick breakfast before loading up. The family was two cars deep, because everyone was going. The girls knew that Craig and Ozias would be there with them, and Toyah and Juan refused to miss this special day either. Toyah and Juan were just as excited about tagging along for moral support. The girls did not mind they felt more like a family when they were all together. "We have a beautiful family sis." said Karmell. "Yes, we do.", Yahtia responded.

Stepping out of the cars, the girls resembled celebrities. At the very least, Instagram models. Other students were looking at them and the whispers began to circulate quickly. Karmell and Yahtia stepped foot on the campus of Grady University, welcoming the speculation and mystery that they were causing. "Damn, y'all ain't been out the car long enough to get your name tags and already the talk of the campus." Toyah said with an eye roll, but had a smile plastered on her face. Toyah told them she was enjoying the celebrity treatment as well. "They must be rappers or something, and in college like Megan thee Stallion. Maybe it's a trend" an already fan favorite said in passing while the girls were getting their paperwork. Karmell and Yahtia laughed and were eating up the attention.

After receiving their schedules and getting their packets with all the information of what a first-year student needed, they were escorted to their dorms. They were staying in Gibson Hall. Karmell had done some research and found out that Gibson Hall was the best hall to be assigned too. First-year students with a high enough GPA could stay in the upper-class student wing, that would allow them a room with a semi-private bathroom, only sharing with a suitemate instead of the entire hall. Yahtia and Karmell were picked to stay in the Mega West Wing, the upper-class student wing. They were assigned a suite and this day was turning out to be the absolute best. They sported thousand-watt smiles, as they walked to their dorm room. The guys had doubled back to get all their things so they could move in.

An hour later, the men were assembling and arranging all the things the girls needed to call the dorm home. Yahtia and Karmell had gone exploring the various meet and greet stations set up for the day. They were met by four wannabe divas named Tonera Jones, Jherika Kelly, Uvoka Wells, and Adreama McCade. They were all sophomores except Adreama, who was a senior. The only thing appealing about these girls were the embroidered shirts they wore because they were members of Sisters of Elegance, the sorority that ran the yard. The golden Es and doves on their hot pink shirts gave that away. Introductions were made and the conversation started to flow, Yahtia had several questions for the ladies. She was able to look past their snarkiness, only because she wanted to be a member of their sorority. Karmell wanted to be included but the vibes they were giving were making her angry low key. "OMG! You two should fit right in, you obviously have what it takes." Adreama stated dryly while looking Karmell up and down. "Yeah, you don't dress like the rest of the freshman dorks that have the nerve to approach us." The fat plump one named Jherika noted. Engaging in more small talk, the wannabe crew gave the girls a flyer about an interest meeting. "My sisters and I would love to have you two beauties join us. We will make the pledge simple and easy for you ladies." Adreama had told them, giving clarity that she was in charge. Adreama clearly was the "head bitch" out of the four wannabes, that is the name Karmell decided she would give them.

Yahtia immediately went in with excitement about the sorority and how they needed to join. Yahtia was spouting off information and facts about them, listing all their positives. "Sis chill. We will join the little girls club." Karmell said with a laugh while dodging Yahtia's swing.

They were standing in a line to get a picture taken with the school mascot for college day. They then met another young lady named Joy White, who was so nice. The conversation between the three flowed perfectly. Joy was a sophomore and a double major and dressed plain but had her own style. Karmell automatically liked her vibe, Joy was genuine and honest. After walking around for another half an hour, Ozias texted Karmell telling her she had been gone too long. Ozias was being clingy today; he was going to miss her more than his pride would let him say out loud. The girls made a beeline back to their dorm room. Upon turning the corner, they heard a loud commotion and saw a circle of students swamped around a girl. It looked as if they were about to haze her. "What the fuck are you even doing on this hall you freak?" They were loud and mean. Yahtia and Karmell heard sounds of a whimper. They walked through the circle to see what was going on but only to find the same fake ass sorority bitches pushing and yelling at the quiet, humble Joy White. Joy was holding her schedule out for them to see that she was in the right place. Fear covered her face, Joy looked so pitiful, that she did not understand what she had done wrong. Joy was desperately trying to fix it, explaining and sobbing, "I made the dean's list and I have a 4.5 GPA. I am in honors classes. I am a double major. I was given the upgrade to be on Gibson Hall by the administration." Joy stated. Joy tried to sound assertive, but her voice came out as a plea, Joy did not like how the girls were making her feel. This pissed Karmell off to the highest. Ripping her schedule and stepping in Joy's personal space, the "head bitch" Adreama hissed, "I don't give a fuck what you did, you belong back on the Alpha wing. You are going to change your room immediately. There is no way I am going to stay on the same hall with you. My sisters need your room ASAP. So be nice and walk your geeky ass back to the Alpha wing." Joy dropped her head in shame and nodded yes. Before Joy could say anything, she felt a push. It was not to her but around her, Karmell had gone into defense mode. Karmell saw so much of herself in Joy, realizing that she was a victim of bullying. "What seems to be the issue ladies?" Karmell asked in the fakest, bitchiest no-nonsense tone she could find. Karmell rushed to stand by Joy's side. Yahtia followed her, standing opposite of Joy and placing a hand on her shoulder to let her know it was ok.

Receiving dirty looks from the sorority sisters, Uvoka responded, "First of all, you need to stay in your place and mind your business." Jherika co-signed, "Look little Ms. Barbie, when we want your help or need you, we will let you know." "Girl bye, what y'all sick asses need to do is leave this girl alone. She's out numbered she can't win against all you bulling bitches." stated Karmell. "Bitches!" said Adreama. "Yes, I said mutha fucking bitches and who the fuck gone check me." Karmell then walked up close to Adreama backing her up against the wall while the other sorority sisters looked with a gaping mouth. "I guess you the so-called bad bitch of the crew. I see you barking out orders and these sluts riding your coat tail fetching behind you like puppies. Well from one bad bitch to another. My sister and I are not scared of none of y'all. For future references you will not be treating this young lady like she's a nobody, this is her hall and that is that." Karma said with hella attitude. Nobody has ever had the courage to put the sorority sisters in their place. "Sis, do you think that's a clever idea to make enemies? We are new here." Yahtia said sadly. "Fuck that shit you know I don't like bullies." The sorority sisters stormed off leaving the hall mad as ever. "So, we meet again, Joy." Karmell said smiling. Joy would not look her in the eye, she was oh so shy. "Yes, it seems we do meet again". Karmell tilted her head to catch Joy's eye. "You are safe with us. We are your friends." Yahtia had picked up her ripped schedule, handing it over to her. "Hey suitemate!" Joy looked dumbfounded. Joy glanced at the schedule and then back at the new girls, a smile spread across her face. "You guys are smart too." They all laughed at that. Putting an arm around Joy, they explained that they prided themselves on being the best at everything. Toyah hugged Joy as soon as the introductions were made. As a mom Toyah could tell the girl needed it. Toyah then ordered the men to get all of Joy's belongings so Joy could get settled in too. "Best day ever" Joy whispered to herself. Joy was so giddy, she had people who accepted her, and it felt good. Before the ladies departed Karmell invited joy to the Lovers and Friends concert. "I don't have nothing but Wal-Mart clothes, you both look like y'all just stepped off the runway." Joy responded. "Girl we do Wal-Mart and Simply 10 too, we just know how to put it together." said Yahtia. "Besides, we are not taking no for an answer, we got you." Karmell said in her big sister voice.

CHAPTER 6
GIRLS NIGHT

The day had finally come for the ladies to hit the road to Atlanta, Georgia for the 'Lovers and Friends' concert. Excitement filled the air for the friend trio and the ladies had a sleepover at Karmell's house. They were up all-night trying on outfits and wigs, getting their best look together. Ozias and Craig were driving them to Atlanta and Craig had given Yahtia a fat bag of loud. It did not take much for them, they were high from one blunt. The ladies giggled and ate the night away. They finally drifted off to sleep feeling good and anxious to hit the road. The ladies had overslept, and Ozias and Craig were knocking at the door like the Feds. A groggy and sleepy Karmell answered the door with a mug on her face. Ozias scooped her up saying, "Give me a kiss with that hot morning breathe." Karmell placed her hands over her mouth and ran upstairs to take off her retainer and brushed her teeth. Joy and Yahtia slowly climbed out of bed and headed downstairs for coffee. Craig was getting an eye full of Joy in her night booty shorts; Craig had to do the man wiggle to keep his dick from rising. It was now 1 PM and the ladies regained their energy and was dressed in no time. Craig and Ozias placed their bags in the car and then off they went.

Their ride to Atlanta was smooth and fun and they arrived at 4 PM, the concert was at 7 PM. Karma and the girls checked into the Hyatt Regency to continue their beauty treatments and change into their outfits.

Craig and Ozias made it known that they were not leaving until they dropped them off at the stadium. "So, babe what are you and Craig going to be doing while we at the show?" Karmell asked Ozias. "I guess we going to hit up the casino about thirty miles from here. You best believe I will be there when it's over to pick your pretty ass up." Ozias then smacked her on the ass and he and Craig left the room so the ladies could finish getting ready. "I can't believe this is me.", said Joy. "Girl you look like a million bucks." Yahtia said loudly, co-signed by Karmell. After they were dressed, the girls start to sing and dance to Destiny's Child's *"Bills, Bills, Bills"*, they had the look. The night was young and full of fun, the ladies pre-gamed with cocktails and a few puffs of Sour Diesel before they left out. Craig pulled up to the stadium giving the ladies front door service. Ozias jumps out the car and kiss Karmell like she was not coming back. "Nigga that's enough you going to ruin her make-up." said Yahtia. As they walked into the stadium giving the poll person their tickets, Joy asked Yahtia, "Do your brother Craig have a girlfriend?" Yahtia and Karmell look at her like she was speaking a foreign language. "What? He cute.", Joy said with a smile from ear to ear. "Let me find out, little miss quiet ain't so quiet after all.", said Karmell. "I get that same feeling between my legs you two get." They all bust out laughing walking to their seats. The lights came to a low beam and the crowd started to scream loud ready for the first performer. Seconds later, Ludacris comes out super hyped off one of his hits, *"My Chic Bad"*. The girls turn up in their section dancing and throwing their hands in the air, feeling the whole concert experience. The next two performers were David Banner followed by Paster Troy and the ladies could not sit down; they were all in and enjoying the concert to the fullest. It was time for an intermission. They gathered their belongings and headed to the restroom, and concession stand for snacks. While waiting in line for the restroom, an old thirsty gold tooth wearing nigga came up behind Joy and grabbed her butt like they were together. "What the fuck! Nigga, please walk away and don't touch me again." "Come on lil mama you are looking sexy as hell, you wanna come sit with me?", the annoying guy spoke trying to have swagger. "Hell to the naw nigga just keep it moving.", Joy said loudly. He then reached for her hand and Karmell and Yahtia immediately went in defense mode and started punching him. "She said go the fuck on nigga." Yahtia and Karma screamed loudly while punching him. His boys then jumped in trying to break up the ladies from whaling on their partner and then out of nowhere Ozias and Craig pop up and smack the guy around. They man handled the other guys. The guys did not want no smoke; Ozias's face spoke death threats. "You wanna be Casanovas better get the fuck out of here." said Craig. "I'm talking expeditiously." Ozias added. Yahtia looked at her brother and Ozias and said, "the casino huh?" "Curse us out later, just know we here now. We're not going to spoil y'all fun, we will be in the next section over." said Craig. "We got two empty seats next to us. Craig want y'all join us since you both are already here." Joy spoke with a soft and sexy tone. "Oh, hell no you two not about to make me a third wheel. Come on Karmell! Let's go, you better get your girl." Yahtia was so serious. Karmell gave Ozias a quick kiss and grabbed Joy's hand and they ran back to their seats. The lights dimmed again, and the next performer came out which was Usher, Lil Jon and Ludacris joined him on stage for their collaboration song "*Yeah*". After hours of show stopping performers and non-stop dancing, T.I. was the last performer and Yahtia went ham singing "*Rubber Band Man*", she had Karma and Joy join in. The three of them was crunk to the fullest. The night had gotten the best of them, the ladies were all tired and worn out. This was the start of a sisterhood for the trio. The ladies had no energy to gather their belongings from the hotel room. Craig and Ozias made the trip for them. When they returned to the car the ladies were shoulder-to-shoulder sleep. 3 AM, they arrive back to Columbia. They all stayed at Karmell's crib, even Ozias and Craig.

The next day around 1 PM, Toyah came beating the door down excited to hear about the concert. After filling her in, the ladies had a heart to heart about going off to school. "Joy how does it feel to be a college student?" Karmell asked. "Sis you know I have no friends at Grady, I'm super happy to have met you two beauties." "Well, I tell you what, we are going to stick together like glue; we will ride for each other no matter what. One band one mutha fucking sound. What we won't do is tolerate any flaw shit or bulling." said Yahtia. "So, let us spend time with our family and get our shit together and be ready to hit the books next week and take this college life to another level." Karmell spoke firm, like a true big sister. They hugged each other tight and departed ways. Before Yahtia left to take Joy home, Joy wrote her number on a paper towel for Craig and placed it on his chest while he was on the couch snoring away. "I see you left my brother a tramp stamp." Yahtia said as they walked out the door. Ozias woke Craig up after he noticed the number superbly written in lipstick. "Wake up lover boy." Craig did a long stretch followed up by a yawn. "Where everybody at?" Craig said on his way to the rest room to release his morning piss. "Karmell in the shower and Yahtia took Joy home." Craig retuned to the couch to fold up his blanket and found the paper towel with Joy's cell number. Joy had kissed the paper towel leaving a sexy set of purple lips. A humongous smiled plastered across Craigs face, he then did the famous Dab dance. "I guess the "Lovers and Friends" concert served its purpose." Ozias said jokingly to his partner Craig.

Only other friend Joy had was Nekendra Blessings. Nekendra was known to her family and friends as Baby Mama, because she had two boys at a youthful age. Joy and Nekendra had been down since elementary school. Joy took the time to see Nekendra before she starts her semester. As Joy walks through the breeze way of Nekendra's building, Joy heard Nekendra screaming to the top of her lungs. Nekendra was begging for the licks to stop, her ugly ass boyfriend, Troy Hall, who was a habitual woman beater, decided to show off his ignorance. Troy would often beat Nekendra just for fun, causing Nekendra injuries and tons of stress. The neighbors had formed a crowd and began to record what was happening, but no one stepped up to call the police. "OMG how long had he been beating her?" Joy asked angrily looking at the crowd while she beat on the door. Troy had the door jammed so no one was able to get in. After minutes of trying, Joy pulled out her phone and called the police. "Why the fuck you call the police? She will be right back with him tomorrow." A skinny woman said while getting a high five from another lady. "Fuck tomorrow. He will be back tonight, driving her car with another bitch riding shot-gun." Another woman added her input, "I don't give two fucks what y'all say, no one deserve to be treated like this. Y'all seven-dollar rent paying bitches ain't shit." Joy continued to beat and kick on the door trying her hardest to get in and save her friend. Joy was screaming out repeatedly, "Leave her alone." The fuck boy was out of breath and the beaten had stopped. The police arrived and Troy was arrested on site. Joy punched Troy then spat in his face before she could make it to Nekendra who was lying helplessly on her living room floor. After the police got a visual of the damage Troy caused to Nekendra, the police roughed him up before placing him in the car. Troy accidently fell down the stairs and busted his head wide open. His face accidently was rammed into the police car window. One of the officers punched him so hard, when no one was looking, knocking his bottom rack of teeth out. The ambulance was called; Nekendra was unrecognizable. Her clothes were drenched in blood and Joy did not want to touch her, because she looked all broken up. Joy cried her eyes out and walked alongside the medics as they placed Nekendra in the ambulance. "Friend you got to leave that nigga alone. Please Baby Mama he is aiming to destroy you. I don't know how much more you can take friend." Joy was so hurt, she silently prayed hoping this would be the last time he puts his hands on Nekendra. Joy called for a Lyft to transport her to the hospital to be with her friend.

CHAPTER 7
REVEALING THE TRUTH

Yahtia and Karmell had been blowing Joy up for the past week. It was Sunday and their first day of class was tomorrow. Grabbing the rest of their things they needed for their dorm, then they both said their good- bye's. Toyah and Juan did the parent thing and laid the law down about partying and boys. They made sure to add they expect them both to make the dean's list every semester.

Grady was only a 45-minute ride, so they had time to play around. Ozias and Crag was dropping them off because first-year students were unable to drive. They headed straight to Joy's house to see if she needed a ride and Craig had a fat one rolled up, letting the girls get faded before they headed off to school land. When they pulled up to Joy's crib, Craig blew the horn for a about five minutes. Joy's niece, Sylvanna, came to the door. "Is Joy home?', asked Yahtia. "She in her room sleep.", The young girl responded. "Come on Karmell lets go get this heffa, she's going to school." Yahtia said as she exited the car. Yahtia walked into the house in search for Joy and Karmell was right on her heels but when they reached her room they froze. Joy was in the dark, with the windows Covered up, and she was snugged tight under the covers. "Girl what the fuck is up with you?" Karmell asked as she pulled the covers off Joy. "Talk to us Joy what's wrong fam?" Yahtia moved in close and noticed Joy had watery eyes, and her bottom lip was trembling. Yahtia spoke softly, "Come on sis and get your things we got class tomorrow." "I'm not going to start until next week, I will catch up on my classes then." "Bull-shit, you don't have to worry about that bullying shit this year I promise you that." "No, it's not that." Joy raised up and gave them the run down on her love and concern for Nekendra. Karmell and Yahtia listened to Joy for an hour before they took control over the situation. "Look sis, you can't save your friend, she is a grown woman with a clear mind. You have done all you can do. If you keep trying to be captain save a hoe that nigga will eventually fuck you up." Karmell went to great lengths of explaining how Joy needs to help her friend from a distance and do not get caught up in her drama. "Now you got twenty minutes to get up and get ready. We will be waiting in the car." Karmell said with a smile then gave her the hug she needed. "Make sure your lips poppin, because Craig in the car looking like he need a kiss." said Yahtia. That perked Joy up quickly when she heard Craigs name that was music to her ears. Joy was tossing her clothes around looking for her Tik-Tok leggings to show off her ass.

Arriving on campus, all three ladies were looking good, smelling like a pound of loud. They quicky sprayed down in their favorite fragrance, 'Strawberry Poundcake', from Bath and Body Works. They desperately needed to cover up the strong weed odor. Ozias kissed Karmell then picked her up and swung her around like she was a small kid. "Nigga put me down." Karmell said laughing so hard that slob came seeping out her mouth. Craig was having small talk with Joy and Yahtia. "Ozias and I are only a phone call away. If any of these niggas get greasy and start getting out of line, y'all better call us ASAP." "Ok big bro, we got this." "I'm fucking serious Tia; I will stomp the yard with these college boys.", Yahtia and Karmell grabbed their bags and headed to the dorm, leaving Joy and Craig talking. The crush was so obvious between the two, the short conversation left them both smiling. Joy went skipping to the dorm feeling mushy and tingly inside. Jherika and Tonera must have had some sense of jealousy because they watched Joy the entire time she was talking with Craig. "That nigga must be slow, or you poisoned him, because he too damn fine for your dingy ass.", Tonera said with much hate. "No, he's not slow he just prefers quality over quantity. Why the fuck you two worried about the way my pussy stroke anyway. Y'all have salvaged enough dicks on this campus already. So let me be great pookabutt." Joy clapped back in her defense. Jherika and Tonera were seconds away from jumping Joy. Joy was ready to fight and right before the first punch could take place, Karmell and Yahtia popped up. "Oh, hell nah let's make this a fair fight, y'all hoe's have no respect. Karmell, you sit this one out Joy and I got this.", said Yahtia. Jherika and Tonera rolled their eyes and walked away. "Don't leave now I got popcorn. I thought you bitches wanted to fight." Karmell was pointing and laughing making them angry even more. "You bitches have learned your first math lesson. one on one is fair fight not two on one.", Yahtia screamed while flipping them the finger. Yahtia and Karmell helped Joy with her things and then headed to the dorm to get their first day of class outfits together.

Morning came around quick for the ladies. They were up at seven am, they all had an eight am classes. Yahtia and Karmell were dressed in the cutest skirts with matching tops and Joy caught on fast, she was not about to be left out. Joy's outfit was a black skirt long in the back and short in front with a burgundy blazer. They all had coffee and donuts for breakfast then headed out for class looking more like professors then students.

The ladies survived the first day of their classes. Joy was catching dirty looks from Uvoka and Adreama all day; they would not dare say shit because Yahtia and Karmell intimidated them to the fullest. Uvoka walked by Karmell changing classes and Karmell walked up close to her and said "Boo". Hopefully, she had on a leak pad because she almost pissed her pants. Yahtia got a good laugh, but she wanted Karmell to pump the breaks on them. Yahtia desperately wanted to be in the sorority. "Fuck that sis we can start our own sorority, we don't need them bulling bitches.", Karmell pleaded with Yahtia. "I know but I been waiting on this since grade school, let's play nice sis and join the squad." "Ok but they better act like they know". Flyers were posted all over campus about sign ups. Joy, Yahtia and Karmell tried to sign up but soon as they placed their name on the sheet Adreama walked over. Adreama had this confused look on her face. "Is this some type of joke?" "Were grown women over here; we don't joke, nor do we play games." said Karmell. "What is the problem?", Yahtia threw her hands up questioning Adreama's approach. "I will be willing to look at you two pledge applications, meaning Yahtia and Karmell. Joy, on the other hand, does not meet our requirements, so we cannot use her." "Why the fuck not?" Yahtia asked. "We are looking for a certain look and high qualifications, and Joy does not fit anything we stand for." "Joy will be perfect for our mascot, no application needed for that." "Really bitch!", Yahtia was close to turning up. "I am leading this sorority. *The Sisters of Elegance* are under my command when it comes to pledging. So frankly it's my way or the highway.", Adreama said before she walked off. Uvoka looked at Karmell and blew her a kiss and Karmell pulled her shirt up like she was about to get some Jerry Springer beads. Karma shook her triple D tits at Uvoka. It was a chain reaction; Joy then pulled up her skirt and mooned her ass in their direction, followed by Yahtia flipping them off with both fingers. The ladies laughed their way back to their dorm room having fun about what they just did. "I told you Sis we can start our own alliance and do our own thing; you see how these chic's are already coping our style.", said Karmell. "Yes, we are a hit around this bitch." Yahtia responded. "That goat face bitch just mad because I saw her sniffing coke off this nigga dick at one of the football games last year. Adreama is an undercover coke head. I did some investigating on her one day when I was bored in class. I have lots of footage of her sniffing lines and partying with the football players doing strange activities. Adreama be so geeked up, some niggas had dogs licking her pussy. It gets better. Adreama returned the favor and had the dogs nut sack in her mouth. The bitch is trifling. Adreama is considered the head doctor around campus, her neck stays in rotation. Niggas be lined up to feed her dick and get their ass licked. I think Adreama the only one out her 4-girl posse that use coke. Jherika, her parents are highly active with her. During home visits her parents drug test her." Joy continued to spill the tea. Yahtia and Karmell had the ammunition they needed to play Adreama like a puppet. "We need this information and then some on a drive ASAP." Karmell said, followed by a hell yeah from Yahtia. "No problem. I had erased it because the students kept taking my lap top last year, but I can easily get it back. My material is backed up on I- cloud and will never disappear." "You the bomb .com sis." Yahtia and Karma said at the same time. "I never had a life, so doing private investigation became my hobby and my major. I can pretty much find any dirt and locate anybody with a legal social security number with ease." "Bitch you are a keeper, go ahead and put it on my brother so we can be sisters for real." Yahtia was so serious.

When the girls got back to the dorms, they changed and decided to have a chill day. They made pizza rolls and fired up some Kush. Ozias and Craig kept them supplied with the best of the best. While they were chilling, they heard a knock on the door. A flyer was slid underneath. Joy picked it up and threw it away. "What was that?" Yahtia asked. "Nothing, just a flyer for one of the Sorority secret interest parties". Everyone froze when realization hit them. "They are inviting us to the party?" Each of them had a confused look on their face. "Shiiiiit". Yahtia drew out the word. "Let's go!" Yahtia started running around getting her outfit together. Karmell just looked at Joy who shrugged her shoulders. "Why you two bitches not getting dressed?" Yahtia quipped. "Man don't nobody want to deal with the SUPER BITCH SQUAD. I don't understand why you all on their tits anyway" Karmell rolled her eyes. With a sigh. "Look sis, I know you do not understand and yes, they are worse than an itch from a yeast infection, but it is just them. The organization as a whole is Grade A. They are nationally recognized and so active in the black community. I do not like the super bitches, but I do want that letter on my jacket. It has always been a dream of mine." Yahtia looked to Joy for help, since Joy tended to have lots of random ass information. "I mean, she got a point." Joy said pulling on the blunt she had yet to pass. *"The Sisters of Elegance Sorority INC* is a great accomplishment to have on your resume. The female senator from Texas is a member. Their connections run deep." Joy stated, finally passing the blunt. Yahtia gave Karmell her best puppy dog eyes. "Sis don't make me beg. I am not above begging, or blackmailing. I think I still have that picture of you in that thing you tried on the other day". Yahtia said with a laugh while running away from Karmell. "You get on my nerves hoe." "If I go you better delete that damn picture." Karma pretended to be mad. In all honesty she was going to go anyway just because it was for her sis. Karmell was dreading being around them bitches tonight. Keeping it cute Karmell wore a Polo body dress with the new gold and pink Jordans and a ripped, short jean jacket. Yahtia had on a Champion shirt outfit with the new red and blue Jordans. Yahtia toped it off with a black terry cloth oversized jacket. Joy sported a messy bun with a bralette top, and some butt lifting leggings. Everyone had on their sneakers of choice. They agreed to be cute but not stupid. The super cunt squad might try something and need to catch a round or two. An hour later the trio walked into the gym looking like supermodel thugs. All eyes were on them. They stared back noticing how everyone was wearing skirts and blouses of some sort. Even the Super Hoes had on matching black skirts and white-collar shirts with pink cardigans wrapped around their necks. "It's giving Stafford wives, vibes in here." Karmell said. "Nah sis, this that single white female flow." Yahtia said. "Definitely mindless bitch behavior." Joy said to herself or anyone who could hear her. More guest began to trickle in. The party was moving along swiftly. Several students approach the girls asking them about themselves and what they were into. "Do y'all plan on joining this sisterhood." A girl asked with her clip board in hand. Karmell turned on the charm and smiled at everyone answering questions in her Miss America pageant voice. Yahtia and Craig liked to pick on her when Karmell tuned into a white girl. After an hour or so, Adreama and the rest of the mindless misfits walked over to the girls, clearly annoyed. "So, who told you about our little party?" Adreama said with attitude. "Clearly someone with taste invited us." Holding up the sign, Joy continued "DUHHH!" Karmell and Yahtia laughed. They were so happy to see Joy taking up for herself against people, especially them bitches. "Whatever, this is an interest meeting and I thought we told you that only two of you were qualified to be amongst us." Adreama said with every ounce of snotty bitch she could muster up. Joy's face fell, clearly hurt remembering what they had said earlier about her. Big sister, Karmell, stepped in immediately. "That's funny because not one of you overgrown, mindless bed roaches are qualified to breath our air." Karmell said getting into their faces, matching their mean mugs. "We are bowing down being nice enough to grace your presence so play nice." "Yeah, before we decide we not playing at all." Yahtia said, standing behind her sister. Clearly intimidated, Adreama had the shit face, so they turned their anger towards Joy. "You think because you aligned yourself with some women of substance you will magically be worth something." Uvoka snapped. "Y'all leave her alone, she is about to cry, just like her whoring ass best friend." Jherika laughed. "Who?", Tonera chimed in. "I know you not talking about Nekendra ass." Just as it registered to Karmell and Yahtia who they were talking about. Joy snapped. They had not seen it coming and for that everyone was slow to react. Joy jumped on Jherika, grabbing Tonera on her way down. Joy's form was not perfect, but she was connecting with their faces. All you heard throughout the gym was a good ole fashion ass whooping. It sounded like something your mama gave you. For every word said there was a blow delivered. "Stop fucking with me", followed by a series of blows. Joy had blacked out. Uvoka and Adreama tried to break it up but when they reached for Joy, Yahtia and Karmell was right there. "Oh No ma'am that ain't finna go down. We will get her but if one of y'all touch her you will get the same treatment your sisters getting." Yahtia spat. "On Big God." Karmell co-signed, mocking what she had heard Ozias say. Their conversation was interrupted with a high-pitched scream. They turned around to see Joy on top of Jherika, she was the one screaming. Joy had two handfuls of her hair and was banging her head against the floor. Tonera jumped on Joy back trying to choke her. Before the others could even react, Joy grabbed Tonera by the back of her head pulling her over. Next thing you know Joy managed to have Tonera and Jherika's heads pushed together. Joy was going ape shit. "Oh Shit!" Yahtia and Karmell grabbed Joy at the same time. "Come on sis let her hair go." Karmell said with a laugh. Once they got Joy off the floor, she would not let go of Tonera's ponytail. Yahtia, being her silly petty self, made a public announcement; laughing so hard she could barely get it out. "Let's take a moment to appreciate whoever did sis ponytail. Her shit holding on stronger than gorilla glue girl hair." This made Joy laugh and she finally let go. "I'm sorry Tia, I hope you can still get in. I just couldn't let her disrespect my girl like that." Joy snot cried. "Girl, fuck them and this sorority if that's how they wanna play it. I don't play about my people, and you are definitely my people, so that makes your girl my girl. SO, FUCK THEM HOES!" Karmell agreed with Yahtia. "What's the story. Why they felt comfortable speaking on her anyway?" Karmell asked.

Campus Security walked in before she could answer. "What seems to be the problem?" Two officers asked. On que, the four little bitches started singing. Of course, they threw the girls under the bus. "Quick send me one of the videos." Karmell whisper yelled to Joy. Joy instantly sent the videos of Adreama snorting coke from a nigga, Bentley's dick, at a kick back. Jumping into action Karmell walked towards the officers and the snitching bitches. "Excuse me officers, I think you need both sides of the story." Purposely waving her phone with the screen out so the video could be seen. Karmell walked up and stood beside Adreama and held her phone so that the video was visible to her only. "Yes officer, as I was stating, this fight was a direct result of bullying, and abuse of power. These girls, although it doesn't look like it, have been tormenting my friend for over a year." The others started to protest, "Ma'am we really don't care. Y'all should probably take this up with the dean or something. We are about to get off and we're instructed to shut the gym down." Adreama stood, terrified, and pissed off. When the officers made the announcement that the party was over. Adreama tried to corner Karmell. "Where did you get that video? And What the fuck do you plan to do with it? You really need to delete it, if you know what is good for you." Adreama demanded. Spit flying from her mouth, Adreama was fuming with the look of kill on her face. With a smile, Karmell took a small step back to give the two some space. Karma then put her arm around Adreama's neck and began to walk. "Let's keep it all the way real. You don't like me, and the feeling is fucking mutual. You don't want us to pledge in your sorority because you know we are highly qualified and over certified. We intimidate you because we are everything that you wish you were. You get off on sucking dicks and sniffing coke, we all about money and looking good. You will accept our applications and you will push them through. You will sponsor Joy as your pledge. Holding up her hand to silence Adreama. Karmell continued, "If you don't, I will make sure that this video and all the others of you doing your magic trick on magic sticks go viral." Adreama was beyond pissed. "Fine, but you delete that now." Adreama said as if she was in control giving an order. "NO, I will not. You must be taught a fucking lesson. You are so mean and so rude. You didn't even say please." Karmell teased. "Once we are in and lettered, we might delete it. Not before. We will discuss the other guidelines tomorrow. Look like you barked up the wrong mutha fuckan tree. I'm about to go back to the dorm and watch some more of this girl gone wild video with my sisters. I give it to you Dreama you were handling them dicks. I can't figure out for the life of me how you kept your jaw muscles moving. Bravo bitch you did that!" Karmell walked off collecting her girls on the way. Yahtia was already on the phone with Craig, telling him everything.

The girls caught a Lyft to the IHOP about fifteen miles from campus. They were meeting the boys because they were surprisingly on the way to "Check" on them. In all honesty, Craig just wanted a reason to see Joy. "Joy I need you to do your super detective shit and get an entire file on Adreama ass. If I am going to black mail her. I need everything to be good and JUICY." Karmell said putting some bacon and pancakes in her mouth. "What are you going to do exactly?" The girls asked. Karmell shrugged. Not sure yet but "Karma is a bitch."

When the boys arrived, they sat down and ate with them. Listening to them recount the events of the night. "Laila Ali over there blushing and shit." Ozias joked. Joy's face had turned red. "I don't know what happened, I was just so mad when I heard her say Baby Mama name. I just snapped." Joy explained that Tonera and Jherika knew Nekendra through her baby daddy. They always hated on Nekendra, because even after having babies early, she was still a baddie and commanded respect. "Nekendra just got caught up with a nigga that don't deserve her. He should be loving her but instead he drags her ass through the mud. Nekendra says its love, but love shouldn't require blood." Joy wiped her tear-stained face and zipped up the jacket Craig had given her. They finished eating without saying much else. After paying the bill they all piled in the car and headed to a room. Karma and Joy were not going to sneak the boys in the dorm tonight because they had early classes. On the ride back they fired up a fat pre-roll and got high as fuck. "I just want y'all to know that Imma get me a man cause what I'm not gonna be is the third wheel to y'all sickening assess." Yahtia said popping her lips. "Who the fuck you finna be with Tia?" Craig and Ozias said at the same time. The girls laughed. "Somebody son. How come y'all get to be hot and ready but I can't?" Yahtia was real hurt. Craig did an Urkel giggle and passed the blunt. "Girl I do not want to hear about you fucking. You are only allowed to fuck with a real nigga. Ozias locked down and I'm your brother, so you single as a pringle." "Soooooo, you not locked down?" Joy asked with an eyebrow raised. The Ooh's echoed throughout the car as they waited for an answer. Joy had not given Craig any pussy, but she knew she would soon. Joy wanted to fuck with him and take the heat off Yahtia. Craig started coughing, he had forgotten to exhale the smoke. "We will talk about this later." Joy said with a knowing look. Craig started blushing. They departed ways from the girls.

On the ride back, Craig had a thought come in his head. "A bro, I seen that shit about Joy's friend, Baby Mama, was hurting her". "Yeah, fam I seen that shit." Ozias responded. "Well, she said the nigga name is Troy Hall and he is housed at the county for now. I'm about to make some noise with my boy Kevie and let him contact his cousin D-Ray. D-Ray is sitting in the county running shit while he awaits trial. Once the word gets out what this fuck boy Troy has been doing, them niggas going to have fun with his ass." Craig spat with confidence. "Sounds like a plan." Ozias responded.

Later that night, the girls were in the living room area of the suite talking and smoking. Karmell had pulled out her notebook and started writing in it. "What are you writing sis?" Yahtia asked. After a minute or so Karmell answered. "We gotta teach them hoes a lesson. They must learn not to fuck with us. PERIOD." The other two nodded in agreement. "We can't stop everybody." Joy said. "Yes, we can, and we will." Karmell handed paper to Joy and Yahtia. "Make a list of any and everybody that has ever done you wrong. We are making KARMA a hitlist." Yahtia laughed. "Bitch is you Karma or something." Karmell just looked at her. "Bitch that's hot, hell yeah I'm Karma. That's my line name too." Karmell then wrote the name down, it instantly grew on her. Karma drifted off for a second mesmerized by the name. "Let's put a mutha fuckan stamp on, we can even pinky swear. We gotta make these clowns pay for fucking with real bitches. I been bullied and treated like dirt since I been able to walk, my own fucking parents even treated me like shit. People have been trying to take me out and shame me for years. I have a big boy list for your ass, and I want them all dealt with accordingly." "You know I got your back sis, so how we gonna do this? Straight vigilante style or what?" Yahtia asked. "What if we come up with a code" Joy asked. Joy had already written one down. Joy was a little nervous to let her sisters know that she secretly had been wanting to do something like this for years. "I have a big payback list too, these people at this school have done everything under the sun to me. I can go on for days telling y'all about my history of being picked on and bullied. I want to be in the driver seat from now on." "We about to make it happen sis.", said Yahtia. Reading the paper, they all agreed. "RED is dead! BLACK & BLUE is bruises with a beat down. PURPLE is the set up and YELLOW is mental health. "Sis, from now on Karmell is your government name, today you have been promoted to Karma. That's the name that fits you.", said Joy. "Damn right!" Yahtia sounded off. "OK I accept. I have some entertainment for y'all check it out." Karma begins to move side to side. Clapping her hands giving herself a beat before she spits a rap:

"MY NAME IS KARMA WITH A CAPITAL K. I'M DOWN WITH OZIAS IN A SPECIAL WAY. HE'S MY MAN AND HE'S HERE TO STAY. I WENT FROM BEING BULLIED, TO THE CATCH OF THE DAY. I'M A BITCH IN A SKIRT AND I KNOW HOW TO FIGHT, DON'T FUCK WITH ME BECAUSE I'M OUT OF SIGHT. ONE THING ABOUT ME I'M NOT WITH NO FAKENESS, I'M ON THE ROAD TO SOME REAL LIVE GREATNESS, I'M KARMA BOSTON AND I'M EVERYBODY'S FAVORITE."

Yahtia and Joy joined in with the clapping. Joy even made a beat box sound. They were dancing and saying, "Go Karma." They were hyped up. "Ok Erika Banks.", said Joy. The three of them continued being silly, dancing around while Joy continued to beat box.

CHAPTER 8
REVEALING THE LIST

The girls spent the rest of the night laughing and making their various hit lists. "Y'all make sure that any and everybody that ever did you dirty get put on the list. Don't worry about the codes as much, this is just our rough draft. Right now, Just make the list." Karma instructed while she made her own list. A few blunts, a lot of shots, and two hours later the girls were wrapping things up. Joy spoke up. "We can double check to make sure that we aren't coding no one wrong or too aggressively." "Or not aggressively enough." Karma chimed in. "Really y'all we gonna do this?" Yahtia asked. The other two said. "YES" at the same time as they went to trade lists. As Joy and Karma went through each other's list and critiqued them, Yahtia started cleaning up. About twenty minutes later Karma noticed Yahtia was being weird as fuck. "Girl what the fuck is wrong with you?" Karma asked. Yahtia looked guilty as sin. "What? I ain't did nothing." Joy laughed and grabbed a slice of pizza. "Says, the girl that has not put her list down. Has gone to the bathroom three times. Cleaned up an already clean room and is currently folding our jackets." Yahtia rolled her eyes dramatically. "Damn bitch! Stalker alert. Ole Encyclopedia Brown head ass." Karma and Joy just stared at Yahtia. She started to pick the invisible lint off the couch in front of her just to avoid her friends' gaze. "Y'all trippin', I gotta pee." Yahtia said turning around to go toward the bathroom. Yahtia just needed to get out of the hot seat. She could not bring herself to tell Karma her secret. "Oh no you don't." Karma was on her ass, getting to the bathroom door before she could lock herself in. Karma blocked the door. "Sista girl spill it". Karma was in her face. Karma's voice had softened, she realized that something was extremely wrong with her sister. Karma needed to find the underlying cause of things. "Sis don't do this. Let me get my shit together I will talk to you." Yahtia started crying and ripping up her list. Karma grabbed her hand and looked at her with unshed tears of her own. "Sis let it go, no judgement." Karma led Yahtia to the couch.

After getting herself together she started talking. "Karma imma tell you because we don't keep secrets from each other. I am really straddled between the fence on this one. Please do not make me tell you." Yahtia cried. Her tears tore Karma apart. "I need to know what is bothering you Yahtia. What is wrong we can fix it together." Karma started crying too. Joy sat down opposite of the girls and just took in the scene. After seconds of silence, nervously Karma said, "Spit that shit out man". Shaking her head Yahtia handed the torn list to her sister. Karma looked at the list and scanned it. "What you mean, Karmelo is stealing the house?" She asked confused. Taking a deep breath, Yahtia started talking. "Craig told me last weekend when I overheard him and daddy talking. Neither one of us was supposed to know, so please don't be mad at anyone." Yahtia began explaining. "You know that mom started the paperwork to legally adopt you after the hospital incident, right?" Karma nodded her head and motioned for her to continue. Yahtia explained that Molly had gotten in trouble for the hospital incident. "Molly was suspended and is currently under investigation for the allegations of child neglect." Karma could not help but to smile at the news. "Well, Molly raised so much hell she convinced Karmelo to get rid of us. Karmelo made some fake documents saying that mom and dad were behind on taxes and foreclosed on the house. Before they ever got the paperwork, Molly had sold the house to a land developer." "What the fuck! When did this happen?" Karma was now crying hysterically, snot flying everywhere. All of this was happening because of her. It was her fault. "No, don't do that sis. I know you are blaming yourself and it is not your fault just because your biologicals are ass wipes." The girls sat and hugged each other as Yahtia finished telling her the tea. Joy sat on the floor just offering comfort where she could.

It was not her family or her fight, but she could not stand to see them hurting. They were her family now. They had a bond that was deeper than the bond itself.

Yahtia reassured her sister that this was nobody's fault but Karmelo and Molly; for that and other things they were on the list. "Dad got his best friend Sandiago Fernandez, a lawyer, to investigate their shenanigans. Sandiago knew off top it was bullshit he must dig deep and prove it. Sandiago has already stopped the eviction. He says when this is over it will be beneficial for us." Yahtia continued, "We aren't going to lose the house, but it was a lot of bullshit that came with what they did. Karmelo and Molly were trifling for doing my family that way. Your dad is a low-down dirty dog that needs to die slow. I have a video of them dumb asses fighting." Yahtia said laughing as she pulled out her phone to show it. Plain as day there was Molly squaring off with Karmelo. World star style. They had a good laugh off the video. After Karma called and talked with Toyah. Karma calmed down. Toyah was still furious that the Boston's were trying this shit. Toyah was simply happy that this was not going to go through; she and Juan had some get back of their own for the criminal matrimony team. Their lawyer had some promising advantages for them. Joy spoke up for the first time. "So, who is Hershey?" Joy had been reading the list after piecing it back together. Yahtia rolled her eyes again "Bitch do you know how to mind anybody else business." Yahtia laughed. Yahtia looked at Karma and told it all before she lost her nerve. "Sis I was so ashamed and hurt when it happened. I shut down and I didn't even tell Craig or Ozias."

For the next hour Yahtia told them about how she thought she was in love with Tyren Williams, the eighth-grade playboy. "When he told me I was cute and he wanted to date me, I just knew I was hot shit. We were a good thing for about a month. Then Rhonda Humphrey happened. Apparently, she couldn't decide if she liked me or Tyren. Back then she was having a tossup between boys and girls. Totally mixed up about her sexuality. The bitch would pick on me and fuck with me because she wanted Tyren. Hershey would spread so many lies about me making me look bad. Hershey told him that I was her girlfriend and that she could prove it. Hershey set me up. Her nasty ass drugged me by putting Roofie in my water at lunch one day. I was on the way to the nurse, and she grabbed me. I passed out. When I woke up, I was in her apartment. Hershey was on top of me. I tried to fight her off, but I couldn't. She violated me. Touched me, kissed me, Hershey had her way with me. Hershey was enjoying herself, not giving a fuck about my feelings. Tyren was hiding in the closet watching with his best friend, Terrell. They watched and recorded the whole thing." Yahtia was crying hysterically. "I cried and pushed her away. I tried to fight but it was like fighting a gorilla. Hershey was putting on a show. Gyrating all on me licking me like I was a lollipop. Hershey then got grimy and pulled her panties down and tried to sit on my face. I threw up all over her and the bed. Tyren came out the closet and started yelling telling me it was over and for me not to ever call or talk to him again. I looked him in the face and asked him to help me. He refused. I was so humiliated. Hershey was sitting there like a big man with her clothes still off and mouth open. Terrell did help me off the bed. He knew that it was a set up, but he would not go against his boy. When I got back to the school, they left me." Karma looked wide eyed. "That was the day Mama T was gonna beat your ass because you did not come home till late that day. Mama T said you smelled like sex and Craig was trying to interrogate you. You wouldn't say anything to anyone." Karma shook her head. "I just could not admit what had happened. I went to the clinic the next day. Remember I told you I needed condoms because I wanted to give Tyren my virginity? It was really because I needed to be checked. That funky bitch touched me. I did not know what her pussy had going on with that smell. I was given a data sheet of what I had in my system; 80% Rohypnol was a positive culture. I tried to tell Tyren a week later. I showed him the proof and everything. He told me I was trash. Tyren called me a dyke bitch and threatened to show people the video. Tyren said he could never be with me he said I was disgusting. That hurt me even more than the actual assault." Karma could not take it. She broke down. "I can't believe I did not know that my sister had gone through the same thing. I'm so sorry Tia." The girls cried it out together.

Joy could not take it. She too at one time was molested and violated against her will. While the sisters were crying and talking it out. Joy started building profiles. Karmelo and Molly Boston, Tyren Williams, Rhonda Humphrey, and the bitch squad. They all had to pay. Joy would not let her newfound sisters suffer anymore.

The next day during class they all were a bit tired a lot had been discovered and just the emotional part was draining. Adreama had been ghost all day. "Joy have you talked to Adreama today?" Karma asked. "No, I haven't even seen the hoe." "Give her a courtesy call to meet me in the cafeteria in 5 minutes or I'm going live." Joy did just that. Adreama did not answer. "She's not answering, you want me to try again?" "Hell, nah sis. The bitch gone learn today." Just when Karma logged on to Facebook, Adreama called back. Joy passed the phone to Karma. "You have 2 minutes to get to the cafeteria, I was just about to go live." "Y'all ain't got nothing better to do but fuck with me." Adreama said very aggravated. "Ain't no fun when the rabbit got the gun." Karma said right before hanging up. Adreama was there in record time. "You can take the frown off your face. You did this to yourself." Karma stated to Adreama. "You have been running shit around here since your freshman year. Your nasty ass can finally take the break you need. Joy is in power now." "Who are you to change shit I will always be in control of this whole damn school and especially my squad." Adreama responded. "So, I see you don't believe in change huh. Joy show our puppy mouth friend how she's been slipping." Joy proceeding with the videos that she had gathered. About 30 seconds into the video, Adreama had a face full of tears. Joy screams out, "Don't cry yet bitch its more." Adreama saw herself having sex with multiple guys and having foreplay with dogs. A line had formed. Several guys with all breeds of dogs on a leach waiting for some of Dreama's mouth skills. They mostly wanted to capture her sick acts on video, you would have thought she worked at the vet. The video was two hours long they only showed her the juicy parts. Adreama stood up and she begged them to stop. "Girl we haven't even got to your Oscar performing debut, sit back down and relax. Would you like a soda? The acid may help break down that dog hair that's lingering in your throat." said Joy. The video continued Adreama immediately put her hand over her face. It was showing her sniffing grams of coke then she starts seizing from an overdose. The frat boys were pouring icy water on her. They kept her in their dorm for days until she had finally bounced back. Karma sits down next to Adreama giving her a 'what you got to say now' look. "Now we know your mom and dad are both partners at the biggest black law firm on the west side of Columbia. They both are active members of Macedonia Baptist Church. Your brother Adam works at channel 7 news; we have Chad the head anchor on standby to air the story if need be; do I need to go on?" Karma asked. Adreama shook her head no. "You will proudly shadow Joy, she's going to be your right-hand girl. You will put her at the top of the list for the sorority and you will let her run the pledges. You will also flood social media with pictures of you and Joy doing positive activities together. "How can I explain this? They will overturn my position if enough members don't agree with the change." Adreama said trying to plead with Karma. "You figure that shit out. You will no longer be friends with your bitch squad. The bully treatment you were so friendly to dish out to Joy, you will now do the same to your bitches and let them see how it taste. A word of advice please don't try no slick shit I will not hesitate to do you dirty. FYI, you need to show up for class everyday with the biggest 'I got a new best friend' smile. You must attend all events, no sick days no excuses." Karma then gave her seven graphic designed T-shirts and explained that she will rotate wearing them as if they were a uniform. Adreama was not allowed to wear a jacket with the shirts, the wording had to be visually shown. The shirts read:

MY NEW BESTIE JOY, NO BULLIES ALLOWED, COCAINE IS A HELL OF A DRUG, BOOGER SUGAR INCORPORATED, I'M ASHAMED OF SOME THINGS I HAVE DONE, KEEP YOUR DOG AWAY FROM ME, and I'M SORRY IF I EVER WRONGED YOU!

CHAPTER 9
SWITCHING THE MOMENTUM

Uvoka, Tonera, and Jherika were all in shock of the sudden dramatic change in Adreama. "Somebody has to be extorting Dreama. She would never be cuffed up with Joy Whites' punk ass." Uvoka sounded off. "The two might as well be bumping cooties how close they have been lately. They seemed to be joined at the fucking hip." Tonera chimed in. Adreama had been avoiding her original sisters. Joy had Adreama attending NA meetings and volunteering at the local animal shelters. Joy was leading the step team practices and barking out orders to the sorority sisters. Adreama had her back on whatever Joy decided to do. "This what y'all ain't ready for, look at this shit.", said Jherika. It was a picture of Joy and Adreama at the county fair with besties T-shirts on full of smiles in a selfie picture. Uvoka screamed out. "OH, HELL NAH, Dreama done lost her fucking mind. We got to get a handle on this." "What the hell can we do? Adreama made it clear for us to leave her alone, she said she would revoke our colors if we continued to bother her." Tonera said sounding incredibly sad. Uvoka was given some pictures of Karma when she was in high school of her hair matted down, and her buck teeth. Karma teeth was big as boiled eggs before her surgery and braces. TJ Riley was one of the bullies that use to torment Karma and felt the need to share this with Uvoka. TJ verbally bashed Karma's name to Uvoka, stating she was a lame and other jealous shit woman say when they are throwing salt. Uvoka painted her own picture of Karma and was going to go after her with full force. Uvoka turned to face Jherika and Tonera, "Are you bitches down with me on this or what?" "I'm staying in my lane, Dreama was very clear for us to leave shit alone." Said Jherika. Tonera said, "I don't know what the fuck to do. I'll holla at y'all later." Tonera grabbed her purse and walked away. "So, I guess we are going to let these retards take over. This campus belongs to us. I'm not scared of them copycat hoes." Uvoka slammed her phone down so hard the screen shattered. Uvoka went from mad to furious. Uvoka then kicked the phone causing it to slide down the long dorm hallway. Joy curiously inquired about the loud thud she heard and noticed Uvoka storming down the stairs looking upset. Joy was about to yell out "keep the noise down people are studying" but suddenly caught visual of a broken phone laying mid-way from her door. Joy's inspector gadget mind kicked in. Joy picked up the broken phone then resumed to her room.

Uvoka recruited a few people to help her with her plan. A mandatory sorority meeting was scheduled to take place in the gymnasium upper-level deck. Members began to arrive. Most members noticed the posted items placed neatly around the wall. Uvoka had pictures enlarged poster size of Karma from grade school to high school. Showing images of how Karma once looked with her teeth and hair. Uvoka had posters attached on the wall of the girls placing perm in Karma's hair in the school locker room. Uvoka also had panties with smeared chocolate in the middle with a written story that the panties belonged to Joy White. Moments later, Adreama and Joy walked inside the gym side by side laughing because Adreama had a case of non-stop hiccups. They both sat down at the table gathering the paperwork they were about to pass out. "Ok ladies Joy is ready to get it cracking let's move closer please. Yahtia and Karma came running in. "Sorry we are late sis." Said Karma. "I will deal with you two later." Joy was firm like a woman of power. Adreama noticed that no one was moving, so she stepped to the back and noticed what the delay was about. Looking at the pictures Adreama blurts out. "Who did this bull-shit?" Karma, Yahtia, and Joy joined the crowd. The three of them laughed it off when they saw the pictures covering the wall. They were totally non-responsive about the prank. "Ok ladies we have a lot of ground to cover so we need to get down to business. No need to waist anymore precious time."

Joy said in her sarcastic voice. Purple Pinky, one of the members and Joy's only college friend before Karma and Yahtia, stayed behind and started taking the posters down and trashing them. She was called Purple Pinky because 95% of her clothes were purple or pink. Her government name was Kaki James. The meeting was conducted professionally, all the sorority business was managed. Before closing Joy put a bug in Adreama's ear. Adreama then made an announcement. "Congratulations to Purple Pinky, she will receive the dues money for the month. She will also be conducting the meetings until further notice." Adreama announced. "What's up with all the changes we deserve to know something?" Jherika said with much attitude. "Changes happen in the world every mutha fuckan day. The last time I checked I was sorority leader and head bitch in charge; that's why I am the one rocking the immunity color necklace. Feel free to turn in your colors or join another sorority, the choice is yours." Adreama said full of aggression. "Purple Pinky gets a big shot out and reward because she was the only one that took the initiative to remove the foolery some ass wipe decided to put up." Joy said still sounded sarcastic. Yahtia then added, "I feel sorry for the party that's responsible." "Meeting adjourned.", said Joy.

The ladies then head back to the dorm to relax. Purple Pinky had sent Joy a text, "I saw Uvoka taping them pictures up." "Good looking fam. Yahtia roll up a fatty bitch." Joy said loudly. "I'm already on it." "I bet you a dime to a dollar Uvoka had something to do with that shit." Karma said calmly. "Yep, Purple Pinky just sent me confirmation seconds ago. That miserable bitch just fucked up. Uvoka is about to be looking butt face ugly. Put some fire on that good and pass that shit." "What bitch?" Karma kept asking. "Just hold your horse's sis." Joy put on her serious face along with her bifocal glasses. The blunt was going in rotation, Joy would do a dance in her seat in-between puffs. Karma and Yahtia knew Joy had something exclusive by her body language and the smacking of the lips. Joy later became slumped over the coffee table focused on Uvoka's phone and her laptop. They heard a knock at the door, it was Adreama. "I just want to clear the air, I had nothing to do with that stunt at the meeting. I have been honoring my word and applying with everything y'all have asked of me." Adreama said in her own defense. "Yes, you have." Said Karma. "We know firsthand who the dummy was." Yahtia said while choking from the heavy cloud of smoke she had just inhaled". "Have a seat, the show is about to begin once Purple Pinky gets here. I want her to enjoy the action pack thriller too." Joy said while giving all the ladies a hive five even Adreama. While waiting on Purple Pinky, Joy poured her a shot of Patron and threw it back quickly. "I'm a bad bitch." Joy said amping herself up. After Purple Pinky arrived, Joy turned her laptop around to face them all then spoke. "Without further ado. Grady's own butt loose stick me hard up the ass Uvoka Wells, presents dykes gone wild part 1." The video was raw and uncut footage of Uvoka getting fucked in the ass (train style) by two twin sisters Carla and Kaila. The twins were part of the Up *Top Divas* sorority, and both were scrapped with 12-inch dildo's knocking the insides of Uvoka's rectum loose. Uvoka was getting her ass devoured like a pit-bull does raw meat. Most of their members were lesbians. Some were feminine gay, but the studs held the most numbers and made majority of their sorority. The way them sister were stroking Uvoka, it is a wonder Uvoka has not been shitting on herself. Uvoka was named loose booty by the ladies. The ladies partake in some shots and conversation. Joy sent a massive forward to all members of Up *Top divas*, and other sorority's as well. "Y'all are not to be fucked with, I'm glad I'm not in the hot seat." Adreama said peacefully. "Since you are the only one to be spared, you need to jump on board with us. We only wanted to teach you a valuable lesson and make you correct your wrongs by shaming you. No one else will get this chance". Karma said and Yahtia was right in Adreama"s face waiting for her to respond. "I'm all in, say less. Thanks for sparing me I really mean it. This was the wakeup call I needed." Adreama hugged Joy with tears flowing down her face apologizing over and over for all her cruel behavior she had displayed towards her. The night ended smoothly, and the sister friends went to bed thinking about their Karma list.

Craig and Ozias had scheduled a meet up with Kevie at the pool hall in the hood. After they exchanged pleasantries and dapped it up like guys do, they made their way to the matter at hand. Craig laid the facts down about Troy and was very critical about how he wanted shit to play out. Ozias put his spin on it and shit was about to get real in the county jail. "So, basically nothing is off limits for this nigga. No delicate treatment, straight slay action." Kevie said waiting for a head nod for confirmation.

Craig gave him a brotherly hug and passed him a quarter pound of Sour Diesel. That was all the confirmation he needed.

Days later D-Ray put the word out to his team of misfits that were down for whatever. Destruction was how they coped in life. D-Ray gave a lay out of how graphic this needed to be. D-Ray had lost his favorite auntie, Niki, behind domestic violence and this was going to be his revenge to honor his auntie, since he could not get the nigga who killed her. D-Ray spotted Troy in the weight room poking out his chest portraying to be swoll and buffed. D-Ray and his gang approached Troy. D-Ray asked him, "Can you read playboy?" "Yeah, I'm pretty friendly with it, what's up?" Troy asked looking confused. "Can you read this article for me?" D-Ray had the article of his auntie being killed and he wanted to see how Troy would react. Troy begins to read the article and stops mid-ways down and asked, "What the fuck you give me this for?" "I wanted your pussy ass to read it since you like to beat woman." Troy then stood up with intentions to swing on D-Ray. Troy was two pieced so hard in the face by D-Ray and four others; the licks were delivered fast like lightning. "Sit your punk ass back down bitch nigga. Was that how you hit on your girl pussy boy?" D-Ray grabbed a hold of Troy's neck with a death grip. Troy had foam seeping from the side of his mouth. The grip was so forceful, Troy could not mutter a sound. The crew then starts to beat him missionary style. This was a personal kick ass moment. Troy was leaking blood like running water. "I want you to answer my question punk. Is this how you beat on your girl yes or no?" D-Ray said with frustration. "NO. This must be a mis-understanding, I love my girl." Troy manages to say in between breaths and the pouring blood. They continued to beat him and dared him to scream out as they twisted his arms and legs. Troy was being choked. Troy continued to pass in and out of consciousness, his bottom lip was ripped off. Troy was placed underneath the weight bench, with his face in the downward position. The legs from the bench were pressed down forcefully against his bottom lip. The severe pressure of all the men caused his bottom lip to rip off and he was left there for half an hour until the medical infirmary staff decided to assist him. Troy was transported to the Columbia Medical Center. D-Ray managed to cuff his torn lip for collateral. The crew showered and changed clothes like nothing happened.

The staff of guards were already notified what was about to take place. Troy had no one on his team not even the staff. Majority of the staff were a group of women that stood ten toes down against domestic violence. The men staff all had daughters. They reflected on their mothers when men would come through with CDV cases on woman. Troy's stay at the county was about to be very un-pleasant.

CHAPTER 10
OOH I THINK I LIKE HIM

" Oh Shit!" Yahtia jumped up realizing she was late for class. She had slept through her alarm. Fooling around with Joy watching re-runs of *Living Single* and smoking all night had her in this position. Joy ass was knocked out. Her smarty pants ass had managed to get the best schedule out of all of them and was lucky she did not have to be in class all the time. Joy's professors allowed her to do most of her stuff remotely because it was mostly research papers. Yahtia rolled her eyes and slammed the door, hoping to disturb her friend's sleep. Karma had left campus with Ozias last night with her "Booty Bag". So, she knew her sister was probably in a dick coma and not attending class this morning either. Halfway to class Yahtia realized she needed to go to the library to print off her thesis paper. Yahtia was in such a rush trying to email her professor, walk, and get to the right place. Yahtia was in her own world and did not pay too much attention to the group of fine ass men that were in the main lobby of the library. Pushing past them, Yahtia reserved a printer and went about her business. Unbeknownst to her; Kross McDonald, a fine ass specimen of a man, set his sights on her as soon as she walked in.

Nodding in her direction he asked, "Hey bro, you see her. You know who that is?" "Nah, I be seeing her and her girls around. I think she with *Sisters of Elegance.*" Rodney, one of his frat brothers answered Kross. "OMG she is fine. All her bitches fine too." Another bruh said. "Special K got that look boys, he about to take her down." Rodney laughed. Kross responded laughing, "Don't worry about me fam. Let us finish business so I can conduct business. You fellas feel me." Even though Kross was laughing, he was serious as hell. The men managed to conclude their meeting without the continuous talk of sexy black women, which happened to be all their weaknesses. When the meeting was over, Kross left his friends and went in search of his "Future", as he called her. Kross knew she was his, he just did not know how he was going to make her understand that. Kross figured she would have to get past the "white boy thing", most women did. Kross was a walking conundrum. Kross McDonald stood 6'5, with red hair everywhere. A true Ginger. His father was a southern white man and his mom a biracial island girl. Even though you would not be able to look at him and tell, Kross was raised in Trinidad by his grandmother. If he got excited enough his accent would come out. His grandmother still lived in Trinidad. Kross left his grandmother's wing when he was seventeen and he came back to the states. Kross wanted to broaden his horizons and finish out his senior year with his father and his family. Kross had the best of both worlds and mastered the art of being a chameleon. Kross could be what and who he needed when he needed to be.

After sweet talking the librarian into giving him Yahtia's information, he set out to find his woman. Kross found her in the computer lab walking toward the printer. Yahtia seemed to be in a rush but was trying to be cute about it. "You are too cute to look so mean; your vibe screams SEXY." Kross said with an accent trying to come through. Yahtia's head snapped up. The accent caught her attention. Yahtia had a thing for a sweet smelling and a foreign accent man. Her eyes landed on the most gorgeous man she had ever seen. "Damn" she whispered to herself. Kross was literally a walking model. Trying to be cute, Yahtia nodded and gave him a small smile and turned quickly and continued her task. Yahtia was so nervous. She had seen this fine white boy at a few of the Greek functions on campus but never said anything to him. Now here he was starting a conversation with her. Before she could continue her inner dialog, Kross was in her personal space. Yahtia was mesmerized by his smell. "Damn he smelt delicious" she said to herself. "You are even more beautiful up close." Kross said with his deep voice. Yahtia crossed her legs because her pussy was jumping at the thought of his deliciousness. "Well, aren't you a sweetheart" she said sarcastically. "I know I look a mess today." Being the bold man that he was Kross pulled the hair tie from her head, releasing the messy bun that was on top of her head. Before she could react, Kross held up his hands in surrender. "No offense, I know you're not supposed to touch a black woman's hair. I like the messy look; I have a thing for hair. Since you my lady, I think you should wear your hair like this." Yahtia was shell shocked. She could not find words. The audacity of this white boy. This deliciously smelling, tall, handsome white boy. "Where are you from?", that was the only thing she could get to come from her lips. Kross smiled, showing his open face grill and his dimples. "Call me. Let me take you out and I will tell you all you want to know sexy lady." Kross grabbed a piece of paper from the printer and wrote on it. "That was my paper." Yahtia said. Snapping out of it. "Unless you needed ten copies, I think you will still have enough to turn in." Kross winked and began walking away, then froze. "Maybe you can give me your number too. That way I can make sure you get to and from class safely." Yahtia was done in that moment. Kross could have asked to fuck her right there in the library and she would have consented. Yahtia scribbled her number down on the same paper and tore it in half handing it to him. "You are too cute when you blush." Kross laid it on thick. Yahtia rolled her eyes. "Your friends are waiting for you." Gathering her things and making sure he saw the way her booty sat in her leggings. In the door of the computer lab, Rodney and a few of the frat brothers were gathered making kissing noises and laughing. "Ignore them love." Kross walked ahead of her to curse his friends out.

Yahtia walked as quickly as she could to the bathroom. She had to collect herself. She called Karma. "Bitch, get off Ozias's dick for a second I need you." Yahtia said as soon as the phone picked up. "Nice to hear from you to Tia." Ozias said into the phone. "Ughhh, y'all get on my nerves." Yahtia shot back, then Karma came on the line. "What's the issue? Where are you?" "Go to the bathroom sis Ozias can't hear this." Karma put her on hold and went to the bathroom, not before she kissed up on her man a little bit. Yahtia childishly made throw up faces in the mirror. "OK sis wassup. What is the emergency?" Karma finally came on the line. Yahtia quickly ran through what had just happened with Kross while she primped herself in the mirror. "Ok Sista, get you some then." Karma hyped. "Girl, I look a mess and he had me stuck like I was in middle school." Yahtia was pouting. "Girl, splash your face with water throw on some lip gloss, shake out those curls for the man. Fix ya titties, toot that ass up, and walk your best runway walk bitch. SHOW OUT!" Karma instructed her sister. After the quick pep talk, Yahtia exited the bathroom and half hoped that Kross and his boys had left. Nope they were still in the doorway. Putting on her sexy, Yahtia strutted to the exit. "Excuse me gentlemen." The men parted like the red sea, all eyes on her. Yahtia walked through like the boss she was, hypnotizing them with her hips. "Damn Special K if you manage to pull that we gonna call you King K." Kross dapped a frat brother smiling extra hard. "Hell, yeah she knows she fine too." Yahtia capitalized on this moment making Kross smile. "Does this number come with an armed escort to class? Or do I need to ask one of these other young men?" Yahtia smirked at the commotion she caused amongst the guys. Kross punched the mouthy one that kept licking his lips at her. "I'm coming baby", a blushing Kross came jogging up behind her taking her bag.

The two walked the yard to the Science and Humanities building. Which in Yahtia's opinion did not take nearly long enough. Yahtia was so comfortable with Kross, she was already in deep like with him. Once they got to her class, he kissed her cheek and walked away. Kross was a ball of nerves and was doing everything he could to make sure she was interested in him. He just hoped Yahtia could not tell that he was nervous around her. Now all he had to do was plan the perfect first date. Kross did not want to scare her off by coming on too strong. Kross knew he needed to make it good.

Yahtia found it difficult to concentrate the rest of the day. She kept thinking about Kross and the things they could get into. Yahtia texted Joy and Karma. "Y'all, I think I got me a man." With the laughing emoji behind it. Yahtia explained to them that he has been calling her his future and his lady since they met this morning. She left out the fact that Kross has been texting her randomly throughout the day. "Joy I need all of his info. Get on your Nancy Drew shit and let me know wassup before I get too excited." Yahtia texted her sisters. Joy did not disappoint either. "Kross McDonald, born and raised in Trinidad with his maternal grandmother, Madeline McDonald, who is wealthy as can be. When he left Trinidad, he then moved to Alabama and lived with his father Kristoph McDonald. His mother was biracial herself and died in a car accident when he was eight. Member of *Zeta Gamma*, better known as *Brothers of Excellence*. Line name Special K. Sis that MuthaFucka is FINE!". Joy sent back. They all agreed that he was indeed fine as fuck, and Yahtia should give him a shot. On paper he was very intriguing and Yahtia could not lie she was wanting to know more about him. Yahtia knew she heard an accent when he was talking to her earlier. On her way back to the dorms, her phone rings. Answering without looking at the caller ID, "Talk to me, make it quick". "Damn it's like that." Kross' sexy voice came through the line. Yahtia just smiled into the phone like an idiot.   After a few seconds Kross spoke, "I ain't trying to take up all your time." Kross quickly added "Yet". Like she would not catch it. "I would like to take you out tonight. Movies in the park tonight. I have something special planned and even though we won't be secluded it will still be private." Yahtia agreed and said her goodbyes. Now to figure out what to wear she began to think out loud.

Karma was at the room cleaning up when Yahtia walked in, "Sis, I got a date." Yahtia said panicking. It had been a while since Tia had gone on a real date. Yahtia had her dudes she would kick it with but never anything serious. Everyone feared her brother and Ozias, so niggas only looked at not touch. Yahtia told Karma and Joy all about Kross and their date night. Yahtia settled for a long black maxi dress with spaghetti straps and pockets. It was that super soft cotton it hugs her curves but not too much. "It's giving the Nerdy Hoe look." Joy laughed as she bounced her eyebrows. "Kross said he likes my natural hair so I'm thinking, twist out." Yahtia said unsure. "Use this" Joy said handing her a bottle of conditioner. It was her own mixture of stuff for natural hair. "It will help make your curls pop and not dry out while you are getting nasty in the park." Joy dodged another swat that came from Yahtia. While Yahtia was in the shower, the other girls got her shoes and accessories together. Adreama knocked on the door then walked in. Putting her bag down. Adreama asked. "What are y'all up to?" "Nothing major, just getting Tia ready for her hot date tonight." Joy answered. "OOOOUUUUU! We got action." Adreama said humping the air and passing a blunt she had just lit. "Who's the guy?". "Kross McDonald." Karma started. "Bitch I know you fucking lying." Adreama was laughing so hard she had tears in her eyes. A towel wrapped Yahtia was looking at her with the side eye. "What's so damn funny." Realizing the girls were looking at her suspect, Dreama calmed down. "No, it's Karma for real. Honey listen, Jherika has been chasing his fine ass since she got here. Tonera tried but ended up having a hoe moment with a few of his frat brothers. They are gonna be pissed when they find out." Adreama explained. Everyone started laughing and thinking of the diverse ways to torture the bitch squad with this information. While they were getting Yahtia dressed, the RA came to the room. She delivered a single flower, and black rose with a beaded necklace. The note was from Kross and explained that it was his necklace and she needed to wear it so she would be escorted to their section. Snatching the note, "Bitch you didn't tell me he was taking you to 'Flex and Chill in the Park'. It is the biggest event hosted by the *Bearded Brothas*." Adreama explained. "They NEVERRRRR bring dates, they are always flirting and carrying on with any and everyone. So, if Kross of all men is showing you off, and lowkey branding you with his charm, then you are SPECIAL. Hands down that nigga nose open for you." Yahtia was all smiles. Yahtia did not say anything; she was on ten with excitement. What Dreama just said made her feel mushy inside. The girls decided they were going to go play chaperone and get some footage just to piss Jherika and Tonera off.

They got to the gate and two men escorted Yahtia to the hill. Kross had gotten an inflatable pool and filled it with blankets and pillows. In the middle was a basket and on top of the basket was another note with six roses. "Sit down and enjoy sexy lady. I will get to you as soon as possible. If you are nice to me, you can have the rest of the flowers." Kross signed the card with his initials. Yahtia took a seat and looked through the basket while taking pictures of everything. Yahtia had to keep the girls up to date on what was happening. She started eating some cookies and drinking a soda that Kross provided in the basket. Kross joined her twenty minutes later apologizing for being late. "What's playing first?" Yahtia asked. Kross took his shoes off and climbed in the pool getting comfortable behind her. "The Goonies" Kross said. They snacked and watched the movie in silence for a while. Yahtia let him hold her and did not protest when he wrapped a blanket around them. All eyes were glued to them; the hate was real. They looked like a hot and spicy seasoned couple. Yahtia figured out early that Kross was petty and liked to show off. They texted each other when they thought people were eavesdropping. Kross made it look like he was kissing and feeling on her while Yahtia laughed at the girls rolling their eyes at them. An hour into the movie the two were in their own world. They were so deep in conversation; they did not even notice when the next movie began to play. Yahtia's phone interrupted the flow of things; it was a picture curtesy of Joy and her detective work. Joy had taken pictures of them hugged up and they were dope as hell. "Look at us, all cute and shit" Kross said looking over her shoulder. "I know right. Look like we belong together." Kross looked Yahtia in her eyes, "Because we do", accent thick. Yahtia had to cross her legs extra tight because his accent made her pussy rumble. The rest of the night went by beautifully; although Yahtia was ready to let her inner freak out, but she decided to play the good girl role for now.

CHAPTER 11
YOUR NOT MY MAMA

After getting several notices from the alarm company about an intruder on her property, Karma decided to take a trip home. Karma had been putting it off because it was just Molly worthless ass. Even though she knew Molly had no way of getting into the house, Karma decided to evaluate things for herself and figure out what the fuck Molly could possibly want at her house. Joy and Yahtia decided to ride along with her. They said they were going for moral support. "Bullshit. You trying to drop in on Craig." Karma laughed while calling Joy out. "Like you not finna take a ride on Big O." Joy shot back. The whole time Yahtia was in her own world texting Kross. They had been heavy since day one and she was feeling him. "Look at this bitch." Joy motioned to the back seat. Yahtia was still oblivious to her sisters looking at her. "OH, MY GAWWDD!" Karma screamed and swerved the car really hard. "What the fuck what happened?" Yahtia was all alert now. Karma and Joy were crying laughing, "If you in love bitch say that" They laughed. "Yall hoes play too much." Yahtia could not help the grin on her face. Yahtia was not sure if it was love but it was something and she liked it. The girls laughed and sang the entire trip. Planning a trip to the mall before heading back to campus. "I need to go to Victoria's Secret; they are having a sale." Yahtia stated. "Suuurree they are" Joy said. Karma was laughing. "Joy like you wasn't ordering shit from Fendi last week just for Craig ass." "Oh, you mean like the lime green set you got for Ozias." "Touché. Bitch. Touché" They were all still laughing when they turned into Karma's driveway.

"Look at this nasty bitch" Karma said in pure disgust. There behind the tree in the front yard was a dirty Molly Boston taking a shit. "EWWWW! That is just nasty." Joy said following behind Yahtia. "Sis we headed to the crib. Handle your business and holla if you need me.", Yahtia said throwing up the duces. "Yeah", was Karma's only reply as she walked towards her front door. Purposefully trying not to make eye contact. Karma was not sure how she was going to handle this, but it was embarrassing to say the least. Before Karma could get five good steps in, Molly rushed her. "OMG Karmell look at you. I'm so glad to see you baby girl." "Please tell me you just didn't take a fucking dump in my damn yard?" Karma was livid. Molly had the sense to look slightly ashamed. "I could not get in apparently the locks have been changed. I could not hold it anymore; I will clean it up." Molly said with a shrug. "Anyway, I have been around here trying to catch you so I can shower and fix myself up." Taking a step back because Molly was in her personal space and smelled like hot garbage and piss. "First and foremost, my name is Karma NOT Karmell. You will see that for yourself very soon. Secondly, nothing in this house belongs to you or Karmelo." Karma turned to walk into the house; she could not stand to be around Molly. All the old feelings of abandonment and torment came rushing back. Molly reached out grabbing ahold of Karma's arm. "Baby please, I'm begging, do not treat me this way. I am still your mother." "Mother, bitch you have never been a mother you lost that title years ago." Karma snatched her arm away with the look of disgust. "You are pathetic, Molly Boston. I never mattered to you; you caused me much pain and embarrassment. When you and that sick husband of yours abandoned this house that was a good judgment call. You and Karmelo left me with no warning. Everything happens for a reason because I now have a wonder family that loves and understands me. Neither one of you cunts have rights to me or this house. The house was put in my name and I'm the deed holder now." Karma said with much confidence. "Karmell, I mean Karma. Please I have not slept in days. I am in desperate need of a shower. At least give me that. You owe me; I did birth your ass." Molly begged. "Girl Fuck you. I do not owe you shit. Go find your scamming ass husband and leave me the fuck alone. Now get your shit and get the hell away from me." Karma slammed the door in Molly's face. Molly stood on the porch crying crocodile tears and making all the unnecessary noise she could to get Karma's attention. "Girl what do you want?" Karma rolled her eyes walking past Molly to her car to get her things. Molly gave the saddest story about how she no longer had a job, and how she was so hungry. Molly explained she had not eaten in days. All Karma could think about were the nights she spent alone trying to fend for herself. Watching Molly and Karmelo eat steak dinners and crab, lobster and shrimp. Molly and Karmelo would even go out eat without her. Karma became pissed all over again. Karma did not realize it, but her eyes became watery. Karma reached into the car and pulled out a subway bag. She stuffed her cookie in her mouth and pulled out her untouched sub. Molly's face lit up like a kid at Christmas. Molly started drooling at the sight of the meal. Karma unwrapped the footlong sub. Molly subconsciously licked her lips. "Oh, thank you sweetie. I am so hungry." Karma smirked while swallowing her cookie. Karma pulled all the meat, cheese and veggies from the sandwich and wrapped it in the plastic bag. She threw the bread right next to the pile of shit on the ground. "Have a shit sandwich. That is more than you ever gave me. Now fuck off before I treat you like a bitch on the street. OH, damn, you are on the street. Have a good day mother dear." Karma walked next door to join Tia and Joy, dismissing Molly for good.

Karma walked in greeting everyone and hugging Mama T and Juan, her real parents in her eyes. Karma mushed Craig like a sister would. "Where's O?" "Dang sis you don't love me no more?" Craig teased, hugging Karma. Mama T was never one to bite her tongue. "What the fuck did Molly want?" Karma told them how Molly had been coming around trying to get into the house. Karma gave them an ear full about the encounter that just took place. Mama T just shook her head. "I said that bitch would need you one day. That is one stupid ass lady." Juan just rubbed his wife. Juan knew how Toyah got about the Boston's. "Toyah calm down baby, Karma handled it." The girls gave them an update on the college life leaving out most of the details. Who wants to tell their parents about how often they were getting dick? "Joy, what about you?" Mama T caught Joy off guard. "Ma'am" "You one of my kids too. So, let me see those grades.

How is life for you? I will beat a bitch about my kids. I will also beat my kids for acting like lil bitches." Toyah said with a straight face. Joy was stunned but gave her an update as well. Karma and Yahtia were trying hard to control their giggles. After seeing all the grades and talking a little longer with the kids, Mama T announced that she and Juan were going on a play date. Her announcement caused them all to make faces and laugh. "Get it mama." Yahtia shook her head at her mom and dad. "You ready chic?" Karma said grabbing her keys and Yahtia followed close behind, while Joy and Craig got comfortable for their "Netflix and chill" session.

The two girls walked into the mall like they owned the place, going about their usual routine. First stopping at Macy's and then moving on to Victoria's Secret. While looking through the sale tables, Yahtia spoke up. "Sis. I think Kross is it for me." "It! Like as in the one? Forever?" Yahtia nodded her head with a grin. "You think white boy gotta strong back? What about the dick sis? You know what they say about white boys." Karma joked holding up a cute leopard print nightgown. "If his dick is small, I'm sure he will more than make up for it with them sexy ass lips of his. Hell, I can nut off his charm and looks alone." Yahtia stated. "White boy is easy to look at that's for damn sure." Karma looked up just in time to see Yahtia texting, undoubtedly Kross. "Damn, King Kross got that pussy gushing all ready. He ain't even smelt it yet." Karma laughed loudly while rolling her eyes at her sister. "Well let's get you super sexy so you can blow white boy mind." The two managed to hit up ten stores in less than an hour. Now they were sitting in the food court discussing ways for Yahtia to make it clear that she was trying to get fucked. Yahtia had to keep it cute without coming right out and saying it. Sucking her teeth, "We gotta go to footlocker. Ozias wants a hoodie." Karma said. "Don't do O like that. You spoil his ass." "Correction, he spoils me. I simply match his energy", They joked. Walking into Foot Locker. "Dolls!" Davie's preppie extra gay voice could be heard well before he came bouncing over. According to him, he was a preppie black girl trapped in a cute white boy's body. Davie absolutely adored Karma and Yahtia. "Oh, I have missed you two around here. How is college life? Any cute men", Davie asked sounded just like one of the girls. Yahtia stepped over to the side, looking at the newly released sneakers. "Hello college girl."

Yahtia knew that voice, it was one she would never forget. It was none other than Rhonda 'Hershey' Humphrey. Turning around with a mean mug so lethal even Hershey stepped back a little. "Don't fucking come near me perv." Yahtia said louder than she meant too but did not give a fuck. Putting both hands up but still laughing. "Don't forget where you came from lil lady. You look good. Smell even better." Hershey took a dramatic deep sniff. "Let's go get reacquainted". Yahtia flipped her the middle finger and began to walk off. Bold bitch that she was Hershey grabbed Yahtia's shirt. Karma slapped her hand hard causing her to let it go. Davie was standing behind Karma like he was about that life. "Damn this my lucky day. I got both my chocolate babies in my presence. Let's go have some real girl time.", Hershey licked her lips seductively. "You are a whole rapist out here fucking up people's lives and shit." Yahtia said gagging at the idea of Hershey touching her again. "Don't nobody want your ugly bumpy, lumpy, cellulite bad body wanna to be man ass. Get a fucking life while you can because you are on borrowed time. Believe that shit." Karma said getting into Hershey face. Recovering quickly from the embarrassment. "I never raped nobody. Any female I touched wanted it. They gave me the pussy with ease. I am a fly ass nigga with mad bitches. You remember how I was digging in your guts. I had you begging and slobbing. OOOH daddy don't stop." Hershey gyrated her hips in the air while licking her ashy ass lips. Having had enough, Yahtia pulled out her Mace and unloaded it into Hershey's face. Karma jumped in raining blows from everywhere. Davie lil cute self even got in on the action throwing his baby hits. Davie's involvement saved Hershey from getting stomped out completely. The girls were so busy laughing at Davie. When security showed up, Davie went into manager mode. Explaining that Hershey was feeling on the customers and being sexually inappropriate. "So, these two were acting in self-defense?", the officer asked. After taking statements, Hershey was handcuffed and escorted out of the store. The girls said their goodbyes after making their final purchases they left the mall. "That bitch is dead." Yahtia texted Joy in all caps for emphasis. Karma was already calling Joy allowing it to play through the car speakers.

Joy answered on the fourth ring. "What's good?". Karma wasted no time. "Get Craig dick out your mouth for a second, Sherlock Holmes, we need your skills." "Is it a Red mission? Tia text me saying its Red." Joy asked. "Nahhh, her as is pink" Karma said. When she realized the girls were waiting for an explanation, Karma spoke. "There are some things worse than death. The bitch will wish she were dead, she will be forced to live in her own personal hell. Pink!" Karma explained. "Her name is Rhonda Humphrey. Goes by Hershey." Before having to say much else, Joy spoke up. "Yeah, I already started her profile after we had our last heart to heart. This is 'Operation HERO'. Check your tablets I sent all the information to you." When the girls acknowledged they received the details, Joy dismissed them. "Take your time coming back y'all interrupted our movie." "Yeah right, finish getting dicked down. We have another stop to make before we come your way." Karma said laughing.

Karma pulled up at Ivy's office, she had called ahead letting her know she was home and needed a session. Ivy was more than excited to see her favorite client. "I'll be back in a few sis." Karma exited the car. Karma had a lot of things she needed to talk out with Ivy. "You good love take your time and tell Ivy I said hello." Yahtia turned on her favorite playlist deciding she was going to cake on the phone with Kross. Having a seat in the lobby, Karma could not help but think about how far she had come. Ivy had become a strong part of her support system. Constantly checking on her and sending her encouraging words and daily inspirational quotes. Karma never told anyone how those messages got her through a lot of days giving her the strength to keep moving forward. The words hypnotize her mind keeping her from relapsing to that dark place of misery. Ivy opened her office door greeting Karma with open arms. "Ok Ms. girl. You are cute, cute." Ivy said. Karma did a twirl. "I mean it. You are wearing happy well, but I can tell something is bothering you so what's up." Karma was always amazed by how Ivy could read her. "We had a conversation a while back about if I ever decided to press rape charges on Hershey that you could help me get everything I needed. Is that offer still good?" Looking at her questioningly. Ivy said, "Yes ma'am I am still here to help you anyway I can." Ivy started typing away at her computer. "Do you need help filing charges or do you just need the paperwork showing that charges have been filed?" Karma gave Ivy the meat and potatoes of the situation adding Yahtia's story and the incident from the mall. "So, you see this bitch gotta pay. Excuse my language." "I agree. You will have everything you need. Just promise me you will be careful. In order to protect you I won't ask too many questions just promise me you will be smart." Karma agreed and gave Ivy a hug. Before Karma left the parking lot, Ivy emailed her the documents that she would need to start her journey to 'Karmalize' Hershey.

While riding back to campus, Yahtia and Karma discussed the hit lists. The focus was on how everyone should be handled. Joy was too busy getting all the details about 'Operation HERO' figured out. "I put Purple Pinky on the next assignment, Operation Shit Storm", Yahtia informed Karma. Yahtia explained that she had mixed a super laxative in chemistry class. Not only will it make her shit uncontrollably until her stomach is empty but anything she tries to eat, or drink will automatically come back up. "This is going to be a magical shit show". They all laughed. "Purple Pinky has to get her to take all of the doses and record the aftermath. Since Uvoka has been depressed about that video being leaked getting her to cooperate will not be hard." Yahtia explained.

Uvoka answered her door with much attitude. She wanted to know who the hell was knocking at her door like she wanted company. When Uvoka saw it was Purple Pinky, she opened the door for her to enter. "What the hell do you want?" "Girl I came to check on you, making sure you alright. Your ass been missing in action lately. I wanted to get you out the house and deliver you from this isolation you have committed yourself to." Uvoka softened a little bit. Right now, Uvoka really needed a friend, she was going crazy. Uvoka could not take being bullied and picked on. Uvoka almost felt bad for the torment she did to others, but not enough to apologize or make amends. "I came with a party pack", Pinky held up the bag. Uvoka tore into the weed brownies and punch, while Pinky lit up a blunt. "Get dressed we are going bowling." "I don't want to be seen. I am tired of people talking shit about my sexcapades." Uvoka said clearly irritated and high. "Girl, fuck who ever got laughs and jokes; own your shit stand tall about it. You like what you like. You did not break no damn law. How you buss it open and drain your rabbit is your prerogative. Besides it's the middle of the week nobody hangs out especially at the bowling alley. We can go to the one on the other side of town so even if people are there you won't know them." After a few minutes Uvoka agreed. Uvoka grabbed another brownie then got up to get dressed. Purple Pinky quickly sent Karma and the crew a text letting them know how things were going. Uvoka retuned with a small square left from the brownie munching away. "Let's Go!", Uvoka was excited for the first time since the ordeal happened. "I feel like tonight things will start to get better for me." Uvoka said in the car. "Sure, it is.", Purple Pinky said while turning the music up praying that the laxative laced brownies do not kick in inside her car.

Purple Pinky pulled into the Bowleramma, the bowling alley across town away from campus. Purple Pinky knew a girl that worked there so she made sure all the bathroom stalls were locked, men and women's bathroom. Now all Purple Pinky had to do was make sure she got the main event recorded. Purple Pinky paid the worker fifty dollars to give her the security footage when this was all said and done. The show started not long after they arrived. While the two were lacing up their shoes, Uvoka farted. "Ooops my bad." "Better out than in", Purple Pinky said holding her nose and activating the cameras. Uvoka went first. STRIKE. "Imma beast at bowling", Uvoka boasted. Purple Pinky just threw the ball because Uvoka had the section lit. Uvoka grabbed the ball and paused. "I need some water." Uvoka said guzzling the water bottle down. Uvoka was midway through her bowl and her ass exploded. Shit went up her back and down her legs. Uvoka stood straight up and started doing the duck walk to the bathroom. Trying to clamp her butt cheeks together and hold it in. No luck the shit kept coming. "Oh my god! Oh my god!" was all she would say while using her hands to try and hide. Uvoka made it to the bathroom and another one ripped loose. Realizing the stalls were locked, she then ran to the men's restroom. That one was locked as well. Uvoka screamed so loud as she went running back toward the women's bathroom. Uvoka hit the floor like a sack of potatoes. Uvoka was in the fetal position as liquid shit shot from her ass. Her leggings were brown instead of black. Her socks and shoes were covered. Uvoka crawled to the bathroom door and just laid there crying. A puddle began to form underneath her.

Uvoka made her way up and walked away with her head hung low. She heard the laughs and saw the cameras. There was nothing she could do. Uvoka continued to fart uncontrollably while she did the dookie shuffle out of the bowling alley. Uvoka had to walk back to campus because she was dripping in shit. She sat down at a bus stop to rest, painful gas still coming from her ass. "Here put these on." A woman said to her. Uvoka looked at the dirty sweatpants then back at the woman. "Don't look like that little girl, you are literally full of shit." Uvoka rolled her eyes and took the pants she was about to slide them on over her shitty leggings. The lady said, "No you need to take them leggings off nobody will notice. You still stink but, hell so do I. At least they will let you ride the bus now. I'm Molly by the way." Holding out her hand. Just then the bus pulled up. "I'm Uvoka. Thank you." As soon as Uvoka got on the bus an old lady sitting in the front shouts out, "GAWD DAMN YOU STANK". Other passengers begin to hold their nose while the bus driver opens the sunroof for air. Tears continued to stream down her face. Uvoka prayed that she made it back to her room without anyone else seeing her or have another shit explosion. For the second time in less than a month Uvoka had gone viral, infamously. By midnight she was the source of several social media memes and had made it on 'The Shade Room'. By the end of the night, Uvoka was humiliated beyond repair. Her face was on the shit emoji and being shared all over social media as "A shitty situation". Uvoka life was falling apart, and it was nothing she could do about it. Creeping Karma at its best.

CHAPTER 12
FIRST IMPRESSIONS

Troy was stable enough to be release from the hospital. His ass whooping was going down in history as the worst to ever take place in the county jail. It took two whole days of fluids before Troy was shipped back to county jail and was placed in the infirmary for further observations. Troy could not speak. His tongue was still swollen, and his bottom lip was missing. Where his plump lip used to be was now 110 stitches and a few staples. Troy would never be able to fully close his mouth again. He was officially deformed and all around jacked up. Troy will scare children for the rest of his life. Mumbling Troy attempted to communicate with the nurse and overheard the nurse tell the CO, "I will be releasing the prisoner in seventy-two hours. He will be going back to gen-pop." Troy did not want to go back to his cell; he knew he was in trouble. D-Ray and his crew were bound to have him a welcome back party, but Troy wanted no parts of it. Tory continued to stall; he felt nervous and had a severe case of the bubble guts.

Craig sent Ozias a message about the girls. He was feeling some kind of way, and suspicious of their activities. "I think they are up to something", said Craig. "What makes you say that bro." Craig explained everything he had overheard Karma and Joy talking about over the weekend. "Well, you know we're their muscle so whatever this 'HERO' business is we down with them". Ozias grabbed his keys, he always down to take a ride. "Let's go see what the hell they got going on." Ozias said sounding curious. Pulling into the parking lot, Craig texted Yahtia. "Get the girls and meet me and Ozias in the gazebo. We need to talk." Yahtia sent the thumbs up emoji and collected the girls. Joy was the first one to come down with Yahtia and Karma a few seconds behind her. Karma immediately walked into Ozias' open arms and kissed him. "Hey bae, what brings y'all this way?" Karma asked. Craig released Joy's ass and spoke. "I kinda overheard you and Joy's conversation that week when you came home. I do not know what operation HERO is. What I do know is, Ozias and I are in on the move. Craig held up his hand to hush the girls before they could protest. "This is not up for debate. We are coming or y'all not going. It's that simple." "Damn baby that was sexy. I love it when you talk business like that." Joy said rubbing on Craig like a crazed sex kitten. "Girl, sit cho ass down." Yahtia rolled her eyes at Joy. Karma sucked her teeth looking from Craig to Ozias and back to Craig. "Ok, since you put it like that big bro let me fill you in on Operation HERO." Karma said. Taking the lead Karma spoke first. "Operation HERO is a mission designed to serve payback to a bitch who deserves much worse." Surprisingly, the guys were all for the payback. The five of them managed to merge all their ideas into one solid plan. Hero was the name of a major sex trafficker from Pakistan. He worked in the United States as a collector. The guys did not feel comfortable letting the girls talk to or meet with Hero. So, they did that part themselves. They had no clue what was going to take place, but they were down to play their part in the ordeal. The girls left to get ready for class while the guys went to meet with Hero. The information was mapped out for Hero to collect his next worker. Before anything Joy and Karma had to hunch on their men. They were freaky like that, just could not get enough. When they all went their separate ways, they agreed to meet at the pizza warehouse at night fall.

Hero was a calm, cool individual and a straightforward businessman. Hero had his hands in everything legal and illegal. If it had a price, he could get whatever direct no middleman. Hero did not talk much just made business moves. The guys appreciated that about him. They delivered the sealed package from Joy using the code word; business flowed smooth that way. The guys met up with the girls who were at the warehouse dressed in all black. Yahtia was about to put a light to the end of her blunt when a black van with blacked out windows came pulling up. Hero jumped out and opened the sliding door and forcefully grabbed a terrified Hershey from the van. She was shackled and gagged face, wet with tears. For the first time in her life, Hershey felt real fear. Karma walked up, "Hey friend, you seemed to have gotten yourself into some trouble. This here, pointing at Hero, is a bounty hunter. He is supposed to take you to the police station for the rape and assault against Yahtia and I." Hershey cried harder. Her sobs were noticeably clear even through the gag. Karma pulled out the paperwork pushing it into Hershey's face. "You are facing 2 counts of brutal rape and assault each worth a maximum sentence of 30 years to life." Hershey's eyes bugged in her head. "Calm down. Hero is our friend. I personally would hate to see a fellow black woman go to jail even if what you did was unspeakably fucked up. So, we paid him. You have a choice. You can go to the police station and face the judge for your crimes, or you can go with Hero."

Hershey just shook her head NO. "Tyren and Terrell have written statements and provided the video of you raping me.", Yahtia interjected. "Yeah, and all your little bitch ass accomplices that were with you when you attacked me, have written statements as well." Karma followed up. "We even have other victims and several character witnesses that have come forward and are willing to testify on our behalf. You going to jail bitch. IF YOU STAY." Karma stressed that last part out. "Or you can go with our Friend Hero and start a new life away from here and get the fuck away from me and mine. The choice is yours, but you must decide now. You have thirty seconds." Karma explained. "Tic Toc Bitch. Kick your shoes off and you will be escorted back to the van and your new life begins. Stay and the sheriff will be picking you up. Makes no difference to me.", Yahtia said angrily. Hershey began to beg and plead for her life through the gag and duct tape, but her cries fell on deaf ears. The girls gave no fucks and had zero remorse for what they were doing. It was retribution for what was done to them. It was KARMA! "10-9-8-7-6-5-4-3-2" Yahtia and Karma counted down loudly while the others just looked on. Hershey kicked off her shoes at the last second. Before she could take her next breath, Hero placed a bag over her head and snatched her up tossing her back into the van. Just like that Rhonda 'Hershey' Humphrey was gone. Hero nodded as he pulled off. "I will send the arrival confirmation within the next 24-36 hours. Nice doing business my friends." Hero tossed an envelope out the window.

Picking up the envelope and opening it, Craig asked, "What the fuck just happened?" "That was some real-life mob shit." Ozias cosigned looking over Craig's shoulder at the crispy blue face hundred-dollar bills. "This is ten thousand dollars." Ozias whistled looking around at the girls waiting for an explanation. Snatching the envelope and fingering the money. "The less you know the better off you will be. Please know and understand that everything was organized and arranged by your girl." Yahtia snapped, nodding toward Joy. Joy winked and blew him a kiss walking up to look at the note and money. "So, walk lightly bro.", Karma laughed at the stuck face Craig displayed. Craig looks scared and turned on at the same time. In all honesty he just wanted to fuck the shit out of Joy right there on the spot. Joy displaying boss moves made Craig's dick hard as a brick.

"Since we done here, get me back to the dorm. I need to get ready for my date". Yahtia walked towards the car ready to see Kross. "What damn date?" Craig asked. His sister going on a date was enough to soften his erection instantly.

Yahtia could have slapped herself for letting that piece of information out. "You hear me talking to you Tia. What fucking date you got?" Craig went after his sister. Everyone else made their way slowly to the car as they watched the siblings go at it. "MY DATE! With MY MAN! Minding MY business! Anything else." Yahtia shot back at him. Yahtia knew Craig would flip out when he found out but damn, she was grown this was a bit ridiculous. "MAN!". Craig and Ozias said at the same time. Karma instantly hushed Ozias telling him to stay out of it. "Why the fuck I'm just now hearing about a damn man. Why I ain't met this nigga?" Craig started questioning his kid sister. "Nigga you did not ask my permission to play in Joy's pussy so why I gotta ask your permission to go on a date. You act like I am getting married. Play fair bro Damn! I am grown you know", Yahtia screamed. Yahtia had started crying but it was solely out of anger. Craig softened his face a little, but his voice was still angry. "I am the big brother, and you are my little sister. I am here to protect you. It's just the way it works. You have to tell me about any man you think you finna be fucking on." Yahtia rolled her eyes and got in the car. There was absolutely no arguing with him. Yahtia listened to all his bullshit back to campus. Craig did not spare Karma or Joy either; he was in full big brother mode. "You two knew this whole time that Yahtia had a man." Craig went in using air quote for the word man. "Y'all did not tell me shit. Joy you talk to me every day and ain't think to tell me my sister was being fast." "Ummm, first check your tone. Secondly, it was not my business to tell. I do not tell her every time you come see me, and every time we go out. So, no need to tell you about her comings and goings. Yahtia is grown and actually very responsible." Joy said. "Fuck all that y'all should have told me. Yahtia around here getting distracted by dick and y'all letting it happen." Karma came to her sister's rescue. Karma could see Yahtia getting ready to spaz and the situation was not that serious. "Craig, don't you think you are being dramatic. Tia got a 4.2 GPA she is already set to graduate with a dual degree. The three of us has the least number of distractions, dick or otherwise going on. Let the damn girl breath. We are not kids anymore." Karma said as delicate as possible. Craig had to sit back as the words hit him. He was being hard on her, but this was his sister. Yahtia had already been through enough shit that Craig was unable to protect her from. "Fine, but you ain't going nowhere until I meet this nigga." Yahtia just rolled her eyes and exited the car. "He ain't a nigga neither." Yahtia slammed the door and walked towards the dorm.

Stuck in the moment, Craig shook his head as realization hit him. "So, sis got herself a white boy?" Craig asked to no one in particular. "By George I think he's got it!", Karma laughed and walked towards Gibson Hall behind Tia. "O, do you hear this shit, Hell nah. Ain't no fucking way." They heard Craig say as he and Ozias walked to the gazebo.

Yahtia was taking her sweet time hoping that Craig would just go home. Every time she tried to get him to leave, they got into another argument. "Sis just get it over with you know him and O not leaving the gazebo until they meet Kross. So, get cute and introduce your white island boy to the bros,", Karma said. Even though Karma was being serious, she laughed trying to lighten the mood. "UUUUGGHH", was all she said as the girls helped her get dressed. By the time they were done beautifying Yahtia she was all smiles. "Damn girl Kross just might be ready to marry your ass you keep showing up like this." Joy joked. Yahtia continued to smile when Kross sent her a message saying he was outside and needed to be buzzed in. Carefully walking down, the stairs in her four and a half inch booties Yahtia buzzed him in.

Kross was dressed to impress. He was wearing a big face polo button up shirt with the sleeves rolled up to his elbows. His jeans were fitted but did not give off the tight leggings look. Polo boots fresh out the box and his hair was freshly done in a man bun. Yahtia admired her gorgeous man eye fucking him as she walked up to him taking the flowers, he handed her. Yahtia's mood instantly changed when she saw her brothers approaching. Noticing her facial expressions, Kross turned around and saw two men approaching them. "OMG! They are so fucking embarrassing." Yahtia groaned to herself. "Kross I would like you to meet my brothers." Yahtia said when they were still a few feet away. "I would love to meet them love", Kross said truly excited. Kross had heard her talk about her family and knew how close she was with her brother and his best friend.   "Yo! Tia. Wassup sis." Craig yelled out being extra hood and mean mugging Kross. Craig knew he was overreacting, but Yahtia was his tender spot. Craig knew how guys acted with a delicate woman. So, in his mind he was justified. "Kross these are my brothers, Craig and Ozias.", turning slightly and pointing with her hands. "Brothers, this is Kross McDonald. My boyfriend." Kross noticed the tension and hostility coming from her brothers. Kross extended his hand for a handshake. After a few seconds Ozias gripped it "Nice to meet you man. What year are you?" Ozias asked making small talk while the two siblings simply glared at each other. Having a silent battle of wills. After brief conversation Kross spoke, "Hey baby, let me speak with your brother right quick. Go put the flowers in some water. I will be ready to go when you get back."

Ozias grabbed Tia's arm and escorted her back into the building. Ozias was going to feel on his girl's booty one more time for the road. As soon as they were gone Kross spoke, "Hey man, I get it. I am a big brother myself. I have two younger sisters and I am equally as protective. I am a junior. My major is Biology with a concentration in Botany. I am extremely good at growing things. My father is a red headed southern gentleman from Georgia and my mother's a fair skinned black beauty from Trinidad. I was raised in Trinidad by my lovely grandmother. I travel between there and the States all the time to manage my properties and visit my grandmother." Kross paused to see if Craig truly heard what he was throwing at him. Kross had done his homework on Craig and Ozias, and he had a proposition for them but did not want to be obvious with it. "Your sister is a great woman and I respect her. We have been dating for a while, but I have not done more than kiss her. All I want to do is make money so my kids will be straight and hopefully me and your sister can retire early back to Trinidad with our businesses. I love your sister. Our connection was instant almost magical." Craig gave Kross a side eye at his last comment. "No not in a sexual way bro, but her conversation is amazing Yahtia has a great business mind. We have a lot of the same goals and I think we can achieve them and more together." Craig nodded, he continued to stare at Kross but softened a little bit. "So, you're not white-white you seasoned white?" Kross laughed at this description. "Yeah, something like that bredren.", Kross said letting his accent slip out. "I'm an Island white boy who likes to grow things with land and connections to the Caribbean.", Craig listened. Kross had threw a line of bait at Craig. Craig nodding his head during Kross tutorial giving confirmation he had his attention.

Craig and Kross seemed like two best friends by the time Yahtia came back down with Ozias in tow. "What the fuck I miss?", Yahtia asked as she watched Craig and Kross give each other a manly hug. "Nothing baby. You ready to go?" "Sis this one is a keeper. You did good." Craig said as he and O walked to their car. "Oh, Island boy, even though you good people. I will still fuck you up about that one.", pointing to his sister. "So, hands off, keep it PG 13, make her smile, and no distractions in her career and we good." Craig started his car smiling like a crack head who found the dope man's stash. Craig began telling Ozias about the connection he was just handed by Kross. Kross was using his family's plantation in Trinidad to grow sugar cane and grade A marijuana. The sugar cane was made into rum and was the families legit business. The marijuana was the family's dirty business but with it becoming legal in the states, Kross was going to be marketing it soon. Kross was no fool he knew he needed to put it on the street before it could be regulated by the government. Then it will be sold for profit in one of the dispensaries which he planned to open with Yahtia. "Bro really got a whole twenty-year plan for him, and Tia and it includes lots of dollar signs and smile for everyone." Craig hyped while firing up his blunt that was left in the ash tray. Ozias was down as usual and thoroughly impressed. "Guess we got a white boy coming to Christmas?" Ozias said lighting his blunt to put in rotation. "Bro roll this." Pulling out the sample pack Kross gave him. Ozias took a big whiff and coughed, "DAYUUMM! If this the shit Kross got, then I know we about to make hella cash." "Exactly. Like I said. Big money and big smiles for everyone". The two hashed out their plan to put this new product on the streets. Brand name: *'Island Blend'.*

In the car the conversation flowed effortlessly between Kross and Yahtia. Yahtia had asked him a second time about his conversation with Craig. Being the straightforward alpha male, his reply was, "Just two big brothers talking about their interests and how to best protect and provide for what they love." His answer or his cologne or maybe both had Yahtia ready to ride his dick right there in the car. Shaking the thought from her head for the moment she just nodded and smiled. Yahtia sent a quick text to Karma and Joy letting them know what Kross had told her and that she was ready to be his "Thotiana". "Mrs. Yahtia La'Shae McDonald sounds perfect." Followed by the ring and water and pregnant lady emojis. Kross peeped the message but said nothing because he wanted all those things with her, but he was going to show her how he felt before he made her feel him.

Yahtia realized they had been driving for a while. "Where are you taking me? You trying to kidnap me?" Yahtia joked. "Shit maybe", Kross said coolly. Giving him the side eye. "I can fight, and I have a taser. Plus, all my people have my location. So, move accordingly.", Yahtia was joking but so serious, and Kross knew it. He loved that about her. Yahtia was so cool and down to earth. "Chill baby I will never hurt you.". "I know", Yahtia smiled because she truly believed him. A few minutes later Kross pulled into the county fair. Before Yahtia could protest he handed her a box. "What's this?". "I knew you would come dressed to kill with your heels. I love to see you in heels you look stunning. I also knew I was taking you to the fair, so I got you some walking around shoes. I don't want you to be uncomfortable or mess up your shoes." Kross explained. Yahtia opened the box and tried miserably to act like she did not love them. Kross had gotten her the all-white with gold trim Air Max 97's complete with some cute footie socks. Yahtia was smiling so hard it hurt. Kross got out the car and walked to her side opening her door. "Let me help you Babe." Accent coming out thick. Kross took her feet in his hands removing her shoes. Kross carefully placed her socks and shoes on delicately. Yahtia watched him intently Yahtia was a good girl but was ready to give him everything right there in the parking lot of the fair. When Kross was done, he took her hand and placed it inside of his hand, helping her to her feet. The two walked hand in hand through the fair talking and laughing about anything that came to their minds. "It's so easy being with you this doesn't feel like a couple of weeks" Kross said to Yahtia. "I know what you mean".

Kross had rented out the Farris Wheel for an hour after closing. He had planned a special picnic in the sky for them. Kross purposefully avoided all food and the Farris Wheel as they had their fun with everything else. "Damnit Kross, I am hungry. I wanted an elephant ear not just this candy apple and now everything is closing". Yahtia pouted. Up until that point Yahtia had been having a blast. "You are so cute when you pout". Kross said. Making her blush instantly. "Don't try to distract me. I am mad. The best part of the fair is the food." Yahtia walked off trying to be mad in peace. While she was walking ahead of him, he sent a quick text to the workers that were helping him with the evening. Kross also snapped a picture of Yahtia in full tantrum mode and sent it to Karma's inbox. Karma had been helping him with some stuff and he felt she would enjoy this. Karma replied. "That's all you bro. Sis is hell when she does not get her way. Straight brat action but she is worth it" That is all the confirmation he needed. Kross ran full speed scooping her up in his arms bridal style. Kross was careful not to let her dress rise too high he does not want the workers sneaking a peak. "Put me down", Yahtia demanded with a laugh. Kross politely ignored her and carried her to the Farris Wheel. "Why are we here?" This ride is closed slow poke. They are going to kick us out man. I have deducted points from your total score for this. You almost pulled off the perfect date."

Kross stood there with his hands in his pockets smiling. He waited quietly for her to realize what was going on. The Farris Wheel lit up and his special playlist started through the speakers. Yahtia looked thoroughly confused for a second. When it dawned on her she almost cried. "You really trying to make a thug cry" Yahtia fanned her face as the attendant opened the carousel door for them. Once they were seated the ride started and when it stopped, they were back at the bottom. This time two men were waiting for them. One spread a blanket over them while the other handed them a basket which Kross took. They began to ascend once more just taking in the view. Once at the top they stopped and Kross opened the basket. Yahtia realized they were in the largest cart. Designed for a small family so they could move around freely. Kross spread an addition plush blanket on the floor of the cart and spread the food out. Yahtia jumped up and down forgetting they were at least one hundred feet in the air. "Oh Shit!" she yelled, scarring herself when it began to rock. Kross laughed loudly at her heavy breathing. Without him giving her the ok Yahtia dug in eating her favorite fair foods.

After they finished eating, they made another full circle to unload the cart. "I'm not ready for this to end", Yahtia said. "It doesn't have to love" The two lovebirds went back to the top and looked at the stars cuddling the entire time. When Yahtia began to shiver Kross pulled her closer and kissed her face. It was a simple gentle kiss. Damn that was a boost to ignite the fire between Yahtia's thighs. Yahtia moaned involuntarily. Before she could talk herself out of it. Yahtia kissed him square on the lips. That kiss was enough to start the hottest sexiest steamiest make out session the two ever experienced. "BABY, we have to stop now if I should remain a gentleman" Kross' accent was strong. "Who said I wanted you to be a gentleman" Yahtia straddled his lap and wrapped them in the blanket. Kross thought for a moment. "I will not be able to stop love" "Good!", Yahtia kissed him again. That was all Kross needed. Kross made love to his future wife at the top of the Farris Wheel cart he was definitely in love. When Yahtia started to tremble with her orgasm he whispered to her. "Hold on for me love I want us to do this together". Kross pushed into her with everything he had, and they came together. Yahtia rested her head on his shoulder and then laughed. "I can't believe I just did that." Kross kissed her face again. "It was a real experience for them both. "If you not trying to be up her all night then we need to go." Kross said already getting hard again. They adjusted their clothes best they could. Yahtia was sure the park attendants knew what they were doing.

The rest of the night went by so fast. They talked for hours about their future apart and together. Kross took her back to his frat house so she could take a shower. They ended up having shower sex. They were like a seasoned couple already knowing how to read each other. Dressed in one of Kross' t-shirts and some sweats, they pulled up to Grady and parked in front of the famous gazebo. Still not wanting to let go they fell asleep holding hands in the car listening to music and smoking. Karma woke up in a panic because Yahtia had texted her saying they were leaving the fair and was on the way back, but Yahtia was not home. Karma checked Yahtia's location immediately seeing Yahtia's dot not blinking, meaning she was on campus. Karma looked outside and noticed Kross' car. Karma walked out in her robe and slides. Knocking on the window scaring the shit out of them both. "Don't mean to end this ghetto love story y'all writing but Bitch we got civics in 20 minutes.", Karma sassed with a smirk on her face and bonnet halfway on. "Girl why you outside looking like somebody auntie all you are missing is a cigarette", Yahtia joked as she exited the car and began gathering her things which were now in a gym bag. "I just finished my blunt hoe now come on you smell like a man and good sex.", Karma said walking off knowing it made Yahtia blush. Kross got out and gave her a hug and kiss. "See you later love. I already miss you.", Kross said as he let her go in the building after her sister. "Yes, I know I got class this morning. I am on the way.", Kross said into the phone. Kross was going to have to go to class smelling like Yahtia, but he did not care one bit.

When the girls entered the room Yahtia headed straight for the bathroom. "I know you want details sis but I gotta get to class.", Yahtia said before closing the door and jumping in the shower. "Oh, it better be good too. I had Joy hack your phone because Craig was tracking your location. Your welcome hoe". Karma said as she finished getting dressed herself. Joy laughed at the two go back and forth but did not offer anything to the conversation. Joy was busy texting Nekendra. Her bestie boo was home from the hospital, and Joy was trying to get to her immediately. "Sis I am on the way what do you need". "Girl I am fine. You will not miss class. I will be here when you are done." "But I don't have to go. I can be to you within the hour." "Girl no. You will not put your future in jeopardy for me. Go to class and then come see me. Love you sis" Nekendra texted. "Ok. Love you too Baby Mama. I'm coming as soon as my classes are over". Joy needed to see her in the worst way. Joy knew her friend was in deep and wanted to help the best she could. She just hoped it was not too late.

CHAPTER 13
YOU MADE YOUR BED NOW DEAL WITH IT

After 36 hours of travel Hershey was escorted off the cargo plane by two of Hero's workers. Hershey was taken to a small room to be readied for auction. Hershey was going to be sold to the highest bidder to do whatever they saw fit. "She smells Hero", Kengiee said with a frown on his face. "Sorry uncle we have been traveling for two days and she wasn't the cleanest when I picked her up. Apply some water pressure to her ass ASAP." The two workers stripped her naked, sprayed her with lye soap. Then hosed her down with a high-speed pressure washer. When Hershey was clean Kengiee slammed her roughly on the table forcing her to bend over. Forcefully without warning he used a fire hot iron stamp to brand a serial number across her right shoulder blade. The iron glowed orange and sizzled when it touched her skin. Hershey screams were so loud they were audible through the gag. The pain was so intense Hershey passed out, but not before pissing on herself. The workers tossed a bucket of ammonia water on Hershey to wake her. Hershey was then taken to the auction room where she was examined and sold. While her buyers were preparing for departure Hershey was placed in front of a camera and projector screen. Hershey looked pitiful and ashamed, but it was a little too late to have remorse. Grabbing her hair roughly Kengiee forced Hershey to look directly into the camera while Hero skyped Yahtia and Karma. Here had sent them the confirmation email about her arrival with the time for the call so they could deliver the rest of their news. "Hey girlfriend, I know your little brain is scrambling right now trying to figure shit out." Yahtia cosigned with what Karma just stated. "Surly you didn't think you could really get away with rapping, harassing, humiliating, and bullying us. You should have known we were coming for payback." The look of confusion and terror was evident on Hershey's face. So, Karma explained. "Yahtia and I did you a favor. Clearly you are into the rough sex fucking, sucking, and raping women. You my dear have been sent to a country where you will be welcomed with open arms." "This time you will not be in control. You will fuck and get fucked on demand.", Yahtia chimed in. "Ultimately we made your sick twisted fantasy a reality. Now you can add sex slave to your list or promiscuity." Karma turned her attention to Hero for a second. "My sister and I would like to thank you Hero, for your excellent service. We will definitely be working with you again in the future. Before we go, I do have one more request. Make that bitch stand up in a corner and sign my name a thousand times, in cursive. Make her sound out each letter too. 'K-to the A-to the R- to the M-to the mutha fuckan A." Karma and Yahtia laughed as the call was disconnected. Hershey was given paper and pen to begin her assignment. As she started tears slowly began to flow from her eyes. All Hershey could hear was her grandmother's voice. "Be careful what you do to people. You got to always be kind and never do harm to anyone because KARMA IS REAL AND SHE IS A BITCH!" As soon as Hershey was done with her written assignment she was escorted to her buyers. They were eager to get her onto her first assignment. A man named Omar Land was waiting for his first piece of Black American pussy. Omar had four sons and two nephews, and they were all infatuated about black American women. Kengiee did not give a fuck who the girls went to. If the buyers' money was green, he would send Hershey wherever she needed to go. Besides, he had already tasted the goods fucking her roughly with his hard two inches of dick. Hershey sucked him so good he let out a load of warm piss in her mouth thinking he was exploding. Kengiee was relaxed. His body went limp from the monster head Hershey delivered. The deal was sealed. The boys had been watching black porn all week waiting for their chance to go deep inside of a Hershey. This was better than Christmas for them.

Back at the county jail Troy was released from the infirmary and sent back to general population. Troy was terrified and with good reason. D-Ray had his crew snatch him up and immediately brought to him. "Look pussy boy, I heard from a reliable source you like to beat women. With those facts your time here will not be sweet I can promise you that." D-Ray spat, giving Troy the evilest glare. D-Ray said, "Nekendra is off limits." D-Ray then took a two second pause, making sure his words were being understood, "If you touch her, go near her, or so much as dream of her. I will personally kill you. DO YOU UNDERSTAND?" D-Ray yelled that last part causing Troy to jump in fear. Troy nodded his head quickly with understanding. "Good. Now you on laundry duty." D-Ray dismissed Troy with a wave of his hand. D-Ray's goons escorted Troy to the laundry room and gave him instructions. Troy had to hand wash all the laundry, making sure everything was ironed and folded. Troy was so scared and ready to be away from D-Ray he happily got to work. Troy would do whatever it took to stay alive that included not contacting his girl Nekendra.

Uvoka slowly crept up the stairs trying her best to remain unseen. She did not want to deal with any ridicule or fanfare about her life. To her dismay Uvoka was spotted by a group of students. Immediately the students started to clown her. "Shitty booty bitch.", one girl yelled while spraying air freshener at her. "Shit monster.", a boy said loudly and laughed pulling out his phone to get more footage of her horrific appearance. Uvoka tried to run but ended up getting tangled in the newspapers and dingy sweatpants Molly had given her. Before Uvoka could get up, the group of students had surrounded her. Squirting liquid body wash on her followed by throwing buckets of water on her too. "Wash your ass", several of them laughed. Fed up with everything and everybody Uvoka turned and left the way she came. Instead of at least going to clean up Uvoka went back to the bus stop looking for Molly. Molly was the only person that was nice to her recently. Uvoka was in need for a friend.

Molly had been homeless for a while now, her clothes looked like old cleaning rags and smelled even worse. Molly slept when and wherever she could and often slept at the bus stop to protect her from the rain.

Molly had become accustomed to eating out of trashcans and begging people for change. Molly sat reflecting on her life realizing she could have done so much better. She had gone from sugar to shit instantly. Molly remembered eating from the finest restaurants and having money to throw away. Molly had reached out to all her so-called friends, but she was denied access. Either by the news of how she mistreated Karma or by her messy divorce from Karmelo's trifling ass. Everyone treated Molly like a villain and would not risk helping her. Karma crossed her mind constantly. The vision of Karma being left home lonely night after night depending on the people next door. Karma had to create her own family because no one in her own house cared for her. Molly was so ashamed and disappointed with herself. There was nothing she could do about it now. Molly could not use her nursing career anymore her license to practice medicine had been suspended due to the child neglect allegations. Knowing she could not ever get caught at Karma's house again or she would go to jail. Karma had made that crystal clear. Deep in her thoughts Molly pulled her arms inside of her ragged shirt to try and fight the night cold air. Uvoka sat down beside her placing an arm around her causing Molly to look up. "Back so soon", Molly grinned. "Yes. I am dropping out. I will never be able to show my face at Grady EVER AGAIN." Uvoka explained dramatically with tears in her eyes. Molly's eyes got wide as saucers. "You go to Grady? Grady University?" "Ummm. Yeah. But like I said. I am dropping out. My reputation has been ruined thanks to a group of preppie wanna be barbie dolls. They ruined my life." Uvoka was ranting in anger just thinking about Karma, Yahtia and Joy. "It's a small world. My daughter goes to Grady. Her name is Karmell Boston. She is a freshman.", Molly lowkey boasted. "Damn it's a small world indeed. That is the mutt faced bitch that ruined me causing all of my problems." "Can't be the same Karmell. My baby would not hurt a fly or cause any problems. Karmell is incredibly quiet and insecure. Child only had one friend her whole life.", Molly explained. "Well, the bitch grew some balls somewhere along the way because she is at Grady running shit with her side kick Yahtia. I have seen it firsthand." Uvoka pointed at herself for emphasis. Molly shook her head. "I did notice a change in her appearance and attitude when I saw her last. Little ungrateful bitch put me out of my own house.", Molly laughed. "She insisted her name was Karma, not Karmell. Whatever that was about. She would not let me shower, eat or even rest up. She cursed me out and then threw me out." Uvoka rolled her eyes dramatically with a snot filled face. "Everybody addresses her as Karma on campus." "I'm sorry but your daughter is a fucking cunt. "Please explain to me how the fuck she put you out your own shit? That shit is ridiculous you don't have to take that Ms. Molly. Fuck her!", Uvoka said sounding amped. Uvoka was trying to give Molly the boost she needed to get revenge on Karma. "Your right fuck her I'm the damn mama it's going to take more than a few threats to keep me off my own property. I worked countless hours establishing that home." Molly gained some momentum. "Damn Right Ms. Molly let's go get what is rightfully yours; there is no way you should be living in these foul conditions. You have a whole house with all the living essentials waiting on you. Judging from your bougie ass daughter you have some of the finer things in life.", Uvoka said. Molly nodded in agreement. "Stop stalling Ms. Molly. What are you waiting for?" Uvoka prompted her loudly. Molly slowly got off the bench and yelled. "Let's go." Molly joined Uvoka and the two headed out to take back or at least get into the house. "What's the worst that could happen?" Molly thought to herself as they walked together.

Joy finally made it to Nekendra. She was nervous and excited to see her. "Hey friend. I missed you.", Joy said walking into the apartment. Joy put her bag down and took a good look at her friend. Her heart broke instantly. "You look good girl. You're healing good too.", Joy mentioned. Nekendra nodded. She was moving slowly due to some pain but overall, she had made a full recovery. "So how is school? And what is his name. Because bitch your hips wide as fuck." Nekendra joked making Joy laugh. Joy did a little twerk sticking her tongue out. "His name is Craig. School is school. You know it's not a big thing to me.", Joy said while pulling out a pre-rolled blunt and holding it up waiting for Nekendra to give her the ok. Nodding her head yes, "Girl I gotta meet this Craig fella. Gotta make sure he is doing my sister right." For the next hour or so Joy enjoyed spending time with her best friend. They talked about everything and everybody. Joy told her about Karma and Yahtia and how they defended her to the school bullies. Joy even told her a little bit about the 'Hit Lists'. "Sounds like you all happy with your new friends.", Nekendra said. She did not mean for jealousy to come out in her words, but Joy heard it. "Don't be like that Baby Mama. You will always be my best girl." Joy gave her a hug. "I know girl. It's just, I get kinda lonely with just me and the boys here alone. Joy jumped up off the couch. "Don't start that shit man. You can do bad all by your damn self. You damn sure can make it without Troy rotten no good abusive ass." Joy's hatred came loud and clear. "I think he has learned his lesson sis; he didn't realize he hurt me that bad. Troy just took things a little too far. He was stressing about his job, and you know his mom recently died". "STOP DEFENDING HIM", Joy screamed loudly while pulling her braids. "That dusty ass nigga doesn't give a fuck about you or my God kids. Him not wanting to work and his raggedy bitch of a mammie dying is only an excuse for you to justify his wrong. That ain't got shit to do with him putting you in the hospital repeatedly." Before Joy could get any deeper the phone rang. *"You have a collect call from,* "Troy". *An inmate at Columbia County jail. Do you accept the charges?"* Joy just shook her head and gathered her things. "That nigga not going stop until he kills you Baby Mama.", Joy cried as she walked to her car. Leaving Nekendra to talk to mumble mouth Troy who was still trying to operate without his bottom lip.

CHAPTER 14
SETTING UP MY KARMA

The gazebo had become the meeting room for the boys and today was no different. Craig and Ozias were not enrolled at Grady, but they were there all the time learning. Kross was the teacher and today's lesson were Geography. Kross was teaching them about the layout of the land in Trinidad. They were scheduling a field trip to the island sooner than later. "Class for today is over just review the information I gave you. We will resume Friday at 7am. I don't have any classes that day so will be pulling an all-nighter so bring lunch. I will supply the greenery." Kross gave each man a brotherly hug before going their separate ways. "Ok professor." Ozias clowned. Ozias had really taken a liking to Kross and considered him family now. Plus, Kross was a straight up businessperson and was always about making money. That was something Ozias would always be able to support, Ozias was anxious about getting the ball rolling; the plan was guaranteed to make them rich. Ozias had already spent his first twenty bands in his head. Rubbing his hands together Ozias and his right-hand man headed home to do some more work.

Dax Riley had been sentenced to six years for the vicious assault on Karma. Dax had served three years of his sentence before he walked away from a level 1 prison yard. Dax was on clean up duty and already had his mind made up what he was about to do. When one of the guards was caught slipping and slacking on the job by smoking and caking on the phone. Dax took full advantage and literally walked away from the cleaning crew, then hit the railroad tracks. When the guard did a count realizing that Dax was AWOL. It was too late. Dax was long gone. Dax had taken off all his prison attire throwing the bright orange uniform in various locations. He was hoping the dogs would not be able to track him quickly. It was hard as hell for Dax to get back to his hood, but he managed to do it. By the time he arrived near his hood he was in a wife beater state boxers and socks. Dax threw his work boots in the river. Staying with the railroad tracks Dax eventually made it to his cousin's TJ house. Hiding in the bushes making sure the coast was clear before he revealed himself.

TJ and her bestie Duchess were chilling on the back porch smoking weed and listening to the Pop Smoke play list. Hearing some rustling in the bushes TJ got Duchess' attention and grabbed a rusty pipe at the same time. "Bitch somebody peeking through the bushes at us". Duchess whispered. "Play it cool and when they get closer, we gonna to start swinging". TJ laid out the plan for her friend. Dax burst through the bush getting tangled and stumbling along the way. The girls raised their weapons ready to strike but TJ recognized Dax and lowered her arm. "Nigga you were finna get beat on. What the fuck are you doing here?" TJ questioned him. Looking at him suspiciously. "I need some clothes quick cuz". Dax said looking around paranoid. "I know damn well your ass ain't escaped. You know how fucking hot it's about to be around this bitch." TJ fussed but opened the back door gesturing for him to hurry and come in. "I know man, but it was the chance of a lifetime. I know they are going to hit my mama and grandma spot, so I need to lay low here for a few days". Dax said going straight to TJ's bathroom. Dax needed to shit and shower ASAP. TJ handed him a razor a hoodie and some sweatpants through the door while he handled his business. "Hurry the fuck up man. We family so they will hit up everybody that is a known associate of yours. We gotta find you somewhere else to go." TJ banged on the door and then went to her room getting her purse.

A few minutes later Dax came from the bathroom ready to go. "Damn you still on jail time", TJ joked. "We can go to my house", Duchess spoke up trying to be helpful. "Good looking beautiful". Dax flirted and then made a beeline for the back door. They all jogged to Duchess house taking the back-alley ways and railroad tracks, so they were not seen. TJ handed Dax a 49ers skully to help camouflage his head. Dax had an abnormally large oddly shaped head. It reminded you of an eggplant on steroids. The trio made it to Duchess house and Dax immediately started telling them about his plan to move to New York. "Cuz I ain't finna be here long. I know I gotta get the fuck on through. I Just need to get me a ticket on that express bus, but before I go I gotta get my revenge". Dax explained passing the blunt back to Duchess. "Boy you sound crazy as fuck talking about revenge. You need to be on a damn bus tonight and hope you don't get caught". TJ fussed. "Nah, that bitch Karmell Boston gotta pay. She the reason I'm in this mess to begin with." Dax felt like he did not deserve to go to jail for what he did to Karmell. Dax blamed Karma for him going to prison like he did not assault her placing her in the hospital. Dax especially blamed her for the shit he had to deal with while in prison. Now he was on the run all for her stupid ass. Dax wanted Karma so bad he could taste her. "Nigga!" TJ exaggerated. "I forgot you had a sick thing for Karmell. Oops, I mean Karma". Dax gave her a strange look. "Karmell is a bad bitch now. The glow up was definitely real for her. She is a whole diva now a five-star bitch". "Her hair, nails, clothes her whole swag is on-point the bitch even got bag and got her teeth fixed, she's on her Cardi B shit cuz. "No more bucked buttery beaver biters." Her and Yahtia are at Grady University running shit. They are local celebrities on campus". TJ gave Dax the rundown of how the girls were living now that they were in college. "They even got bitches around campus copying their style and trying to be down with them and their crew".

TJ went into overdrive explaining not leaving anything out including the shit with Uvoka. "We need a car. I need to case the school so I can snatch my prey", Dax said. Revenge heavy on his mind. All Dax did was think about how he would fuck Karma and release his kids into her mouth. Dax planned to piss on her again too. "You ain't saying shit fam. We can give crackhead Kim a crisp twenty for her whip", TJ said ready to make a move. The jealousy in her overpowered her thoughts. TJ could not wait to put Karma in her place. At least that is how she looked at it. On the way out of the door Duchess did not move. "Are you coming hoe"? TJ spoke. "Let's go rain on these bitches' parade". "Nah bitch.", Duchess wasn't feeling this plan, but she didn't let them know that. "Imma stay behind and see what the hood talking about. I can keep y'all posted about the police." "Good idea" Dax said as he and his cousin made their way to Kim to secure the car.

During the ride to Grady, they mapped out a plan going strictly off emotions. Nothing was solid but they went with it. Dax was in deep thought about taking Karma to New York and fucking her everyday making her have ten of his kids. TJ parked in front of the Alpha building; they begin people watching. Knowing she would eventually see someone she knew. Dax sat slouched down in the passenger seat, waiting. They did not have to wait long before TJ spotted Kross. TJ remembered him from a frat party with Uvoka. Kross had some good ass weed and he was cute as fuck too.

Kross was on his way to see Yahtia, but TJ cut him off. "Hey. Can I ask you something right quick?" Kross met her. "What's good? What you need?" "I know you probably don't remember me, but I met you a few times at a frat party and copped some killa green from you". Kross gave her a look. "Nah. I have no idea what you talking about fam, but if you are looking for some smoke it ain't hard to find. The shit be everywhere you gotta get your hunt on Kross said excusing himself." "NO actually I'm here to see my friends Karmell and Yahtia", TJ said. Kross was listening carefully now. Kross felt like something was off with this girl, so his antennas were up. "Yeah, I know them. What's your name? I can ask the RA if she can give me their room number for you". Kross said as he gave her a wink. Turning on the charm so she would not think he was plotting on her even though he was. Thinking she had hit the jackpot on the first try. "That would be great. My name is Sonya, and my cousin is Ronald. We grew up with them and are trying to surprise them with a visit so don't tell them OK". "Oh, for sure I'm sure they will love the surprise". Kross said, heading to the dorm. "Wait right here let me work my magic for you" making TJ blush. As soon as Kross was inside the double doors he called Craig and Ozias letting them know what was going on. "Shit definitely suspicious bro. I get all kind of bad vibes from these two. The dude just sitting in the car looking crazy with a humongous ass head." Kross gave the description of the car and tag number he was being very observant. Craig and Ozias hit the highway on two wheels racing to the campus. "Stay with the girls fam this is a set up I know it". Craig said as he hung up.

Kross ran up the stairs two at a time and beat on the girl's door like he was the Feds. "Who the fuck is it?" Joy snapped snatching the door open with a bat in hand. "Oh, it's just you", she said as Kross let himself in immediately holding up his hands in surrender. All three of the girls had weapons ready to strike. Kross shook his head and laughed at them. "Yall got some company downstairs". Kross told the girls everything that had transpired. Joy tapped into the security cameras and zoomed in. "TJ and Dax gotta be". Yahtia yelled. Karma grabbed her Glock; she was ready for war. "Dax supposed to be in jail but I'm about to send his ass straight to hell". Kross stepped in her way. "I can't let you do that. Craig and O are on the way to handle it. Y'all sit pretty and let us oversee this". Yahtia was all smiles. "Y'all heard my man. We ain't going nowhere". "Damn bitch at least take him to the room before you blow him". Joy said making a hand mouth gesture. In the meantime, Joy looked up Dax on the inmate search web site and found out that Dax Riley had escaped earlier that day. The entire Columbia police department was on the hunt for him. "That nigga is gunning for me I see. I got a trick for his ass" Karma said. She quickly produced a plan for both Dax and TJ.

Craig pulled up on two wheels coming to a screeching halt. TJ knew something was not right when she saw Craig. So, TJ bolted before Craig spotted her. TJ and Dax pulled up at Burger King a few exits down they had to regroup. Neither of them expected for Craig and Ozias to still be around the girls. "Them punk ass niggas still stuck up their ass I see". Dax said pissed the fuck off hoping that their cover was not blown. The two ate and re-strategized.

Normally Craig and Ozias waited at the gazebo but this time they walked straight to the room. Once inside the girls let them in on what was really going on showing them the pictures of Dax and TJ. They informed them that Dax was officially a wanted man because he escaped. Craig logged into Facebook and saw all the posts confirming Dax's escape. "I thought this nigga learned his lesson about fucking with the family", Ozias said. "Apparently not but he will", Craig said while typing something in his phone. "Hey Kross, didn't you say we needed a runner to and from Trinidad?" Kross confirmed with a nod. "Yeah, they gotta be expendable". Kross said, "OPERATION YOU GONE LEARN TODAY! Joy informed Hero the new business at hand. While everyone was attentive Craig laid out his plan for Dax and TJ. "These mutha fuckas going to be a help to us before they both take the long ride". Bet, Ozias said. "I hope we catch these bitches before the police do." Ozias really wanted Dax to pay for everything he did to Karma and everything he thought he was going to do. "Joy you set that shit up yet". Craig yelled. "10-4 daddy" Joy yelled out. After sealing a deal with some Dominicans in California. Hero made his way to South Carolina to see his new favorite people.

It was finally release day for Troy. His time had been postponed because of an escapee but today was the day. Troy had been sneaking and calling Nekendra and now he would finally see her. Before he could walk out a free man D-Ray planned a little going away party for Troy. Every night for the past week Troy was on his knees getting face fucked by every man that played the sex game left-handed. Troy was made to suck and swallow; Troy received a blow to the head for every gag. Most inmates started to complain. The bottom lip being missing took away the feeling they were chasing. So Troy was forced to use his tongue to lick and eat ass. Troy was gangbanged and humiliated, but he did not fight it. Troy took pride in it because he knew he was going home. With a ruptured asshole and no bottom lip. Troy was wheeled out of the jail and dumped in the front of the station. When he was able to get himself together. Troy called a taxi and made his way home to his Nekendra.

CHAPTER 15
RIGHT PLAN. WRONG BITCH.

Molly had produced the brilliant idea to purposefully trigger the alarm repeatedly. Molly knew from experience that eventually the police would stop coming and the alarm company would come out to investigate the "malfunction". "Ms. Molly you sure this gonna work". Uvoka asked for the umpteenth time from their hiding spot in the bushes. "Shhhh! Yes, it will work. The hard part will be for us to convince the alarm company that we belong here, and its ok to let us in." Before Uvoka could ask any more questions Molly silenced her. "Here help me with this child". Molly had Uvoka help her put on the dress they stole from a neighbor's yard. "I can't look like I am homeless when they get here", Molly explained. Sure, enough after the tenth trigger the two of them watched the police officer call the alarm company. The officer explained that there had to be a glitch in the system. "You will notify the homeowner correct", the officer verified before he left. Less than thirty minutes later a black utility van pulled up with 'Secure Us' on the side. "Show time". Molly mumbled hand combing her hair hoping she did not look like she felt. Molly approached the heavy-set black man who appeared to be sleepy or high. Molly smiled inside and out. If he were sleepy or under the influence this would be easier than she thought. "Hello sir. I am Molly Boston the owner. My daughter Karmell Boston is co-owner and the account holder for our alarm system. That child of mine took my keys by mistake and went back to school. I triggered the alarm trying to get in. I was at the neighbor's house trying to contact her when the police came out. Do you think you can help me out sir?" Molly explained giving her best mommy dearest impression. "I understand ma'am. I can certainly help you with that I need you to verify the date of birth for the account holder and give me the past word. I will also need you to contact her for me", Rico the security man said. "9-16-99 is her date of birth. Past word Ms. King. Molly blurted out to Rico. Molly knew her daughter was in love with Ozias King and every girl at that age claim ownership of their man's last name. Unfortunately, Karmell is in class now. That is why she hasn't returned my calls or showed up to let me in." Molly started doing the pee-pee dance. Molly did have to pee she needed him to feel like he had no choice but to let her in. Rico gave her a side eye and slight hesitation. "I understand. Here is my card with all my information on it. Please give me a call if you have any more issues tonight." Rico flipped the security override switch and disarmed the system. "Do you mind calling your daughter one more time just so I can tell my boss I tried everything?". Rico gave a small smile. Molly agreed. When she picked up the phone Molly did not know what to do. luckily, she remembered Karma's old phone number she had in her room upstairs. Molly dialed the number praying that it was still in service. When it rang until the voicemail came on. Feeling relieved. "She still is not answering". Rico nodded and let himself out. Rico figured that Molly would reset it when she needed.

Molly played her part all the way to the end, holding the phone in her hand pretending to have reached someone and waving to Rico. Once he was out of sight, Molly called for Uvoka to come in. They both stood speechless for a few moments before rushing around neither one knowing if they wanted to bathe or eat first. Molly took charge directed Uvoka to the downstairs bathroom while she went to what used to be her bathroom. The ladies took their time taking a bath and a shower. Uvoka cried in the shower just thankful to finally have all that dried shit off her. They did not really speak to one another as they indulged themselves. Uvoka made sure to rub down in oil and use deodorant. When Uvoka found a pack of toothbrushes, she acted like she hit the lottery. Molly went to see what all the commotion was about she found Uvoka in Karma's room. "Ms. Molly what are we gonna do when we leave here". Molly started crying.

"I know we have to leave but I don't want to go back to having nothing". Molly comforted her and pulled out a track suit for her. "We will be ok. We must take some of these things with us". Molly said pulling down two MCM duffle bags. Molly wiped her face free of tears. remembering when she bought them just to shut Karmell up about being bullied.

After getting dressed and packing the bags with a few changes of clothes and toiletries the two set their sights on the kitchen. Not wanting to make it too obvious that they had been there. The two decided against cooking a big meal and settled for sandwiches and things that could be heated in the microwave. It was a comfortable silence between the two while they feasted on cookies, chips, hot pockets, and bologna sandwiches. Before Molly reached a full belly she munched on some salt and vinegar chips and turned on the TV. Deciding to have a movie night camping in front of the 70-inch plasma screen TV. Molly went straight to Netflix. "That's what I'm talking about Ms. Molly Netflix and chill". Uvoka propped her feet up and reclined in the overstuffed lounge chair. As soon as Molly clicked on Karma's profile on Netflix the TV froze then it shut off by itself. Confused as hell Molly attempted to cut it back on only to get a 'WARNING'. Notification flashing across the screen saying unauthorized user. Scared out of her mind Uvoka snatched the remote and turned the TV off. "Ms. Molly I think it's time for us to go".

Karma had been getting alerts from the security company all day about the alarm being triggered. Karma eventually got a phone call letting her know that the police saw nothing each time they did a wellness visit and seen it was clearly a glitch in the system. "Well, how soon can this be fixed? I don't like my house unprotected", Karma said to the representative. Karma had a gut feeling that something was off about these alerts. Accepting that the security company would fix everything she went on about her day. Now she was getting a notification that her Netflix account was being accessed from home. "Something ain't right". Karma said to Yahtia and Joy. Karma called the customer service number for 'Secure Us' and immediately asked for a supervisor. "Hello this is Sal how can I assist you". "I need to know why my alarm is not set for armed. I have reason to believe that there is an intruder in my home". Karma yelled into the phone. The manager Sal apologized and placed her on hold to see who responded to the issue earlier. "Ma'am I just spoke with our technician Rico he stated that he disarmed the system for your mother. She called you to verify this before he disarmed it. That is what his report is saying." Before the manager could say anything else, Karma was on his ass. "I did not give any one permission to disarm my system! My mother is a scammer and manipulator. My mother is a low life, a trouble making conniving bitch". She is not allowed on my property EVER." The supervisor was livid. Sal apologized repeatedly for the unprofessionalism his technician displayed. Sal begged for Karma not to leave them as a customer. "Sir right now I don't have time to deal with the sloppiness of your company. I do need for you to activate the Power Lockdown that I recently upgraded to". After giving her credentials and verifying her safe word Sal activated the feature. At the same time Joy was logging into the camera system so they could look around for themselves. "In the future, please understand that I am the only person who can authorize anything on this account." Karma gave a new safe word for him to add then hung up in his face. "Joy tell me what you see". Karma asked. Already knowing that the super sleuth was already on it. "Oh snap, you are not gonna believe this shit". Joy pulled the footage up on her tablet. The three girls watch Uvoka, and Molly run around the house trying to find a way out after the lock down.

Uvoka ran to the front door just as the bars came crashing down locking in place with a loud click. The same thing happened to every other door and windows too. "What the fuck is all of this?" Uvoka cried, but Molly was speechless herself. Molly had no idea what was going on, but she did not like it. She felt trapped. As the two of them held each other listening to all the power locks click into place they cried loudly. Deciding to fuck with Molly and Uvoka. Karma suggested for Joy to access the security voice speaker. "What the fuck y'all bitches doing in my house?" Karma yelled causing Uvoka and Molly to scream. Spinning around and staring, not knowing where the voice was coming from. Uvoka spoke first. "What the hell?" her voice trembled. "Ms. Molly?" "Nah Bitch. Fuck Ms. Molly and your shitty ass too. No need to keep shaking the bars, only I can unlock them". Karma aggressively taunted them for the next two hours. Karma played with the lights and the thermostat. Karma raised the temperature in the house to 95 degrees. Karma then remotely turned the stove on too. Once the women started to sweat. Joy turns the air conditioner to sixty, that begin freezing them. The lights flickering was getting to them both, but Uvoka was on the verge of breakdown. "STTTOOOOPPPPP!" Uvoka broke down pulling her own hair out. Uvoka's crying would not stop. The lights stopped and the TV came back on, but this time it was a text screen. "I told you Molly to stay the fuck away from me and my house. I told you that if you came back, I would send you to jail. Now you will be taking poor Uvoka Wells with you". Molly shook her head in disbelief as she read the messages out loud. "Please Karmell just let me go and I won't ever bother you again". Molly pleaded aloud hoping Karma would show sympathy. "I should have just taken my ass back to my dorm room, but NOOOOO I had to make another stupid decision". Uvoka was literally beating herself up about this. "Yeah, bitch you should had taken your shitty but fucking ass home". Karma said loudly laughing through the speaker. Karma turned to Yahtia, "Tell Mama T and Juan to go keep an eye on things until the police get there". "I'm already on it sis". Turning to Joy Karma stated. "Inspector Gadget, I need you to trigger the fire alarm. I'm going to add fuel to the already hot fire and scare the piss outta these bitches some more?" Joy nodded her head and went to work. "Watch me work" Joy boasted as she typed away on her computer. Karma called the fire department and informed them that her alarm was going to sound off, but it was just a drill. The fire chief alerted all surrounding fire houses so no one would come out. On que, Joy set off the alarm. It sounded like a fire truck was in the living room with them. The lights began to flicker again with the alarm sound from hell. Just when they thought it was over. Two large clouds of fire extinguisher sprayers shot from the stove and ceiling. Covering them both fully. This was it for Uvoka. She was in the fetal position on the floor mumbling and rocking. When Toyah and Juan got to the house the girls cut the alarm off. When Toyah opened the door Molly rushed over. "Let me out please!" she was pulling on the bars and begging. "Your dumbass going to jail. You can get out when the police get here, not a moment before. According to the girls I have about 5 minutes before they get here". Toyah said. Toyah used the next five minutes to curse Molly out for old and new. "You and that worthless husband of yours are going down. You cannot escape the consequences of your actions. I promise you that. Karma is a bitch". Juan said just as the police pulled up.

Toyah met the officer in the driveway with Karma on facetime. "Officer this is my mother Toyah Beeks. The women in the house are intruders. They both tricked my security company into letting them inside. I have video footage of them stealing and damaging my property. I need them arrested and I want to press charges". Karma explained to the police. As soon as she finished talking to the police. Karma called and lifted the Power Lockdown. The bars immediately start rising effortlessly. Molly rushed out the house and tried to run but was football tackled by an officer and handcuffed. A female officer retrieved the bag she was carrying and read her rights. Molly dropped her head in shame and cried. Molly was thinking to herself about all her wrongdoings and trifling actions. Molly hated she fucked up towards her own daughter. Molly felt her world crashing down she felt gut-wrenching bad and begin to vomit. Somehow, Molly knew shit was going to get worse. When the officer attempted to apprehend Uvoka she went limp. "We need a bus. One of the perps needs medical attention". The officer called in. Both women were arrested and charged with breaking and entering, trespassing, identity theft, malicious damage and mid-night burglary. Karmelo happened to be riding past while this was taking place. He was very curious to know what had happened, but he would not dare stop. Karmelo almost felt bad when Molly's eyes locked with his when she was bending down to enter the police car. Karmelo knew someone would eventually call him with the news. Karmelo Boston kept driving, with no intentions of helping his wife.

CHAPTER 16
PAY BACK AIN'T ENOUGH

The ladies put together an itinerary for Hero. The package was left in a lockbox at the airport. That had become their usual way of exchanging information. The crew took extra precautions to not become traced are affiliated to Hero. Hero never needed too much guidance just a basic plan he always understood the assignment. This assignment was going to be much like the one with Hershey. It was easy money for everyone involved. The crew sat in the dorm smoking on some new new Kross had brought in. Classes were cancelled because of a small covid outbreak. So, the girls were doing all their assignments virtual to stay ahead of the curve. The munchies kicked in hard after about three blunts. The hunger pains always hit different when you were smoking Kross' shit. Not being able to take it any longer. They decided to hit up their favorite wing spot 'Dripping Sauce.' After ordering their usual with an extra 10-piece wings to go. Everyone dug in. Being slightly satisfied, they started secretly going over the plan. Craig felt like Ozias should take the lead on this mission simply because Karma was the target. Kross sat back and listened. Kross was shocked hearing about the past missions. The girls shared about how they had been holding each other down since elementary school. This made Kross love Yahtia even more. It was something about a bitch in the streets but a lady in the sheets that took him out. Yahtia was his little sour patch kid, and he loved every bit of her wild side.

Joy licked her fingers and then wiped them off before looking at her phone. Hero texted her needing the location for Dax and TJ. Joy had hacked TJ's phone and her location was being shared to her tablet. So, they always knew her exact location. Joy sent the coordinates to Hero and got back to her crew. They sat around and laughed with each other. Everyone was coupled off. Yahtia did not feel like the third wheel anymore. She was all about Kross, and he was all about her. They wrapped things up at the wing spot and headed to the liquor store. The idea was to have a couple's night and handle business at the same time. They set up at the pizza warehouse as they waited for Hero. While they waited, they started playing Drunken Uno. After about an hour or so Ozias went to change clothes. All black everything. Ozias had tools attached to multiple chains hanging around his neck. Ozias looked like a sexy psycho rapper. A buzzed Karma was excited just looking at him. Ozias noticed her licking her lips and he winked at her. "Wait till later love." Ozias whispered in her ear and kissed her face with an open mouth, leaving her face wet.

Ozias prepped the table with more tools of destruction and torture devices. "Before I forget, here". Handing Karma an envelope with the payment for Hero. He did not want to waste any time when it came to Dax. Ozias felt like he failed Karma because Dax was still a problem for her. Ozias would not fail a second time. Karma began getting prepared as well. Karma was sick of Dax and TJ. They both came hard at Karma for years, for no reason. Karma was determined to put an end to the shit for the last time. "Don't you dare hold anything back Karma. Make sure TJ remembers who the fuck you are and why fucking with you was a mistake". "UNDERSTOOD". Ozias waited for an answer, Karma nodded yes and begin cracking her knuckles. Ozias was in his zone, and he wanted Karma feeling froggy too. Ozias continued with the pep talk; He knew how to get Karma crunk and ready for war.

Everyone was feeling good they were buzzed, and the adrenaline was flowing. Now they just waited for Hero to hand deliver the honorable guests. They did not have to wait long. Seconds later Hero pulls up in a flatbed tow truck with a Lexus jeep hooked to the back. Everyone was a little confused until they realized that the Jeep contained, Dax, TJ, and

Duchess. "Damn he smooth. Nigga repoed the car with them in it." Kross laughed as everyone got into position.

Hero released the car, letting it fall to the cement floor. The guests had plastic bags over their heads, taped tightly around their necks. There was a quarter sized hole for breathing but with all the layers of duct tape it was damn near impossible to get a full breath of air. Craig and Ozias grabbed Dax, slamming him to the ground. After Craig stomped on his chest, Ozias wrapped a cord around his neck and drug him to the opposite side of the warehouse. The ladies did not hesitate, they removed TJ and Duchess from the car and began doing their own dirty work.

Ozias tore the bag from Dax's face but still left it tapped around his neck. Dax sat there breathing hard just thankful for air at the moment. Feeling something hot underneath him, Dax tried to stand up. He was held in place by Kross and Craig. Ozias had set a fire underneath the milk crate. "Bro you are literally about to fire his ass up." Kross joked while holding Dax in place. Ozias would squirt tiny amounts of alcohol on the fire making the flames higher. The fire burned hotter and faster. The team was satisfied with the burnt flesh smell coming from Dax ass. "I think he shit himself." Craig frowned his face up. Forcing him to stand up Dax was pressure washed with ice cold salt water. Dax screamed from the pain of the salt but was happy his ass was no longer burning. While Ozias delivered some vicious body shots Kross, and Craig got the next torture devices set up. Another bag was placed over Dax's head and secured tightly around his neck. Then gas was poured into the breathing hole. Dax anticipated what was about to happen and tried with everything he had to get away. Kross tossed a lit match into the hole and yelled out, "Fire in the hole."

The guys watched Dax run around screaming trying to put the fire out himself. His hand was tied so there was nothing he could do. "Damn that was the best Stop! Drop! Roll! I ever seen executed." Kross said while laughing. Ozias turned the hose on again this time aiming for his face. Craig removed what was left of the melted bag and looked at a half-drowned Dax. "What the fuck is wrong with you pussy boys?" Dax sputtered, trying to catch his breath. "Pussy boy," Kross' accent came out strong as he kicked Dax in his ribs. "Mutha fucka you are not in no position to be getting aggressive", Craig said followed with another vicious kick. This combination had Dax spitting blood. "Instead of your dumb ass chasing some pussy or leaving the damn country. You escaped jail just to fuck with my lady. That was the dumbest decision you ever made." Ozias was pissed all over again. "You have failed to realize that Karma is a bitch. A bad bitch at that. Karma just so happens to be my bitch." Ozias punched Dax in the side of the face causing him to spit out a tooth and more blood. "Fuck you and that beaver mouth hoe. I was gonna leave town but not before I made that bitch eat my dick." Dax spit blood at Ozias, clearly not giving a fuck. "Glad you feel that way playa." Ozias strapped Dax to wooden bench while Craig and Ozias tagged teamed him. Pistol whipping him violently. Dax was getting hammered repeatedly across the face. His teeth were flying out one by one. Thick slimy blood continuously poured from his mouth. Dax became unrecognizable within minutes from the brutal beating. When it was over Dax was laughing and smiling a now toothless grin. Ozias was even madder now because he felt like Dax was winning. Ozias wanted him to beg for mercy and cry for his mama. Ozias turned it up a notch. Stripping Dax naked and tying him to a wooden support beam. Ozias, Kross and Craig whipped him slave style. As soon as Dax yelled out his first cry lemon juice was squirted over his back. Then the whipping started again. When the skin on his back split open into gapping wounds. Sea salt was packed in between each opening. Dax was still trying to hold out on screaming in pain. Until Ozias nearly drowned him in green rubbing alcohol. Dax looked like he was having a seizure from the mixture of salt and alcohol in his wounds. Dax fainted from the pain. Kross begin to pressure wash him again then started over with the salt and lemon juice in the wounds. Dax cried out for his mama and the lord so many times they lost count. Kross then topped him off with the rest of the gas and lighter fluid giving his wounds some extra marinate. "Apologize bitch" Ozias yelled. When he did not speak soon enough Craig hit him with the whip. "I'm Sorrrrrryyyyyyy." Dax cried out with a hoarse voice. "Again" Ozias ordered. Craig did not stop this time until Dax was involuntarily throwing up Dax body was in shock. "You will beg for my girl's forgiveness. Bitch ass nigga. You better pray she has mercy because I don't." Ozias dragged a half dead Dax over to Karma. "Hold up bro I been itching for a lil action" said Kross. Kross took a Philips head screwdriver and jammed it into the back of Dax hand causing the screwdriver to go straight through. Kross then proceeded to do the other hand. "This is how we send a I'm not fucking playing with you message back home." Kross added. Karma just stood there astounded by what she was seeing.

Dax was made to say "I'm sorry for ever disrespecting a beautiful woman like you. I do not deserve to breathe the same air as you. I am at your mercy" Everyone looked at Karma waiting for her decision. "I am Karma. I don't know who Mercy is." Karma said as she delivered a karate kick to Dax face causing him to fall backwards hitting his head on the concrete hard. Dax was barely alive. While he laid there body completely motionless. The men did exactly what he did to Karma years ago took a piss on his head relieving every drop they had.

All the girls were turned on by the show the men put on. They were not going to be out done. They started slow fucking with Duchess and TJ. Now it was time to get down to business. "My turn put me in the game coach." Yahtia yelled snatching the bag from TJ's head roughly. "Yes, let us get this over with. I'm ready to be fucked and sucked." Joy chimed in while stirring a concoction. "We had a simple plan for you, but I see you upgraded your package to the deluxe combo. Since you wanna ride or die with your people and prove that blood is thicker than water." Karma shrugged her shoulders putting on a pair of gloves. "Let's get it cracking bitch." Karma put a super perm mixed with Nair all along TJ's hair line while Joy poured a mixture of honey and sugar water throughout her head. The mixtures started to drip down her body. Yahtia made sure to rub Nair on her eyebrows and across her eyelashes. TJ cried and tried to cop a plea. "It wasn't me or my idea. Dax put a gun to my head and forced me and Duchess to help him. "I did not want to go please believe me." Joy shook her head. "Damn this bitch got no loyalty. She is selling out her own damn cousin to escape Karma." "Fuck that ugly bitch I owe her an ass whipping anyway. Ion give a fuck who idea it was." Yahtia popped off throwing a bucket of water on TJ just to activate the perm and the Nair. "If you even try to move. I will stab you in your titty and cut your nipples off and make you swallow them like a Xanax." Karma spat. Joy began pouring a pale of fire ants on TJ. Involuntarily she flinched her fight or flight skills kicking in. True to her word Karma stabbed her in her titty as promised. "Bitch I said don't fucking move." TJ cried out. "Please get these ants off me. I will do anything you ask me to. Just please make it stop." The ants were everywhere, and the bites were turning quickly into welts and large knots in her head.

Karma had a flash back of what TJ did to her back in the day and smeared perm across TJ's face. Some got in her eyes and mouth, but Karma did not care. "You remember this bitch? How the fuck does this feel?" Karma screamed. After TJ continuously begged for the torture to stop. Yahtia used the same pressure washer with ice freezing water to hose her down. Spraying most of it in her face causing her to gasp for air. Yahtia did not rinse her head thoroughly making sure to leave most the mixture in. In a few hours TJ would most likely need Rogaine after this. With a 100% chance of being completely bald. "It burns." TJ cried. "Very soon you will be a naked mole rat", Joy said. Karma grabbed TJ by what little hair was left and pulled her to the other side of the warehouse to join Dax. "You two bulling mutha fuckas are gonna stay here for a few weeks until you start work". Craig stated. Letting Kross explain exactly what they would be doing. "You can stop whining and complaining. You are going to go on a little vacation. We are going to send you to Trinidad instead of the Feds." Kross teased. "You will make that trip a few times. Each time you will be bringing back precious cargo." Kross ran down what they needed to know. Kross added how they would get in and out of the countries and bypass international customs. "Each time you will be given a route and you will make each stop on the route; our people will manage the rest. If you decide you wanna run off with our shit you will be hunted down. Not before we find your mamas and make them pay for your bullshit. Understand" Kross demanded.

Karma began to speak. "You both are wanted felons at this point," showing them the news reports on her phone. "TJ you are wanted for aiding and harboring a fugitive. Dax you are a dangerous escapee so if either of you decide to not play by the rules you will be locked up and then we will come get you from prison. The torture will be deadly. You are being watched at all times and you will not leave until Hero is ready for you." They both shook their heads in understanding. "Nah use all of them words y'all had a little while ago. We don't understand head movements." Ozias said. "Yes" they said dryly. Karma corrected them quickly making them say "Yes Ma'am." "Good glad y'all understand the assignment. Now this five-pound bag of dry dog food should be enough to hold you animals until we return. Oh, and if you get thirsty the toilet is in the back flush and drink." Yahtia smirked at Karma. "Damn bitch a real Hennessy fountain huh."

Karma tried hard not to laugh but Joy laughed aloud causing them both to burst in laughter. As they made their way out of the warehouse Yahtia stopped, "I almost forgot" holding up a black dress. "Your mama wears a size twelve right. They about to be matching on the front row for some flower bringing and soul singing. Don't make me drop these dresses off." Yahtia threatened and walked to the car with Kross close behind her. "We have no issue with you" Karma addressed Duchess. She had been standing there silently crying hoping to be spared. "You can be dropped back off where you were picked up from or you can stay here and ride this wave with your friends." Karma said giving Duchess and ultimatum. "Drop me back off please. I won't say shit to nobody." Duchess cried, trying hard to steady her breathing. Grabbing her arm and pulling her into the car. Joy told her. "That was a million-dollar decision, good girl. "Please know you are not hard to find, so a final word of advice. Snitches get stiches."

The ride back to campus was full of laughs as if nothing happened. They tossed Duchess out in her front yard like she was a newspaper. Barely making a stop. The crew was all into each other playing footsy with their mate and begin to get touchy feely making the ride home a make out session.

CHAPTER 17
UNFOLDING THE TRUTH

A few weeks after Troy's release Nekendra was still nursing his crusty ass back to health. Troy was all fucked up. He could not hold his shit in. If he passed gas shit would fly out his ass full speed. Nekendra never complained or made fun of him. Troy was pissed about his condition and he cowardly blamed Nekendra. Troy was extremely jealous of Nekendra. Nekendra's dedicated worth ethic and being a lovable person made him evil inside. One day they were watching a comedy show and everyone was laughing. The joke was about the dudes' big lips. Troy in his twisted mind decided that Nekendra was laughing at him and that was enough to push him over the edge. Determined to wipe the smile from her face Troy started beating on her again. Troy criticized everything she did and turned everything into a heated fight. Nekendra would fight back but he did not fight fair. Troy would wait until she was not expecting it and jump on her, he would punch her from behind like a bitch ass nigga. Nekendra kids were so confused wanting to help their mom. The kids did not understand why a man would do such harsh things to their mom. They were even more confused on why she kept taking him back. Nekendra needed a friend desperately but did not call Joy because she knew how Joy would take things the extreme. She knew not to call her sister Za'Drea either, because Za'Drea would come pistol ready on go mode, with her trigger finger itching. Nekendra was not ready to let him go even though she was tired of the situation. In the meantime, Nekendra did what she was comfortable with. She isolated herself in her apartment hiding from all her friends and family.

Molly and Uvoka were both sitting in county. Uvoka told the judge that Molly gave her clarification that she owned the house. Uvoka explained that Molly had given her all the clothes and things that was recovered. After agreeing to undergo a psychological evaluation Uvoka would be released after two weeks. Molly did not get off so easy. Molly had other pending charges. All the swindles she did with Karmelo were catching up with her. Four couples had lost everything behind the Boston's. All the couples were out for blood. The judge issued a warrant for Karmelo hoping to have him brought in sooner rather than later. The public defender that was representing Molly, Kyle Sanchez reached out to Karma to discuss the case. Kyle gave her all the information hoping to get some sympathy from her. Kyle was aiming for Molly, to at least walk on the breaking and entering charges. Molly had written a statement shifting all the blame to Karmelo for the fraud cases. If Kyle could get her off on the breaking and entering Molly would go free. Karma had no sympathy and hung up in his face. Karma was very curious to know about all the shit her dad had been participating in. "Karmelo Joel Boston born 5.28.79 social 456-98-0845. You should be able to find everything with that right." Karma asked Joy. "I need everything on everybody he ever associated with dig deep and spare nothing. Joy this bastard hiding something I feel it." Karma said with a confused and concerned look. Joy was already typing away. "Sis if he has shit stains, we will know about it. Just give me a blunt and a few hours." "My girl," Karma high fived Joy.

Yahtia was sick to her stomach she was covered in chill bumps just hearing Karmelo's name. Yahtia grabbed her jacket and walked out before anyone could notice her face. Yahtia knew her secret was getting ready come out and a part of her was relieved, but the other part was terrified. Yahtia thought back to all the disgusting things Karmelo made her do as a child. Yahtia had blocked most of it out and moved on with her life. Things were hard for her not to tell Karma about her dads' sick ways. Karmelo just do not stop with the crime Yahtia thought. Him trying to steal her parents' house topped off his fuckery. Yahtia felt as if her past was coming back to bite her in the ass. Yahtia wiped her eyes free of tears and met Kross at the donut shop for coffee and donuts. Trying to put a smile on her face before he arrived, but she could not. As soon as Kross laid eyes on her he knew something was wrong. When he asked Yahtia broke down crying. "I don't know how to manage this. You will leave me. I don't want to lose anyone in my family." Yahtia cried on his shoulder. Kross went ahead and ordered her favorites and walked her to his car. They sat at the park, and he just held her while she cried. Kross knew that she would let it all out when she got ready. Kross also knew that whatever hurt his woman was gonna die slowly and painfully.

Things were heating up; Karmelo's associates and co-workers were all leaving him messages about the FEDS. "Thanks bro. Molly bitch ass snitched and gave a fucking statement on me. So, it's a must I get missing for a little bit." Karmelo said to one of his associates and scamming partners Luke. No one knew where he was going that was for the best for him. Using a fake ID Karmelo bought a train ticket to Wisconsin to meet up with Carlita, a Latina hottie he met on Tinder. Karmelo was no slow leak, he felt someone would hack his information and try and track him. Karmelo was scared shitless he figured he could wiggle his way out of the scamming. Karmelo knew if anyone found out about his twisted fetish for younger girls he was finished. Karmelo tried deleting and burning every shared evidence he had that connected him to any of his victims he just hoped it was enough.

Joy typed furiously at her keypad. She was dumbfounded and sickened by what she found but she needed to verify all the information before she shared anything. Joy refused to give this kind of information without having straight facts. Karma ordered food and rolled some fat blunts. Karma felt like shit was about to go left and she did not want to be sober when it did. Karma was tired of her fucked up ass parents. Karma and Joy sat in silence passing the weed and working. Two blunts and three hours later Joy finally spoke. "Sis grab that bottle of D'usse and call the boys. Get Yahtia and Kross too. We need all hands-on deck". Joy said and tossed back a double shot. "What the fuck going on." Karma asked getting loud. Joy stopped her with a hand. "No disrespect sis but right now I don't need you yelling at me and for once I need you to listen. Get everyone together I do not want to say this bullshit more than once. We need the family here for family matters." Joy's face said everything. Karma knew it was serious the only time she ever seen Joy this serious was about her friend Nekendra. Fearing the worst Karma called everyone letting them know what Joy had said. "Look I don't know what the fuck Joy found. I just know she said bring your ass and be ready to move when you get here. Apparently, it's some fuck shit that will affect the family." Karma said almost in tears. Less than an hour later everyone was coming in. Craig and Ozias were sprinting up the stairs and ran into Kross and Yahtia who were being all lovey dovey. "Ewww y'all are sickening." Ozias said pushing past them. Followed by Craig saying, "get a room." The four of them walked into the dorm. Yahtia looked at Joy and her tears came flooding back. "Damn it Joy why are you so fucking good at what you do." Yahtia went to her room and slammed the door. At that moment Joy understood just how bad this was going to get, and she took another shot.

Craig pulled Joy to the side and tried to sweet talk the information out of her, but she was not budging. "I will only say it one time and I won't say it until Yahtia is ready so make yourself comfortable." Craig got an attitude knowing that Joy hated when he was mad but even that did not work. Joy usually was the calm one. Now she is bossed up refusing to be bullied. "Look y'all please be patient. I love y'all and yes y'all will all know what I know. This is different so, get mad scratch your ass everybody gonna wait. Smoke Drink Fuck whatever but I ain't saying shit." Joy walked off. She knocked on Yahtia's door then sent her a text. "Sis let me in we can talk first then I can let everyone else know or you can, but you know they have to find out." Tia snatched the door open and pulled Joy inside. Yahtia even shut Kross out which was not like her. Yahtia broke down and told everything to Joy happy to finally be getting everything out. Joy did not interrupt she just listened and held her friend. Joy cried with her and reassured her that she was not alone and was loved. "Nothing is your fault, and nobody will judge you. It is a must we tell them because that bastard must pay. It wasn't just you." Joy told her everything she found. There had been about fifteen victims that she found and most of them were in the neighborhood they grew up in. Joy had even found evidence of him buying child sex slaves. "Karmelo is a sick bastard."

Yahtia came out of her room holding Joy's hand. Yahtia found Kross and just hugged him. Kross was so nervous. He had no idea what had his girl hurting but he needed to make it right. Joy began to speak but Craig interrupted her. "I need answers and I need them now." Craig demanded. Joy rolled her eyes. "Stop being a little bitch please. This is not about you and if you shut the fuck up for just a second you will get your fucking answers." Joy snapped. Yahtia and Karma locked eyes and then looked back and forth between their brother and their friend. "Damn bro, guess you need to shut the fuck up". Karma laughed. Everyone joined in on the laughter even though Craig did not like being the source it felt good to everyone to laugh. "As I was saying. Mr. Karmelo Joel Boston is a pedophile, rapist, money launderer, real estate scammer, and the list goes on and on. Karmelo has successfully swindled families out of their properties for years. Keeping what he wants for himself and selling the others for his own personal gain. I have located four other families that he did this too. It was the same set up he tried with Toyah and Juan." Joy said pointing to Craig and Yahtia. "From what I can tell Molly was in on everything including some other underhanded deals. The worst of the worst is his pedophilia. I have located fifteen young girls that have been photographed, molested, or raped by Karmelo and some of his associates." Now it was Joy's turn to cry. Joy had the attention of everyone in the room they knew something was lingering in the air and just waited for it to be put out there. Joy could not bring herself to say it aloud, so she focused on all the other victims. Joy felt like she would be violating Yahtia if she spoke on her individual experiences. Knowing why Joy was struggling to get through her presentation Yahtia stood up and joined Joy in the middle of the room. "One of the victims is me."

Before she lost the nerve Yahtia went into how everything happened to her. "Back when we were in elementary school when I would sneak you clothes and stuff." Yahtia spoke to Karma but loud enough for everyone to hear. "Karmelo found me sneaking out one night and told me he would have me locked up for breaking and entering unless I let him take pictures of me. After that it did not happen for a while. The next time it happened I caught him taking pictures through my room window and this time I was naked. I called myself going over there and cursing him out, but he kissed me. I tried to leave but he hurt me and threatened to hurt you." Yahtia cried but she managed to get the story out with all the details. By the time she finished everyone was crying. Kross hugged her tight and refused to let her go. Kross was livid, and everyone thought he was holding it together for Yahtia but Yahtia just being in his arms was the only thing keeping him calm. Kross promised himself and the Almighty that he would avenge his love.

After what seemed like hours Craig spoke after wiping his tears away. "Imma kill that fucker slowly." Karma chimed right in. "Nah bro imma melt his dick off with acid and make him eat his balls." Ozias patted her letting her know that he had her back no matter what. Kross let it be known right then. "I don't care what y'all do to him, just know that his blood belongs to me." Kross words left no room for debate. Sure thing, Craig and Ozias should rightfully feel some type of way and want pay back; Yahtia was their whole heart. They both were hurting and sadden by the news and wish they would have known sooner. The hate is real for the men. Karmelo had unknowingly signed his death certificate when he messed with Yahtia. "We got your back bro", Craig said accepting Kross as a man. His sister's man. Craig would give him the honor and respect to discard of this man in his own way. "Just make sure he suffers." Silence filled the room. It was a comfortable silence even though one of the family had been hurt they were alright and cherished that moment together.

CHAPTER 18
ON THA MOVE

Joy checked the police database for any leads and information she could find on Karmelo and his case. "Damn, bitch your mom has no love or loyalty. Molly wrote a statement on Karmelo and is waiting for him to be found. Says here if they catch him, she will testify against him and she will walk free". Joy notified everyone. "Slimy bitch was always good at covering her ass." Karma spat in disgust. Karma hated Molly increasingly each day. It made her sick to her stomach that she was created by that woman. "If nobody else deserves to stay in prison she does. Molly should not get to walk away from any of this especially because she knew about it all." Karma fumed. "We will think of something for her sis. Molly will not go unpunished. Karma's rules." Joy said hugging Karma making her smile. "The police are actively looking for Karmelo, and they are doing surprisingly good right now. Should I help them? Or?" Joy dragged the question out. Joy could update the police database so they would think they found the information that Joy actually found. "Makes no difference sis, just know he got to pay, we're going to handle this shit our way. Karma is a bitch in a skirt. Remember" Karma announced, and everyone agreed. "I knew that I was just making sure. I tracked him to Wisconsin, but his trail has died there. So, I am still digging." Joy said going back to her laptop to work. Yahtia called Hero filling him in on the situation and what they needed him to do. As usual he was ready, willing, and able to assist his new favorite crew.

Joy was frustrated as fuck. Karmelo is paranoid as fuck, he has gotten rid of his phones and computer so his location could not be tracked. Joy decided to switch tactics she printed out the last twenty phone calls and text conversations. One number and conversation stood out more than the others, so she focused there. "Jackpot" Joy said aloud while working. Joy did a trace on the number that had called Karmelo the most in the past 72 hours and found that it belonged to a Carlita Gomez. The two had exchanged several messages discussing how eager they were to finally meet one another. Going on a hunch Joy ran Karmelo's credit card again. Joy kept coming up short, so her fingers were crossed, and she was praying for a miracle. "Look at God. I got your sick ass now bitch." Feeling like a champion Joy finished tracking her prey. "The dumb ass used his card on the Uber app to get from the bus station to Calita's place." Joy explained to the crew while sending Hero the coordinates of Karmelo. "Now all we have to do is wait. Hero will pick him up and we can get started on creating his own personal hell." Joy said with a sick and twisted look in her eye. None of them knew the plan in its entirety but they did know he would pay with his ass, and eventually with his life for all the crimes committed against the family.

Joy looked at her phone for the first time in what seemed like forever. She noticed several missed calls from Nekendra, so she sent her a text. "Wassup Baby Mama you good? I been busy but if you need me, I am there." Joy sent. Joy was not ignoring her best friend, but she had a lot of other shit going on now and did not want to hear about anything related to Troy. Nekendra responded, "Yeah I just miss you sis." Nekendra needed to talk to Joy about what was going on. Nekendra knew that Joy would be pissed but she would at least listen. Not only had Troy started back beating her, but he had also been messing around with another woman. When Nekendra confronted him about it, he flipped and whipped her ass pretty good. Nekendra now had bruises on her face and arms. Nekendra was certain that at least one of her ribs were broken. To add insult to injury Troy left her for this mystery woman. "She is more woman than you could ever be, you nothing ass bitch." Troy slurred with his missing bottom lip as he walked over Nekendra's beaten body. The new couple has been seen publicly in the hood. Troy made sure to flaunt his new boo thang in her face. You would think Nekendra would be relieved that he left, but she was not. Nekendra was heartbroken and desperate for his love. Her attachment to Troy was unnatural and unexplainable. Joy just hoped Nekendra would understand someday before shit is too late.

Uvoka was released from the county jail after twenty-five days and an extensive psychological evaluation. The psychologist decided that Uvoka needed additional assistance mentally she had to continue treatment at the Department of Mental Health. "Ain't shit wrong with me man," Uvoka insisted as she was walked out of lock up. While being processed out the officer handed her the clothes, she was arrested in. Which Uvoka was so grateful. At least she could be cute and homeless. When the lady handed her the MCM bag she had stuffed at Karma's house Uvoka froze. At first, she thought it was a set-up, so she was hesitant taking the bag. Not knowing if the lady was being nice or if it was a mistake. Uvoka quickly shut the fuck up and got the hell on through signing all paperwork agreeing to mental treatment. Uvoka walked away from the detention center with nowhere to go and no one to call. As luck would have it, she found a twenty-dollar bill. Uvoka thanked God and made her way to McDonalds. Ordering a large Big Mac meal with extra sauce. Uvoka took a seat by the window and charged her phone while she ate. Uvoka was in deep thought about her life and what her next move would be when a group of kids caught her attention. They were all wearing Grady U hoodies. It was a long shot but if it were possible Uvoka could salvage her semester by doing a medical withdrawal and then transferring schools. At least then she would not be homeless. Uvoka logged into student portal only to find that she had already been given a withdraw fail and had been removed from housing. Checking her emails Uvoka found out that her belongings were at the campus police station and must be claimed within thirty days or they would be donated. To make matters worse Uvoka owed Grady University eight thousand dollars. She had property damage and her classes had an outstanding balance. Uvoka finished her food unable to even cry anymore. Uvoka took a deep breath realizing that her life was over, and it was all thanks to Karmell "Karma" Boston and her band of bitches.

With nowhere to go, Uvoka sat in the window at McDonalds just pondering life. Uvoka was void of all feeling. If "I don't give a fuck" was a person, it would most definitely be her. Scrolling through Facebook she stumbled across the sisters of Elegance page. Going through the pictures and reminiscing about when she and her crew ran the school and the sorority. It hurt to see Karma Yahtia and Joy with the shield and colors on. Uvoka damn near spit her drink out when she saw a picture of Adreama looking cozy with their sworn enemies. Tonera and Jherika were nowhere in sight. Now she was pissed. Adreama had switched up on the crew and she needed answers. Uvoka slid into Adreama's DM, "Hey bitch you look cute with your new besties. What's up with that?" she sent. To her surprise Adreama was quick to respond. "Don't we though. Pink and Black looks good on us. What do you want?" Uvoka did not expect the attitude but was ready with her own. "So, you the opps now. Who would have ever guessed it? I guess its fuck us and every woman for themselves. What does that bucked tooth bitch and her goof troop squad have on you to make you, their puppet? I need to know because you would never stoop this low for anyone. Not publicly anyway." "Oh, I thought a homeless bitch with a shitty attitude said something." Adreama clapped back. "I should be your least worry; your priorities are all fucked up." "You might want to get with the program because you are fighting a losing battle. These bitches will crush your soul with pleasure." "Fuck you Adreama! I can expose your bitch ass with so much shit." Uvoka texted angrily. "Girl I was exposed to my lowest the shit you know is small things to a giant, go wash your shitty ass I can smell you through the phone. Have a good day." Adreama finished her text then blocked her once best friend. Dreama was not about to get back on Karma's bad side she had learned her lesson, and Uvoka had to do the same. Adreama still partied but she was now a casual coke user she no longer sucks and lick the nut sack of dogs. Adreama stopped tricking and became more conservative and classier. If Joy continued to keep her embarrassing videos from leaking and ruining her life Adreama would gladly be their lap dog. If Uvoka knew what was good for her she would leave well enough alone. Jherika and Tonera both left Grady after seeing all the damaged Karma Joy and Tia was causing to their once squad. They both knew they had secrets that would ruin their families and it was not worth it to them. The two often thought about revenge but killed that thought when they discovered the power and committed loyalty Karma had.

Karmelo stepped off the Amtrack wearing grey Nike joggers, fresh Air Force 1s, complete with a Nike hoodie and skull cap. Karmelo looked around with his duffle bag in hand looking like good money. Carlita quickly spotted him. She was relieved that he was as cute as his profile picture on Tinder and judging by the print in his pants she would be able to have some fun with him. Carlita flagged him down and gave him a hug. They embraced and touched like old lovers instead of internet sneaky links. Carlita drove them to her place where she had already set everything up for him. Karmelo sat down on the lounge chair making himself comfortable. "So good to finally lay my eyes on you sexy." Karmelo complimented a blushing Carlita. "I need you to do me a favor though" Karmelo said smacking her butt. "What do you need Papi?" "It's my ex, back in South Carolina. She went to the police with some bullshit story. I think she has a private investigator following me". Karmelo explained. "So, I need for you to find us another place to stay and get rid of your phone. I can't have her finding me by tracking you." Carlita was giving him the side eye because his story sounded crazy as hell. Karmelo saw that she would need some convincing, so he pulled out three crisp hundred-dollar bills. "This should be enough to cover the loss. I swear I am not trying no funny shit with you love. I just can't risk being found." Karmelo slid the money into her bra and caressed her body with his other hand. Karmelo was not above seducing a woman to get his way. This was a "by any means necessary" kind of situation. Carlita relented after kissing him and feeling his dick for herself. She just had to see what it felt like. "Ok Papi. You are safe with me. Let me call my friend." Carlita said but paused when she saw the panicked look on Karmelo's face. "Don't worry baby she is like my sister she is with whatever bullshit I'm with." Carlita put him at ease with a wink. "Hola Chica. Me and my new boo headed your way for some fun. We are staying at your spot though." Karmelo had a big ass grin on his face not only did Carlita smash the phone to pieces, but she laid the groundwork for him to have a threesome. How lucky could one nigga be? He thought to himself.

Carlita was all over Karmelo, and the two stumbled into Martina's basement damn near fucking with their clothes on. "Damn bitch you started the party without me". Martina interrupted as she closed the door to the rest of the house. Martina lived in her aunt's basement, but it was more like a studio efficiency apartment. Martina had everything she needed, and never had to go into the rest of the house if she did not want to. "Of course, not baby we just warming up." Carlita kissed Martina on the lips. Karmelo's dick was brick hard instantly. Carlita knew Karmelo had a money stash based on the story he was telling her. She had already planned to rob him, but she wanted the big bucks and not his pocket money. Sex was always the way to a man's wallet, so Carlita played on his sexual appetite. Carlita was no dummy she and Martina had done this a few times. Martina followed Carlita's act knowing that something good was going to come from it. Plenty bomb ass sex and most likely some money. "Oh my, looks like your friend is ready to play with us." Martina said dropping to her knees. The two sucked Karmelo off quickly giving him their best impression of Super Head. When Karmelo's dick exploded, they swallowed every drop and then fixed his pants for him. Karmelo was in heaven his body was relaxed because of that he lowered his guard. Pulling a wad of money from his sock he gave the women a stack. "Go get all the party supplies you think we might need. Food too which I want need because I will be feasting off you two beauties. I plan to keep us in motion for the next day or two." Karmelo flirted, but his twisted mind was thinking of all the kinky shit he could do to them with little to no resistance. They took the money promising to return quickly.

Karmelo waited until he thought they were gone before he went to the shower.

"Bitch what's the move are we partying then making a play or is he just a play?" Martina asked. "Shit, it can go either way. I think he definitely down to party." Martina continued counting the stack of bills in Carlita's hand. "Bitch if he will hand us this money for a party, I know we can get more just got to figure out where he got it stashed. With the way he is talking he is holding a lot of cash on him right now." Carlita said from the driver's seat. "It got to be in that duffle bag he was holding on to it too tight even when we were tag teaming him." Martina noted. "Let's go get Bo and Hammer" Carlita said turning down the next street. "If he willing to buy me a new iPhone 13 and hand out hundreds like toilet paper, he has some long money and I want it". Why we need Bo and Hammer dusty assess sis"? let us just play this out." Martina suggested while texting the dope man. Martina planned to get higher than the moon tonight. "According to his story he is in some type of trouble, so I don't know how long we have until some shit pop off. I plan to have all his money and be long gone away from him in case the law is on his tail." "I don't do the law." Carlita schooled her friend finding a park in the back of the local bar they frequently attending. "Bitch I ain't friendly with the mutha fuckan law either. Martina said co-signing on Carlita's comment. After meeting with their dealer and doing two lines of crushed Percocet's they entered the establishment.

Carlita and Martina sat at the bar directly across from the pool tables where Bo and Hammer were hustling some poor souls in a game of pool. Bo and Hammer were some ruthless Latino thugs that would do about anything just because. So, with the promise of money the girls were certain they could get them to do their dirty work with Karmelo. After the game was over Carlita called the men over to her. "What the fuck y'all sluts want?" Bo asked drinking the rest of Carlita's beer. "Handsome that is no way to speak to a lady." Carlita said looking at him. Those two had a love hate relationship it was weird, but it was them. "We got a job for you two" Carlita went on to tell them about Karmelo. "What the fuck that got to do with us? I mean why can't you just fuck him then take his money? I'm not really in a robbing mood." Bo laughed signaling for the bartender to hand him a beer. Martina paid for a bucket of beer and waved the crisp big faces across Bo and Hammer's face. "We not really trying to do all that we trying to get this money. Y'all can fuck around and find out what this tag team feel like. Maybe even get a few dollars too." Martina said seductively. The boys were all in now. Hammer shifted his dick in his pants he had a hard on from Carlita licking his ear. They took the bucket of beer to the back room; they all partake in snorting a jumbo line of Percocet. The women explained the situation and the set up. The four left the bar together with a plan to get paid and laid. "What a fun night this is turning out to be huh

Bo?" Hammer laughed as he pulled off in his sunshine yellow Hummer truck.

The girls entered the basement first purposely leaving the door unlocked. Karmelo let out a breath he had been holding when he saw Martina with pizza boxes. Carlita sat the drinks and party drugs on the table. "You been missing me Papi?" Carlita started up. The plan was to get him busy. Then the guys were going to come in making it look like a robbery. This way if police were after Karmelo the four of them could not be linked to one another. "Hell yeah. I got nervous thinking you two beauties left me high and dry." Karmelo pouted palming their ass. "Never" the girls giggled as they prepared three shots and a few lines. Karmelo did not want to do a line, but he did pop two pills. He was never a fan of putting shit up his nose. The three were deep into a make out session when Bo and Hammer made their appearance in the basement. Karmelo was pinned underneath the women so he could not see the intruders until it was too late. Bo pushed the girls to one side and Hammer delivered two hard blows directly to Karmelo's face causing his nose to leak blood instantly. "Damn them down south boys bleed like bitches". Hammer laughed as he zipped tied Karmelo's hands and feet. Karmelo was dazed but he was conscious, so he heard everything. "Damn I fucked up". Karmelo whispered to himself. Karmelo remained quiet hoping and praying they would not find his money. His hopes were killed quickly when Martina and Carlita emptied out his duffle bag finding the coffee can filled with hundreds. It was thirty thousand dollars inside the can. That was money Karmelo had swindled people out of was being taken from him. "Found it". Carlita announced already dividing the money between the four of them. Hammer punched on Karmelo for fun trying to see how much damage he could do while Bo repacked the duffle bag. "Imma sale all this shit. This rich nigga got style."

Once they got everything, they wanted the men threw Karmelo in the back of the Hummer with the girls and they pulled off. "Next time don't trust a big butt and a smile". Bo laughed. "Yeah, I hear these two are poison with some good pussy." Hammer joined in on the jokes and laughter. They drove to Kenosha and tossed Karmelo out on his ass.

Karmelo did not move until they had been gone for about five minutes. Karmelo did not want them to turn around and strip him like Hammer had suggested. Karmelo had four thousand dollars in his shorts under his pants. One thousand went to the ladies for the party supplies. Karmelo was feeling lucky he was not searched. After limping for a few hours Karmelo spotted a shopping center. He desperately needed a phone; Karmelo slowly walked to the Metro PCS kiosk buying a prepaid phone. "Hey where can I find a liquor store and room"? Karmelo asked the clerk being careful not to show how much money he was holding. Karmelo managed to find the Minimart and a motel. Karmelo nervously checked into the roach infested motel watching his surroundings close. Karmelo spent the rest of the night trying to find a way out of his mess, that he foolishly allowed his dick to get him into. Karmelo had underestimated Carlita thinking she was young and dumb. Karmelo gave himself a pep talk about how he had to take control of this situation. He then drunk two bottles of cheep store wine and passed out. Hero had some difficulties finding Karmelo. The tracking information he received from Joy was not accurate. Hero sent Joy a detailed text about his dead end. Joy rolled up a blunt and proceeded to find the glitch. Her findings show that Carlito has a new phone number. Joy tracks her down then forwarded Hero the added information.

Hero had four teenage girls with him to take back to Pakistan to become sex slaves. He felt he could multitask and manage that buyer while he manages his favorite crew. Hero finds Carlita at a local bar getting ready to walk out with two black men. As Carlita and the men turn the corner of the bar Hero stabs the two men in the side. The men hunched over then Hero grabs Carlito and threw her in his van and drives off. Carlita did not scream or fight. "Who the fuck are you"? You didn't have to hurt my friends it's enough of me to go around." "Don't flatter yourself if you knew my line of work you would watch what you say." Hero said with a thick accent. "I'm looking for Karmelo Boston he was last seen with you. Where is he"? "That nigga was acting strange. He appeared to be in some trouble back in South Carolina, my girlfriend and I had him robbed." "He was beaten up by the same men that robbed him, we all had him followed thinking he would circle back." "He purchased a phone from the shopping center parking lot and that was the last time I saw him." Carlita explained looking at Hero as if she wanted to fuck him. "You hurt my two men they were about to fuck me, so the least you can do is become my substitute". When Carlita was done talking she was naked rubbing between her legs breathing heavy in heat. Hero thought to himself how he could place her in the back with the other girls and give her a free ride to get more dick than she could manage. Hero whipped out his 13-inch dick and he mouth fucked her slamming his dick past her tonsils. Carlita gagged for air she could not breathe. Carlita had a thick monster dick down her throat. Hero roughly placed her head flat against the front seat of the van he forced an arch in her back and rammed his dick in her ass. Hero then fucked her silly Carlita was on a roller coaster ride scared for her life. Carlita begins to vomit, Hero was riding that ass non-stop. Hero continued for a full hour Carlita was begging Hero to stop. Hero was in his groove, stroking and pushing deep ignoring all the screams and cries. Carlita had no idea what she was getting into she bit off more than she could chew. Hero was well experienced in the sex game. Sex to him was like lacing up your shoes totally normal. Hero finished her off like a mortal combat game. The girls in the back begin to cry they wanted no part of what was happening in the front seat. Hero exploding what felt like an ounce of cum inside Carlita. Hero then threw her out the van like a bag of trash and headed to the shopping center.

Hero had given the sales rep a bogus story about his injured brother. The rep remembered Karmelo, and she gave Hero the number to the phone he purchased. Sending the information to Joy she had his location within minutes. Karmelo was at the Sizzle Inn motel a block away. Hero stepped inside the motel in go mode. Hero gave a description of Karmelo to the borderline high clerk behind the desk. Hero slapped a big face on the counter and said he needed the key to the room. The clerk snatched the bill and passed him the key to Karmelo's room. Hero opened the door with his gun in hand Karmelo was on the bed sleep with his mouth opened wide and head tilted back. Karmelo was so relaxed until Hero jammed his extended Glock down his throat. Karmelo eyes almost popped out his head. Karmelo tried to jump up but was overpowered by Hero. "Don't fight it because I will shoot you." Hero then realized that that Karmelo was a familiar face. Hero knew him as Monty someone who was a frequent flyer with buying young sex slaves. Monty was a high paying client that loved to photograph and sex underage girls. Hero gave Karmelo instructions to get up and walk to the van calmly. Once they arrived at the van Hero gagged him then placed a bag over his head. Hero wrapped Karmelo in duct tape until he felt he was unable to move or break free. Hero then tied him down to a wooden bench in the back of the van on the opposite side of the girls. Hero reported his newfound information to Joy. Hero gave full length details of what Karmelo has done as Monty. Karmelo had well over a thousand transactions delivered by Hero living out his sick fetish.

The crew headed to the pizza warehouse to check on their guest. Dax and TJ were coming along well as expected. They smelled terrible and looked malnourished. Dax was doing push-ups when they open the door. TJ was bent over holding her stomach covered in blood from her period. "Damn y'all mutha fuckas stink." Karma said while holding her nose. Craig went and grabbed a bottle of dawn dish detergent out his car he squirted them down then Joy hosed them down. "That hoe need some summers eve that dish detergent not going to cut that smell." Said Yahtia. "Dawn is for grease." Karma yelled. "I'm doing the best I can." Craig said laughing. "Joy make that bitch open up her ass cheeks and hose her thoroughly she smells foul." Yahtia said loudly talking over the water hose spraying. Ozias brings in another bag of dog food and drops it on the floor next to the two dog food bowls. Dax and TJ back was against the wall they tried to escape a few times and the security crew that was on shift had to chin check them back in line. The two finally realize they were there to stay until Karma and the crew saw fit to release them. When Dax notice the crew setting up for torture, he then broke down apologizing for trying to escape. Dax cried like a bitch begging for them not to torture him anymore. Dax was already burnt like a piece of toast and had been beaten worse than Clubber Lang did Rocky Balboa. TJ followed his lead begging Karma too; TJ cried her heart out trying to get sympathy. "Shut the fuck up and swallow that shit how I had to. Bad bitches don't cry." You have bullied dozens of girls in school now look at your ass, this is uno bitch the shit has reversed back to me." Karma stated as she rolled up her sleeves and smacks TJ across the face. "Did your funky pussy ass have pitty on me when I begged for y'all bitches to not fuck with me." Karma must have had a flash back because she spazed out on TJ picking up a chair and bashed her across the face repeatedly. Yahtia then cracked her orange juice bottle across her face. Joy wrapped a towel over her head and squeezed it tight causing her to gasp for air. They all three then gave her some kicks to her chest while laughing at her ass. Karma and Joy lifted TJ up in the air and slammed her down through a table WWE style. "I know we didn't come for this, but that bitch struck a nerve." Karma said walking off fixing her wig.

Kross had several high-tech torture devices ready for Karmelo. The crew finished setting up. They all decided to leave and wait on Hero to drop off their prize.

CHAPTER 19
NOTHING BUT A SPERM DONOR

Karmelo had so many thoughts floating through his head. Trying his hardest to figure out what the fuck was going on and who wanted him captured. Karmelo knew the line of work Hero was in, so he knew somebody paid for his capture. Karmelo could not figure out who. Not yet anyway. Hero sent the thumbs up emoji to Joy. "It's show time people." Joy said with a big bubbly smile. The entire crew all jumped up like the house was on fire and sprinted to the car with excitement. They all had a heart full of rage and they were anxious from the long wait. Karmelo had been the topic of their discussion for far too long they were about to put this whole situation to sleep. The crew made their way to the back to pizza warehouse in silence. The blunt was going in rotation when Karma passed the blunt to Tia, she noticed she was crying softly to herself. Karma wrapped her arm around her. "It's about to be over sis, let that shit out." Hero pulls up first, seconds later the crew came swarming in. The security pulled open the warehouse gate and the crew walked in going in different directions for different shit. Hero dumped Karmelo on the floor. Hero had to quickly back up because Kross immediately went Hank Aaron and begin beating Karmelo with a metal baseball bat. Kross swung heavy hits with all his power bussing Karmelo across the back and face sparing no body parts. Craig and Ozias joined in with body kicks and stomps they beat him to a pulp. Stripping him naked and tying him to a chair was the next step. Snatching the bag off his head Craig looked Karmelo in his bloody eyes. "You sick mutha fuckar. I hope you didn't think you were going to get away with what you did to my sister." "I wish I would have known about your molesting ass years ago; I would have saved a lot of girls from getting hurt, because I would have eliminated your ass execution style Craig said with pure hate." Ozias spit in Karmelo's face and walk away he became emotional thinking of Yahtia being abused in that way. Karmelo had no energy to talk or scream or even move at this point. Karmelo was holding on by a prayer. Joy came over with a big metal foot tub followed behind her was Yahtia with a rolling cart. On top of the cart was a giant pot with twenty pounds of boiling grits. His feet were placed in the tub while Tia and Karma poured the grits on top. He tried jumping up between screams only to be knocked back down with a blow to the head by Craig and Ozias. His head flopped down in his chest; he had passed out multiple times. The crew looked confused thinking he was dead. "Wake that bitch ass nigga up it ain't over don't take no pity on his ass he just my sperm donor this bitch means nothing to me." Karma spat. Kross backed everybody up and he pointed at Yahtia to do her she needed this closure this was the only way Yahtia would fight back from these nightmares. Yahtia walked around Karmelo for a few seconds, she then starts to talk about how he ruined her life as a child. Yahtia went deep with the graphic details of how Karmelo had his way with her then acted as if his sickness was her fault. Ozias was about to run over and pound on his ass some more, but Kross stopped him. "She got this bro". Karmelo could not mumble a word he knew his life was over. His thoughts were kill me already, but that would be too easy for him. Yahtia continued to talk while putting on a pair of gloves. Yahtia had a bag full of rusty nails. She took the nails out one by one and hammered them across his neck. Karmelo's screams were low his voiced was strained. Yahtia made her way to his arms and kneecaps. Yahtia then took a large head nail and hammered it into the inside of Karmelo's ear. Yahtia made the crew jump with that one. Yahtia took the smallest nails and forced them down his penis hole one by one. Yahtia pulled out a homemade but plug with spiked tips that she showed no mercy by plunging it up his ass. Yahtia then stomped his ass forcing the spikes to go further. Yahtia was riled up moving in victory. Yahtia did a dance move to let her crew know she was back. Yahtia was enjoying herself her voice and acts became more aggressive and direct. Moving on to her last play. Yahtia gripped his mouth opened and fucked his mouth with a shitty 12-inch dildo. Using all her strength jugging in and out his mouth. Karmelo already had bodily fluids leaking from all ends. But this was massive. Karmelo continued to vomit non-stop. Karmelo showered the entire floor with vomit, blood, shit and anything else that leaked. Hero was tuned in and was amazed by the damage control this crew could do. Hero then had to take the girls out the back for a few minutes to give them water and a donut and let them use the rest room. When he took them out Joy and Karma noticed how young they were. Their hearts melted instantly. "Oh my gosh, they are babies." Joy said softly. Craig whispered to Joy. "Mind your business we don't need no ugly trouble." We don't know what this man has going on or do we want any smoke with him." So let him conduct his business and move on". Yahtia then joined the rest of the crew Kross hugged her and so did Craig. "It's done sis we don't have to mention this ever again." Said Craig. Yahtia stepped over to Joy and Karma who had a shuffled look on their face. Karma whispered to Yahtia how those girls were going to become sex slaves. Yahtia felt bad she wanted to save those girls. Pulling Kross to the side asking him for advice on how to make a play at Hero about saving the girls keeping them from going to Pakistan for sex slaves. "This is the kind of man you don't fuck with, but for you fuck it." Kross said being unsure of his next move. While Hero had the girls in the back using the rest room Kross briefed Craig and O on the proposition he was about to hit Hero with. "My sister got your ass whipped fosho, this man might fuck around and kill us all." "I'm sure the deal is already sealed; this man is not about to negotiate with us." Craig said nervously. Craig gave Joy a mean look then motioned for her to come to him. "Why the fuck you had to get them started"? I told you to leave well enough alone damit." Hero was returning to the van to load the girls back in. "Now that my job is done, I will be leaving you all for now. As always nice doing business with you." Hero said as he extended his hand out for a shake. "I need to run something by you before you bail out." Kross spoke firmly. "You mentioned to us guys that you had a fight club over in your country." "Yes, my partners and I make lots of money are you interested in joining forces"? "Not exactly." Why don't you take this scum bag off our hand and let us keep the girls here not for anything sexual we only want to save them." My lady just went through an emotional roller-coaster with this sicko from what he did to her as a kid. Yahtia would like to give these girls a chance at life by doing a good deed for them." Kross waited patiently for a response. "I can defiantly do that, but he would only generate money in the fight club. I will be missing out on money in my sex business. I would need something in return any female would do." "I could easily make you an offer, but I have people in higher places I have to answer to. Coming back empty handed will discredit my character. So, give me something and they're all yours." Hero explained slowly so they could understand his words through his accent. "I have the perfect person for you." Karma blurted out. Let us put you in a hotel for tonight and you can let the girls stay here at the warehouse with our security and we do the official trade off tomorrow around sundown. "You kids are damn lucky I like how y'all move and operate. "Joy has saved my ass a few times providing me with professional courtesy when I ran into some hiccups." So, it's only right I pay it forward." "I need a bag of whatever I smelt the security guys smoking and a big booty black chick with a wet mouth. The throat skills need to be superb, Hero said then grabbed his dick giving clarification of what he just asks for." The guys started dapping him up like he was one of the boys. "Damn we never knew you could speak clear English, but you fluent around this bitch I see". Ozias joked. "We will deliver you a head banger shortly." Craig said. He was relieved that it went smooth. Craig took a mental note when Hero mentioned Joy helping him out on a few of his runs.

"Sis what's the move"? Tia asked. "I'm going to drop the charges on Molly and have her released and act like all is forgiven and then drop her ass off with Hero. Kill two birds with one stone." "Whoop there it is". Said Joy. Yahtia, Joy, and Karma went to untie the girls and give them a pep talk that they would be free after tomorrow. The ladies spent time talking with the girls and they managed to make them smile. Reassuring them they would regain their childhood back and have nice girly things that girls should have. Karmelo was laid out on the cold cement floor half dead. Hero searched the pockets of his bloody clothes and helped himself to what money he had left in his pockets. "He will not need this where he is going". Hero stated while entering his van. "Hold up fam I got one more thing I need to do." Craig come help me really quick". Karma spoke. Karma had a large amount of Hydrofluoric acid mixed up ready for use. Karma placed on her protective gear and signaled for Craig to place Karmelo in position. Craig kicked Karmelo flat on his back and kicked his legs spreading them far apart. Karma was going to make good on what she said she was going to do to Karmelo. Karma poured the acid on Karmelo's dick and watched it melt away, his dick was fuzzing like an Alka-Seltzer. Dax and TJ had front row seats to the horror show they both set Indian style on the cold floor while security stood close by. They both were scared shitless for their life. Dax glanced over at TJ; his eyes was full of tears "I think we have fucked up cuz." That was all he could say. TJ burst into tears and begin to vomit. "The next mutha fuckar that vomits in here will catch a beat down, one of the security men Curry said.

Craig and Karma returned to the car. Yahtia and Joy curiously wanted to know what just went on. "Don't worry I got it all on video." Craig said as he passed his phone around. The crew loaded up the car to go manage business. During the car ride it would not be them if they did not smoke. "I want to thank you all for the support and having my back. I am so sorry Craig for not telling you." Sis chill you don't owe me no explanation its done and over with." Craig said as he blew her a kiss because he was in the front seat and could not hug her. "I ask all of you this one favor because I cannot relive this again. Please do not tell mom and dad." Everyone was silent but they were in total agreeance. The thought of Toyah and Juan finding something so horrific out about their baby girl would kill them. Kross held on to Yahtia tightly he then whispered in her ear; "I'm going to make you, my wife."

CHAPTER 20
THE PROCESS

Karma had a meeting with Molly's public defender Kyle Sanchez. When they met, she handed him a signed notarized statement of her dropping all chargers on Molly. Kyle went over the process and gave her confirmation that Karmelo would be going down for all the other charges when he is apprehended. I'm going to process this paperwork and your mom will be out within the hour." The nerdy public defender said to Karma.

Karma contacted Ivy about some resources pertaining to the girls they were saving. Ivy found a group home that would be perfect for the girls. Ivy explained they needed to produce a name and birthdate if possible and get much family history and background as they could. Karma was concerned because she knew these girls had no family and probably did not know much. "That will be ok we just have to gather this information for our records and make since of who they are". Ivy explained. Kimmie Jones age 10, Irma Buttons age 12, Candice Williams age 15, and Shavon Moss age 9. The girls were processed in and excited about being around other girls and not sweaty old men desperate for sex. Yahtia, Joy and Karma all went shopping buying the girls what they needed and more. Kross and Ozias wanted to splurge on the girls as well they bought sneakers and purses. The entire crew wanted to give the girls a warm welcome. It was their duty to make the girls feel good in this world and for them to live comfortable as kids. Karma later picked Molly up from the county jail. "OMG I'm so glad you had a change of heart Karmell I meant Karma" "Don't make me take your ass back in there. You know my name don't try me again." OK I'm sorry DANG." "Let us not do this. I want us to spend time together I'm starving how about Outback a juicy steak would be so nice"? Molly said trying to be convincing. "Sounds good you buying"? Karma said being sarcastic. Molly dropped her head. Where are we going? You passed the exit to the house." Molly questioned. "You been through so much so I'm sending you and dad on a vacation." "Karmelo is a wanted man you need to turn his ugly ass in he was about to let me take the blame for all his shit." Molly spat. Karma pulled up at the warehouse full speed she did not want to spend another second with Molly. Hero was already in position. Karma stepped out the car she then spoke loudly. "That's her." Hero opened the passenger car door. He pulled Molly out the car by her arm. Hero turned her around as if she was about to be handcuffed. Hero tied her hands tightly; Molly begin to scream and fight. "What's going on Karma"? Help me please." Get off me, get off me, Molly continued to scream out. Molly had a set of lungs on her she was getting louder and louder. "I am going to have to gag her." Said Hero. "She belongs to you no explanation needed." Karmelo was already in the back of the van and seconds later so was Molly. "Hey fam thanks again for your generosity. Hero gave a head nod. The bitch may be useful to you. She's a nurse you may need her in the future for your wounded fighters." "Good looking." Hero pulled off to take his passengers to Pakistan. Karma paid the security guys and she left as well.

Karma, Tia, and Joy had been going through their list dealing with the smaller fish. Making good on their promises they had planned for everyone. Karma had printed a name so many times on her list Joy had to ask her what was up with that. Urban Watts was his name. He out of all people gave Karma the most hell. Urban was a code red to the highest power. Urban would break in Karma's house in the middle of the night and force her to have sex with him and his cousin and sometimes his younger brother. Molly and Karmelo were never home so sometimes they would be there for weeks at a time. Urban would make her go steal him beer and cigars which she never did because she always had money around the house. Karma would get a crack head to purchase the items for her.

Karma had to take baths with Urban and suck his dick throughout the day and night. Urban even made Karma eat other females' pussy while he and a group of delinquent's watch. Urban beat Karma and would kick her out of her own house to sleep in the cold sometimes the rain. This went on for almost two years. It finally stopped when Karma moved in with Yahtia and her parents. Karma could not dare fix her mouth to tell Yahtia Karma was embarrassed about it. The things she had to do to basically stay alive was gut wrenching. The average person could not have survived all that Karma has been through. From day one of her attacks none of them has never been her fault. Karma could relate to Yahtia holding such a big secret about her dad. Karma knew the pain all too well. Urban was next up on the list. Karma's mind was going hay wire she was so anxious to destroy this creep.

Kross called a meeting for him Ozias and Craig. It was time for him to share his secret weapon and introduce his silent partner his boy Art Jefferies. Art had been doing small runs bringing in product form Trinidad. Art could only do so much because he was handicap. Art had limited use of his lower body and a stutter speech impediment. The product Art delivered was always helpful. Art had been trafficking lots of product through the states. A handicap superhero to all the dealers. Art had a permit to have two ounces of the strongest medical marijuana allowed. If he ever ran into any turbulence with the law that was a decoy. Now that Dax and TJ were going to be moving product Art would go along because he knew the route and exactly how to maneuver. Art would micromanage the two. Art loved when Kross gave him a big boy assignment and a little control.

Art family is well connected with money and power same as Kross. Art has access to yachts speed boats and small air crafts. Since his boating accident left him, paralyzed Art became obsessed with becoming a pilot. This helped the team tremendously. Art was only able to bring in what product he could on his power chair. Art had to use commercial boats and planes to ship the bulk of the product. Now that Dax and TJ are on board Art had his medical marijuana papers duplicated for safety reasons. Art will become the driver while TJ and Dax got the big loads to the boats and planes. To sweeten the deal Ozias becomes a pilot so that multiple shipments could come in at once. When dealing with the boarder army police, your whole organization must tip toe around and be extra careful about any moves you make. Too many trips or any nervous energy could cost you a prison sentence. Craig and O purchased some land by the pizza warehouse for private air strip. It was the perfect plan; they could also store product until the dispensaries became licensed and up and running. Art flies to Trinidad with Dax and TJ to do a walkthrough of the routes. They all come back successful. Art explains to them how and why things will be different when they do it themselves. "Y'all will not be flying commercial you will be in a plane with me." Art continued with his tutorial feeling in charge. Art has a special handicap plane, designed, and equipped for his purposes. The first time they go on the airstrip in Trinidad they were stopped by local police, and they were searched. Dax and TJ were scared to death. Dax had on a Bob Marley dread cap with the dread locks hanging down. Dax looked like a real Jamaican. TJ was quick on her feet; she starts to cry and holds her stomach. She talks extremely fast in English knowing they would not be able to understand her. All the police thought they heard was" the baby is coming." The police get scared and tell her to be careful and go on. They tell Kross and Art about the scare and they make a point to pay off police to help secure the route for all other trips. The police made extraordinarily little money so they would ignore whatever was asked of them especially coming from a member of the McDonald and Jefferies family. Americans often say bands will make you dance, but in Trinidad land will make you dance. Two success trips later the crew had enough product to set up the dispensaries that were pending and enough to supply their buyers. They decide to take a month off and get their business in order.

The men had started a business savings making investment moves. Kross was working with the contractors on both dispensaries in Miami and New York. Kross also purchased property on the southside of Columbia for Yahtia to open her group home. Kross was surprising her with the news over dinner and a movie later tonight. Ozias planted his seed in California. His realtor came across him a building with much space in a high traffic area that attracted tourist. Karma helped him with his layout. Karma was extremely extra having the contractors add two secrets rooms with a hookah and cigar lounge on the opposite side of the dispensary. Karma secretly contacted the realtor and sent her an extra five grand through Zelle she knew that money talks and bullshit walks. Karma was aiming for a complete product in forty-five-days, putting the contractors in overdrive.

Joy had ten missed call and twenty emails from the Dean of criminal justice Dean Landrum. Joy could not help wondering what was so urgent. Her and Craig were out at Best Buy purchasing her a new laptop. Joy was so excited about the many upgraded features she was gaining with her new device. Joy knew she needed to respond to Dean Landrum, but she was a computer geek at heart, so she blew him off to set up her laptop and explore her features. So, the Dean had to wait she would see him tomorrow in class were her thoughts. Joy and Craig made it back to the dorm. Karma and Ozias were laid up in Karma's room smoking a blunt and passing love licks. Yahtia and Kross were caked up as well. After getting relaxed Joy dives in on her new device. Transferring all her information adding security codes and activating her fingerprint entry which she loved. "Damn, am I going to get any loving tonight." Craig pouted. "Boy hush I got you bae, this want take too much longer". Don't make me take that shit back to the store". Craig said being jealous because Joy was giving her laptop her undivided attention. "Don't make no threats because I will cut you off from getting this WAP." Joy gave Craig a wink while she motioned her tongue licking up and down. That put Craig at ease he grabbed his dick then sparked up a pre-rolled blunt while watching his lady enjoy her new device. Halfway through the blunt there was a light knock at the door. Kross and Ozias both headed to answer at the same time. Ozias stood behind Kross with his gun in hand Kross looked out the peep hole then he waved for O to stand down. Kross opened the door, and it was Dean Landrum. "What's up Dean what bring you to the dorm"? Kross asked. "Bae who is it'? Yahtia said as she entered the room and seen Dean Landrum. Yahtia started choking and hide the blunt behind her back. "You kids don't have to hide your fundamentals; I partake in a little weed blowing occasionally myself". Dean Landrum explained. That is why Kross opened the door so freely he knew the Dean was cool. Kross kept the Dean supplied with a lunch box of edibles and pre- rolls. "I'm here to see Joy about a serious matter is she here"? Yahtia tapped on the door and told Joy she had a visitor. Joy and Craig both came out looking confused. "Ms. White I have been calling and emailing you, but I never got a response. I hate to pop up on you like this, but I have something important we need to discuss". "OMG what's wrong Dean it sounds serious"? "Yes, serious but not bad it is impressive news to be exact". "Do I resume here or do you want to step in the hallway". "You may resume these are my sisters and brothers from another mother. This big hunk of love beside me is my future baby daddy". Joy stated with excitement. "Let's take this to the table". Dean, have a seat". Dean Landrum pulled out this thick packet he handed it over to Joy. "The top Forensic scientist criminal justice university in Denver Colorado selected you out of thousands of candidates. They are offering you a full paid training to come collaborate with them. They want you on their payroll while you train and finish school. You will get your credits and graduate early just by accepting the offer". "Wait I haven't applied to this school. How did they pick me over all the others"? Joy asked. "You have been helping them solve crimes and cold cases online. The criminal groups that you are in has been the staff at the university. You have been providing them with so much evidence against the toughest criminal cases. The school has checked out your credentials and with my high recommendation of excellence they want you and only you". Dean Landrum said with pride. Yurzele Martin is the lead Forensic analyst who will be getting you started with all you need to know". "You will have to relocate to Denver if you decide to take the offer, or should I say when you take the offer". "Yurzele will be contacting you in a few days. Yurzele want the newfound information to marinate in Joy's head for a while". "This package has all you need to know about the school and city of Denver. Joy sat at the table with her mouth open trying to digest what was just offered to her. Karma and Yahtia pushed Craig out the way and gave her the biggest hugs. "Bitch you going". Said Karma. "Hell to the yeah she is going. Yahtia cosigned. "I knew you was a bad bitch with the technology, but my girl is the mutha fuckan GOAT". Yahtia said amped up. "Congratulation baby. "Your phenomenal don't you ever forget that". Craig said as he finally got his hug in. "Y'all calm down this a lot to process in thirty minutes. "I'm happy and all but Denver I don't know". Joy said. "OH, BITCH YOU KNOW". This is not negotiable". Yahtia was being aggressive. Everybody was talking at one time it sounded like they were at an NFL game. Craig scooped joy up and carried her back in the bedroom then shut the door. Craig was about to help his lady relax. Craig undressed Joy then devoured her pussy sucking her lips loose. Craig made love to her forgetting about the others being only a room away. Joy was feeling ecstatic her moans turned into pleasure screams and Craig grunts made it sound like a sex movie was going down. The others were being petty and listening outside the door. "I ain't mad at her, toot that thang up Joy." Karma teased while Yahtia did a hands on her knees dance. Ozias and Kross looked at their woman and gave head nods. That meant go to the room and get in position since y'all want to be nosey.

CHAPTER 21
MONEY IS THE MOTIVE

Yurzele called a meeting with Joy, so she could convince her into taking the offer. "Hello Joy. Glad you could make it," Yurzele greeted Joy as she walked into the office. "I invited you here today to impress you with the importance of an offer like this." Yurzele wasted no time getting to business. She did not have much time, and she needed Joy to accept. Yurzele did not hold anything back, explaining to Joy what life would be like with the FBI. "Consider this an exciting adventure for the next chapter in your life. You are a young black woman, with a dual degree. Honors graduate, and you were handpicked by the FBI. You will be making six figures from the start." Yurzele put on her best sales pitch. Not just to butter her up, but because Joy was deserving. "This will require a lot from you mentally and sometimes physically. Overall, it is demanding work, but you can manage it. I have seen your work. Besides, I will be right there with you." Yurzele stopped talking as Joy stood to her feet. "This is my dream, and you are totally convincing." Joy extended her hand for a handshake. "I am accepting the offer." Joy knew she had hit the lottery with this job. Joy would be a fool not to accept. "Wonderful! I thought I was going to have to beg you and do my James Brown". PLEASE, PLEASE, PLEASE." Yurzele joked showing she had a since of humor. She was not above begging. Yurzele and Joy sealed the deal with a handshake and a hug. The remainder of the meeting was spent going over the specifics of the job and the duties required. By the time, the meeting was over Joy and Yurzele were like old friends. They finalized the meeting with Joy signing the official paperwork accepting the job as a Forensic Computer Analyst for the FBI. In ninety days, Joy was to report to Denver Colorado for training. "Congratulations Joy! This is exciting for the both of us. Our adventure will begin in just ninety days" an excited Yurzele said as joy left the office.

Craig reached out to Kross. He needed his brother's help, for business and personal life. "Yo! Kross. Let me holla at you for a sec," Craig walked up on Kross, who was sitting on the couch. "Wassup bro?" Kross responded giving Craig his undivided attention. "I know Joy about to take this job and I ain't letting her go for nothing" Craig stated. "Dude I know you not about to interfere with her career" Kross said side eyeing Craig. Craig hit him with a stale face, "Nigga is you retarded? Joy is the best thing to ever happen to me. I'm just not tolerating her being all the way in Colorado without me. So, I want to open a shop there. Legit Shop." Craig relaxed his face just a little, stressing the words 'Legit Shop.' Kross questioning him had him a little pissed, but he did not go off on him. Craig had to go legit completely. His future wife was going be working for the big PO-PO and he would not jeopardize her career like that. "Gotcha bro. Imma hook you up with my boy Keith. He has been working with for me and my family for years. He can manage everything you want done. You know I got your back too" Kross wrote down a phone number and handed it to Craig. "Fasho. You think he can get me started in buying a home too?" Craig asked pulling out his phone to call. "My boy Keith will make it happen as long as the money is right" Kross told him. Craig hit the call button and walked off. Craig did not know how much time Joy had left before she shipped off, so he told Keith he needed everything ASAP. Keith understood the assignment. Craig had two possible locations for his business, 'Exotic Smoke', by the end of the day. Keith also found him the perfect house and was set to have renovations and additions made the following morning. Keith was the best agent and land developer hands down, if you gave him a vision, he would capture it all through your story. Keith was worth every dollar Craig spent.

The dispensary in Miami had been up and running for weeks, and business was booming. Sales were through the roof, and the shipments could not come any faster. You know when black folks find that pressure, they tell everybody. Word of mouth was the key to building a business, and it definitely paid off for the guys. People from all over were touching down in Miami, not just for the fun in the sun, but for that Island Funk. So, with this kind of clientele, it was easy to open new locations. With Craig going to take over Colorado and now Ozias' place was about to take off in Cali. That made three large dispensaries black owned. Ozias thought he would need a few months to be up and running but with Karma doing her magic tricks, it was only a matter of weeks. Things were smooth sailing. Karma was in with helping the crew with the décor virtually. Karma was a genius with business ideas. Karma added a kitchen to the building to extend the amities. Fresh THC infused food, treats, edibles, and drinks. Pre-rolls were going to be KING KONG strong. Karma also added private smoke rooms available for small gatherings. Karma always was going to step when it came to Ozias, she was his boss lady and oversaw any business pertaining to her man.

Uvoka was doing any and everything to get by. Lately she had been prostituting. Her latest trick was an old wino named Smitty. Smitty lived out of an old van on a ratty mattress. It was warm, and he would often feed Uvoka. In exchange she had to do freaky tricks with her mouth, but it was better than sleeping on the cold ground. Uvoka found a toy water gun, which looked like a real Glock. "Set it off in this mutha fucka" Uvoka sang to herself. She got the idea to become a stick-up kid. Uvoka was nervous but managed to successfully rob two corner boys. Uvoka used those hundred dollars to check into a low budget hotel for two days and get some food. Deciding that she would not be a victim or turn tricks anymore. Uvoka went back out playing the part of a stick-up kid. Uvoka knew it was not the best idea, but she did not realize she is dancing with death. Uvoka managed to get away with a few stick ups, and she was eustatic. One night she was on her way to her hotel room, and she came upon a group of boys. "One more time for the road" she told herself. Uvoka was planning to go from town to town, robbing the local corner boys. She figured it had to be better than staying here. Uvoka ran up on Ziggy and his partner Will, with her water gun. Will and Ziggy were shocked at first but recovered quickly. Before Uvoka could demand any money from them, they knocked the gun from her hand. "Bitch you trying to rob me with a fake as toy", Ziggy was furious. The boys did not give a fuck that Uvoka was female. They stomped her until she was a mere of a second away from being lifeless.

The owner from the corner store called 9-1-1. Ziggy and Will took off running when they heard sirens, leaving Uvoka for dead. The ambulance rushed Uvoka to County Hospital, where she had to have emergency surgery. Ziggy and Will left Uvoka with three broken ribs, severe bruising all over her body, a broken collar bone, and a crushed ankle. The EMTs notified the hospital staff that Uvoka was homeless. They could tell from her smell and her lack of identification. The nurses used at least ten packs of bathing wipes to clean her for treatment. Once she was stabilized and medicated, she was given a bath. The nurses refused to deal with the smell. The doctors had to reconstruct Uvoka's ankle, so she was in constant pain. Uvoka had swelling in her spin, so they kept ordering X-Rays to check for spinal damage. Uvoka was ready to give up. She let the drugs take her mind away while the doctors patched her up.

Troy was feeling himself. He was flaunting his new bitch and still running over Nekendra every chance he could. One day he got himself arrested for being in possession of a stolen car. Due to his extensive record, the judge did not hesitate to sentence him with the maximum of nighty days. Troy begged the judge for mercy. "Your honor I know I did wrong but please send me to another jail. I will go anywhere. I will do anything. Just please don't make me go back to the county" a terrified Troy cried. The judge banged his gavel and ignored the pleas for mercy. During the admissions process Troy cried like a baby. He broke down again when he saw D-Ray. Troy fell to the ground and grabbed on to the officers' leg trying his best not to be put back in the block. "Don't be no bitch now. You like to hit women right: the officers tossed Troy like a rag doll. Troy landed at the feet of D-Ray. "Didn't we have an agreement. D- Ray asks as he kicked Troy hard in the gut. "Didn't I tell you to stay the fuck away from Nekendra?" D-Ray waited for his response. Troy was stuttering and stumbling all over his words. Troy was scared shitless. "Damn homie. You are shaking like a stripper on amateur night." One of the inmates said while laughing. "So, you're a boxing champ with Nekendra, a real live Evander Holyfield. Let me see your skills." D-Ray positioned himself in a fighting stance putting his guard up signaling for Troy to do the same. Troy knew this was a lose-lose situation. If he fought D-Ray, he would get his ass beat. If he didn't fight, he would get his ass beat. Reluctantly Troy put his guard up, with tears running down his face. Before he was in position good, D-Ray bitch slapped him to the ground. Troy was mad with himself for the whimper that came from his throat. It sounded just like the women that he beat on. Troy took that ass whopping and everything that came with it. Troy's face was cover in spit from the goons hawking it in his face, after his brutal beating D-Ray doubled his dick sucking and ass eating duties.

Troy was the jailhouse hoe. D-Ray was pimping Troy out to everyone, even the guards. Troy could not eat or sleep without permission. D-Ray would give him a rotten apple and toilet water after dumping his food in the trashcan. Some days he could get his tray, but he had to eat it off the floor. Life was hell for him. Troy was called for a visit one Sunday afternoon. His new boo Evvie had come to see him. Evvie was worried and confused. She did not understand why he hadn't reached out to her. Evvie was all smiles when she saw Troy walk through the door. Her face fell flat when she realized he looked like a walking zombie. "What is wrong baby?" a concerned Evvie asked. She noticed the cuts and bruises on his face. The scars from his lip had been reopened. Troy was a scary sight for sure. Troy picked up the receiver but did not say anything. He was too ashamed. He could not bring himself to tell anyone what was going on. Evvie asked him question after question. "I will go to the warden about this just tell me what happened. Who did this? I know you are innocent love. I am going to have reporters here to expose this place" Evvie was going off. Before Troy could bring himself to speak. Two inmates walked up and dropped their pants. Troy looked up at them and audibly cried. The men pointed to their penis and waited. Troy could not refuse them because he would have to pay D-Ray. He knew the back would be in blood. These inmates had paid for a 'two for 1" special. Troy grabbed both dicks and went to work.

Evvie was horrified. She tried to run from the visitation center, but the guard couldn't open the door. He held up a sign, "YOU MUST WAIT THE FULL 30 MINUTES!". Her back against the wall, Evvie watched in horror as Troy served two men porn hub style. When the timer went off and the gate opened, Evvie ran straight out of the visitation room, never looking back. When she reached the car, she threw up, unable to get the images out of her head. Evvie stopped by the Rape and Crisis center. She told them she had been assaulted and needed a full physical. Evvie wasn't downplaying women that actually went through sexual assaults, but she had to make sure Troy hadn't given her anything. When she got home, Evvie took a bath trying to clean the images from her memory. She changed her number and trashed everything that belonged to Troy. Evvie did not want any explanation or anything else to do with him, or his jailhouse homosexual tendencies.

On the other side of the world, Karmelo and Molly were introduced to their new line of work. Night after night, Karmelo had to fight. He gave it everything he had but the fights were causing him major damage. Karmelo was simply nice in the ring and he often danced around entertaining the crowd, but the back-to-back fights caused severe exhaustion. Karmelo's once handsome face was now unrecognizable, from multiple facial injuries. After countless fights, and broken bones, Karmelo had to be placed on bed rest. "The next fight will surely be his last if this keeps on going" Molly informed one of Hero's men. "Isn't it your job to keep him alive?" the goon answered with a raised eyebrow. Molly just nodded her head. That was the deal. "Keep him alive for me to make money and maybe I will limit your dick sucking." Hero said to her. "I understand that, but I am not God. The next blow to his head is surely going to kill him" Molly repeated to Hero. She did not want to go back to being a cum rag, but she could not keep Karmelo alive if he did not get the proper rest. Hero got an idea in his head. "Fine you have your time. But if he dies before this next fight, YOU WILL WISH YOU WERE DEAD AS WELL." Hero threatened Molly. Hero knew she was right, but he could not show her any remorse. Hero needed her afraid of him. "I understand" was the only response Molly had.

Hero made the call to Kross. "Kross my man. I have good news for you" Hero spoke into the phone. He explained to Kross everything that was going on with Karmelo. "I know you said to keep him alive, and I have done that. It is only right that I leave the kill shot for you" Hero waited to hear what Kross had to say. Hero felt like the crew was his distant family, they were so much like him. "Say less. I will send you the details of our arrival soon. Just try to keep him on this side. I want to be the one to send him to hell." Kross thanked Hero and hung up. Kross rubbed his hands together like birdman. His mind was running a mile a minute. Kross was planning to give Yahtia the best gift of which he could think of. Kross knew his girl and her girls were no stranger to this life, so this gift would get him plenty of baecation pussy. He was going to let her see Karmelo die. Hero called all his high roller friends. He was going to market this as 'A Death Match.' Karmelo had made a name for himself as a fighter, so most people were betting for him to win against the unknown newcomer. Hero made sure to place several bets, using everyone in the crew's name. Hero placed the bet on the kill shot. They would split a big jackpot once Kross landed that last blow. When he was done placing bets, Hero took a red marker and crossed out Karmelo's name. There was no coming back from this.

Molly was in the house where they kept all the women. She notices a familiar face when she was putting on her lip stick for her date. Her lips had to be poppin for this client he like his dick sucked with ruby red lip stick on his woman. The young girl was Hershey. "How in the world did you get all the way over here? Doing this?" Molly asked her, concerned. "Same reason as you" Hershey replied. Molly nodded her head in understanding. Molly walked away with a slight ache in her chest. Her maternal instincts were getting to her. Molly remembered what Hershey had done to Karma, and it made her sick to her stomach. Molly cried to herself, as she realized how bad she failed to protect her only child. Molly sat beside Karmelo's half dead body. Molly was lost in her own thoughts. She could not believe Karma had sold them into sex slavery. Molly was a prostitute, for free. "When did our daughter get so powerful?" Molly whispered to Karmelo. Karmelo shrugged his shoulders in pain. "Her new name definitely fits her Molly said as she stroked Karmelo's head." Molly dried her wet face, with the back of her hand. "Karma" Karmelo huffed out. "That bitch is ruthless" Karmelo attempted to get comfortable on his worn mattress. Molly nodded her head in agreement. Molly knew she deserved everything that she was going through and then some. Truth is she never wanted kids and ended up resenting her own daughter, which was the only justification she had. Molly let her tears fall as she spoke to an unconscious Karmelo. "I never loved her and now I am paying for it. I knew I was supposed to, but I just did not. My pettiness would not let her receive love from other people either. I did this to myself. I know what you did too. We deserve all of this." Molly said, sulking in her and her husband's misery. "Til death do us part." Molly laughed humorlessly. "That is real shit" Molly said in a low tone, wiping the blood coming from Karmelo's nose.

Over the next few days everyone is hustling. They each were dealing with their love lives, as well as the expanding businesses. The girls also had graduation on their minds. "Sis! We are legit boss ass bitches." Karma said to Yahtia, out of nowhere. "Real shit! And we got boss ass niggas." Yahtia did a little dance and Karma laughed, co-signing with her. The two continued to talk, enjoying each other's company. With everything going on they had not really had sister time lately. There was a knock at the door. When the door swung open that interrupted their conversation. "Better not be no baby making going on in here" Mama T could be heard, but Juan was the face that greeted them. Now that everyone was self-sufficient, Mama T and Juan were like newlyweds. Mama T stepped from behind her husband as the girls hugged her. "Mama we know the rules" Yahtia laughed. "You better young lady. I see how you be all in that boy face" Mama T faked fussed. "And don't think I don't know your fast ass be in Ozias face every chance you get." Mama T turned the heat on Karma. Holding their hands up in surrender. "We just trying to be like you Ma." This made Mama T laugh. Toyah loved her kids, biological and otherwise, but she was not ready for grandkids. Not yet anyway. "Where is my son in law anyway?" Mama T asked, speaking about Kross. She knew her daughter was in love, and she was rooting for her and Kross. She dreamed of the day Yahtia getting married, but she could not tell her that. Toyah needed her daughters to be strong and independent first. Then they could be a wife and mother.

The boys had been out playing basketball and came running up the stairs of the dorm. "I know y'all got better manners than to run in these people building making all that damn noise." Toyah opened the door fussing. All three of the men stopped dead in their tracks. None of them dared to speak, until she started laughing. "Gotcha" she said, opening the door wider so they could come in. It was like a small family reunion. Toyah made the boys go wash up. "Eww y'all stink. Go wash and change clothes." They looked at each other and then back at her. Craig started to speak. "Ma how we gonna…" Toyah raised her hand like she was about to slap him. "You ain't got to lie Craig. I know y'all be over here laying and playing with these girls. Go in your woman's room and get you a change of clothes. Then go wash your ass with the hygiene stuff I know you keep over here." Toyah said with her hands on her hips. Everyone looked guilty as hell. "GO!" Juan spoke up. "We know what y'all doing but y'all all know the rules. We ain't stupid or slow." Juan grabbed his wife' s butt feeling like a college boy himself. Joy walked in just as the guys finished changing. "Hey everyone" she ran and gave Toyah and Juan hugs. Joy loved them like she was their daughter, and they never treated her any different than Yahtia or Karma. "I'm glad everyone is here. I have some news" Joy couldn't contain it anymore. When everyone had given her their attention she proceeded. "So y'all know about the FBI job offer right. Well, I went to talk to Yurzele and she gave me all of the details" Joy dragged on. "Baby spit it out" Craig rushed her. "Well, I took the job. I leave for Denver in 90 days" she got out. Joy knew everyone would be happy and support her decision, but she did not want to hurt anyone's feelings. She had begun to question her decision. "That is impressive love" Craig kissed her. Everyone else joined in on congratulating her. "Sis is the FEDs now" Karma joked hugging her.

Juan and Mama T made everyone get dressed for dinner. "This cause for a celebration. We as black people love to eat and celebrate." Juan said sounding happy. The crew tried to decline, telling them to go ahead and they would all get together later. "Ahh No you don't. Y'all can hunch later. Right now, y'all come eat with me and ya Pops." Mama T snapped. "Mama really. Hunching?" Yahtia whined, as she and everyone else went to change for dinner. "Don't be trying to be fresh neither. I'm hungry damn it" Toyah yelled out at them. "Pops get your wife. Why she cock blocking" Ozias dodged the swinging arm from Mama T. "I'm not in this" Juan stepped back. Juan knew better. If he said something in the kids' defense, he was not going to be hunching later. The last door slammed and all you could hear was giggling. Mama T just smiled. She knew that this was one of few moments she would have like this for a while. "I mean it!" she yelled. "WE KNOW MA. GRAD THEN GRANDS" everyone yelled in unison. Juan doubled over in laughter. If anybody could whip some kids into shape it was his wife. "Mrs. Beeks you are something else" he kissed her lovingly.

The family decided to go to Carrabba's Italian Grill for dinner. They ate and laughed. Reminiscing about the past and thinking about the future. "My babies are just growing up so fast" Mama T wiped her eyes. Juan decided to call it a night after that. He knew the tears were just the beginning, especially because she had been drinking wine. "We will see you all soon. Congratulations again Joy" Juan said as he escorted his wife out of the restaurant. Kross paid the bill and they all left.

Not wanting to separate just yet they all went back to the dorm. The residential advisor stopped caring about the boys being in the dorm, because they were always there. They also paid her to erase the cameras. The crew kept the party going by sparking up a fatty and opening a bottle. "Just for you baby" Craig popped the top on a bottle of *Armand de Brignac*. "Ok now" Joy did a little dance at the sight of the cute Ace of Spades bottle. This bottle was the hardest champagne to come by, since Jay-Z featured it in, his video. Everyone is having an enjoyable time, but Yahtia seems lost in thought. "Bro let me holla at you" Karma pulled Kross to the side. "Tia been stressing or acting weird around you?" she asked him. Kross was not going to say anything at first but decided he needed to tell someone. "Yahtia has been fighting in her sleep and crying for no reason. Hell, I kissed her while she was sleep and she woke up screaming NO" Kross was heartbroken. He did not know what to do or how to help his future wife. "I don't know what to do sis. How do I help her get through this" Kross said defeated? "Bro she been doing the same thing when she is here. And when I ask about it, she brush me off or catch an attitude." Karma filled Kross in on Yahtia's nightmares and change in mood. "He gotta die bro. That is the only way. He gotta die." There was no need to specify who

"He" was. They both knew. "Say less sis. Imma make sure that nigga stop breathing." Kross passed the blunt to Karma. "But you stand down. Let me handle this one." Kross gave her a knowing look. Karma laughed. "Glad you said something because the wheels in my head already started turning. You know how I do behind that one." Karma pointed at Yahtia, who was still zoned out. "Facts" Kross said, as his own wheels began to spin. Killing Karmelo was not the issue. He needed it to be witnessed by Yahtia, so that she could have closure.

The idea came to him instantly. "Fellas" Kross waved them over. Kross filled the guys in on his plan and they contacted Hero. The guys all had somewhat of a romantic gesture planned for their women. They decided they would do it together. "We are going on a family baecation" the guys announced. That got the girls attention. "Ok where we going?" Joy asked, hugging on Craig. The guys told them the plan. "Each of you get to pick a place, any place. We are all going to go" Ozias explained. "I get it, so we all get to tag along to each other's dream vacation!" Karma surmised. "The first stop in Trinidad though. I want to show y'all the island as tourist." Kross said kissing Yahtia on the forehead. The girls started planning and shopping immediately. The men had to make plans of their own. Kross finally connected with Hero and was ecstatic with the news he received. Kross filled Hero in on the plans, "I will give you more travel details when we get them. I need your help setting up transport to your location. I know it is a secret but the whole crew has to be there" Kross expressed to Hero. "No problem my friend. Hero was about to secretly set up some bets for the crew. Hero knew how good the money flowed in the fight industry. No one had to know Kross was about to destroy Karmello.

Yahtia had been visiting the girls regularly. One day she stopped by and saw that the girls were all upset. She asked them what was wrong, and they told her about a few of the workers being mean to them for no reason. After looking around and getting negative feedback from some of the girls at the group home. Yahtia decided she had to open her own place. Yahtia told her mother about the girls and the conditions they were dealing with. "Ma I just don't like it. They deserve so much better than what that place is doing. They are not doing therapy or nothing. It makes me angry" Yahtia vented. "What you wanna do about it then little girl?" Toyah asked. "Imma open my own group home" Yahtia said with a big burst of energy. Toyah started to protest but she noticed the enthusiasm and passion covering her daughter's face as she talked about it. "Baby I will help anyway I can. That is a great idea" Toyah hugged Yahtia. "Glad you feel like that. We're having a meeting with Ivy" Yahtia grabbed her mom's hand and headed for the door.

They pulled up at Ivy's office on two wheels. If Yahtia, had it her way she would be opening the doors to her group home tomorrow. After hearing the details Ivy was sold. "I am all in. Just tell me what you need" Ivy smiled. She was proud of Yahtia. Yahtia was never officially a patient, but she would come and vent from time to time. Toyah was looking at her daughter, wondering what could have sparked a passion like this. "It's a shame that it takes tragedy or trauma to inspire goodness and healing." Ivy said while going through the girls' journal entries.

That statement spoke to Toyah. In that moment she knew her daughter had been a victim. That was a pain Toyah had never felt before. Toyah cried and blamed herself, but she never once spoke of it. Toyah made her peace with God and left it at the altar. She did not want Yahtia to relive anything. Toyah decided to stay focused and help Yahtia bring her dream to life. Toyah doubled down on all her efforts to get this group home open. Toyah was backing her daughter 100%. Toyah made herself busy with designing a program and shopping for the building. Toyah did not allow herself to think of the things that had driven her daughter to this point in her life. Toyah knew her kids were up to something, she felt it in her soul. Toyah knew the code of the streets, and the love her boys had for the girls. So, it was understood that whatever, or whoever hurt Yahtia was dealt with. Toyah never asked for confirmation because the less she knew the better. Plausible Deniability.

Working hand in hand with Ivy, Toyah had produced a great therapeutic program that would allow the girls to heal and move on with their lives. While working at the office with Ivy, a call from the doctor's office came in. "Thank you for your call doctor. Can you please fax the results?" Ivy requested. The results from the girls' physicals were in. Viewing them made Ivy sick to her stomach. "There is a special place in hell for people who abuse kids." Ivy spat looking at the results. All the girls had suffered broken bones that had never set back properly. At least two of them would have to have their bones rebroken so that they can heal correctly. All of them had been sexually assaulted and neglected in every viable way. The eldest girl, Candice was pregnant and had severe vaginal scaring. "This is just sick" Toyah cosigned Ivy's sentiments. Ivy decided right then that all these girls would have the same type of notebooks that she had given Karma. Ivy could read a person better when they put their inner feelings on paper. "Hey Yahtia, is Karma around you?" Ivy made the call to inform her and Karma about her decision. Ivy explained her plan of action Ivy wanted these girls to release the bottled-up anger and see who hurt them the most. "Give it a few weeks so they can actually have some content. "Go ahead and get them started now. Give them some pretty color pins and highlighters and colorful notebooks." Karma said. Karma knew that would put the girls deep in thought because it worked for her. "They are headed this way." Ivy shook her head and laughed, as she told Toyah about her conversation. "What did you think would happen?" Toyah joined in on the laughter.

The girls were interrupted with a call from Kross. "Bae, I need you to meet me asap! I just sent the location to your phone" Kross said and then hung up. Yahtia tried calling him back, but he did not answer, so she sent a text. "Can it wait love? I was on my way to Ivy's office. It has to do with the group home?" Yahtia was desperate to talk to Ivy about the girls in person, but Kross insisted that she come now. Rolling her eyes, "Come on sis, I gotta see about my man then we can slide to the girls." Karma smiled knowingly and followed her out of the door. Kross finally answered the phone, "Babe don't be mad. It will not take long I swear. I need to put a smile on your face." He flirted into the phone. Yahtia blushed and told him she was on the way. When she pulled up, Karma riding shotgun, Yahtia realized the gang was all there. Her anxiety kicked in quickly. "Oh my God. What happened? What's wrong?" Yahtia rushed over to Kross. Karma was right on her heels, but she did not say a word. Kross kissed her into silence. "Eww. Y'all got plenty of time for all that." Karma chastised them. "Girl let my boy do his Rico Suave shit." Ozias grabbed Karma and stuck his tongue in her throat to shut her up. Craig and Joy just laughed at their friends. "Babe I know you have had a lot on your mind, and it has been causing you not to sleep at night. I know you want to save the world and I plan to help you." Kross said, turning Yahtia towards the building. Yahtia was stuck for a second. "This is all yours. The paperwork in on the way. All you have to do is name your LLC." Kross waited for his words to register. "What?" Yahtia started crying. "You are an entrepreneur. Your group home is officially open for business!" Kross picked her up and spun her around. Yahtia screamed so loud as she jumped into Kross' arms, raining kisses all over his face. "Oh My God. Thank you Thank you Thank you" Yahtia said in between kisses. Kross walked Yahtia into the building where he had a table set up. There was a pair of ribbon cutting scissors and a bottle of champagne. "Consider this your pre-ribbon cutting ceremony love" Kross kissed her again.

Yahtia cut the ribbon and they all began to celebrate. "Ok now! My sis is a mutha fuckan entrepreneur Boss in this bitch!" Joy yelled out. "What's the name sis?" Joy asked once everyone had a cup in their hands. Yahtia shrugged her shoulders. "No clue" Yahtia said. "Girl what comes to your mind, give us the first thing and roll with it." Karma advised. After a few minutes Yahtia spoke. "Girls of Redemption!" Yahtia spit out. "Hell, yeah sounds good to me sis. "GIRLS OF REDEMPTION IT IS!" Karma yelled out and they all raised their glasses high. They made a toast to all their businesses moves and investments, ending it with a "GIRLS OF REDEMPTION!!"

CHAPTER 22
KARMA DOES NOT DISCRIMINATE

Yahtia and the girls hit the ground running. They managed to get the LLC paperwork fast tracked. So Yahtia had her licensing framed and hanging in the building already. Toyah already had the decorations and furniture set up. The girls were transferred over and now clients at GIRLS OF REDEMPTION Group Home LLC. Ivy had already started their treatment plans and their notebooks. Everything was going quickly and smoothly. After countless hours of work Karma and Yahtia go to visit the girls. They had a lunch date planned for them. Before they all left. Karma and Yahtia read the girls' notebooks. Sadly, they all had comparable stories. "Sis they are so much like us" Yahtia started to cry. Karma noticed that certain names had been written multiple times and some circled. That was something she had done a few times in her own notebook, Karma did not like the feeling that came with it. Karma started paying close attention to Candice's notebook. The name Ezra had been written on every page. Karma made a mental note to ask about this person.

Over lunch Karma and Yahtia took turns telling their story to the girls. They explained how they were bullied and abused by men and women. Karma used her story to encourage the girls to speak their own story. "Have any of you thought about what you want to happen to the people that hurt you?" Karma asked. Kimmie was the first one to speak up. She was the talkative one out of the girls. "I want all those bastards to die." Kimmie stabbed her fork into the plate for emphasis. "Those are really harsh words coming from a ten-year-old." Karma responded. Stabbing her own fork down mad from seeing Kimmie's aggression. Karma fully understood where Kimmie was coming from. The memories of the pain took her appetite. "She not lying we have been passed around like a phat blunt, from city to city. The shit we been through is HARSH." Irma said dramatically, putting her arm around Kimmie. Shavon spoke up next. Shavon gave her account on her situation, she was beaten the most for always trying to escape. "I will never go down without a fight" Shavon slammed her fist on the table. Everyone had stopped eating. They were too busy talking and exchanging stories. Karma and Yahtia listened, trying to keep their own feelings in check. Karma sent a text to Yahtia as the girls kept talking. "Sis they are good girls. They have hopes and dreams just like kids raised in a two-parent home. Yahtia nodded in agreement. After getting the rest of their food to go, the girls were taken back to the group home.

Karma had gained a lot of knowledge about the girls over lunch. All of them were sold to the highest bidder, into the sex trade. Their only crime was being born to crack addicts with bad parenting. Their parents never gave a fuck about them they only cared about getting another hit. Candice would have to deliver the baby because termination would only make her vaginal scaring worse. Candice was labeled considerable risk by the doctor, due to age and trauma. Candice was scheduled another appointment and Yahtia and Karma agreed to go with her for support. They refused to take away her right to know about her body. Prayerfully she would be healed enough to push the baby out. Only time will tell.

Art had set up the last travel for product. Art was planning to get a triple load that would put the entire team above the map. Kross and Craig went to the pizza warehouse to give the instructions to TJ and Dax. The two were excited about making a move. They had been sitting in the warehouse eating dog food needing a bath desperately. "This will be the last run, so do us proud. Make this shit happen and you will be set free". Craig said smiling. TJ and Dax gave a head nod and were jumping for joy in the inside. Art, Ozias along with TJ and Dax they all hit the road to go manage the load. They made it to Trinidad with ease. They were in two big body jeeps, which was taken apart frame by frame to hide the product. Every part of the vehicles was utilized. When the men were done Ozias and Art waste no time in leaving. They by passed many army police, but they were not bothered. They made it back to the planes safe. Both Art and Ozias were doing their pilot thang. TJ and Dax un-loaded the jeeps then loaded up the planes with product. After all packages were secure, they were ready for take-off. Ozias explained to Dax and TJ that they would be driving the minivan that was parked a few feet away, because the plane was over capacity. "Just drop the van off at the mall on Two Notch and ill have somebody scoop it up." Ozias explained. "If you love your family, you will take everything you have seen to the grave." Said Ozias. "Trust me we will not violate y'all ever again. Thanks for letting us live and not shipping us away with that foreign man." Dax said trying to be friendly. TJ could not be still she was so anxious. She was first to the van. TJ got on the driver side and placed her seat belt on turning up the radio moving her head back and forth. Dax was still trying to hold conversation with Ozias. Ozias walked off to start his engine to his plane. TJ blew the horn for Dax to hurry up. "OMG cuz, I thought they were going to kill us." TJ said loudly. "Yeah, me too, but when we touch down, I can't let this shit ride they did us dirty." Dax said with a mug on his face. "Nigga you have lost your damn mind fuck that shit you on your mutha fuckan own. I'm not dealing with them goons." "Fuck you then just drive." "Nah nigga fuck you we barely made it out alive look at us we both all fucked up looking a mess. Did we experience the same shit I'm confused?" TJ was pissed at Dax for even thinking about retaliation. After hours of driving, they both needed a restroom break. They stopped at a rest stop and did their business. When they proceed back on the highway moments later a state trooper was stopping them. Dax begin to sweat he yelled for TJ to keep going. TJ ignored Dax and pulled over. Dax was looking for somewhere to run. Soon as Dax opened the door the trooper was at the door with his weaponed drawn. "Place your hands on top of your head sir". Minutes later more state troopers came for back up. Dax was immediately placed in the trooper car. After figuring out Dax was on the most wanted list the trooper dispatched the police to pick him up. TJ was being questioned she was tripping over her words and acting extremely nervous. "We had a call that this vehicle was engaged in trafficking drugs, would you know anything about that ma'am?" The state trooper asked. "No sir I was just forced by my cousin to drive him around in this van." The police showed up with two canines the van was searched and ten bricks of heroin, and six bricks of coke and Thirty grams of molly was sniffed out by the canines. Kross did a big trade off with a couple of his buyers for the hard drugs. The van was packed down with the drugs by one of his cousins who also made the set-up call to the police. With the quantity of drugs that was recovered along with their prior drug records. Dax and TJ will never become exposed to daylight again. Karma has stuck again.

The crew meet up at the warehouse to rush and unload the product and ship it off to the dispensaries. The product was equally divided. The men wrapped up business at the warehouse and Karma, Joy and Yahtia along with Mama T were putting some final additions on the group home. Ivy found five more girls that needed a place to stay the girls were six, fourteen, fifteen, sixteen, and seventeen. The group home was designed to house twelve girls. Yahtia had dependable and trustworthy staff she made sure their background was squeaky clean. Yahtia knew Mama T was in charged so Yahtia knew she could relax and not worry about any under minding bullshit. Karma pulled out the primary copy of their list as they walked out the door, she then showed the girls that TJ and Dax name had a big red check mark beside it. "Mission accomplished." Said Yahtia.

Karma could not get out of her head the name Ezra. She knew it was a secret behind that name Candice had written down so many times. Karma explained to the girls that she wanted to swing by the group home and talk with Candice. Karma just had to see what she could find out about this Ezra. When they arrived at the group home Mama T had a concerned look on her face when she spotted the girls walking up. "What are you three doing here"? "We just came to talk with Candice." Karma said in a low tone. "Look honey I didn't birth you, but you are my bonus daughter. I know when something is fishy." "Ma ain't nothing wrong we just want to give her a pep talk." Said Yahtia. "These girls are on a schedule and you three are not going to disrupt their sleep time. Y'all have ten minutes." When Candice spotted Karma, Joy and Yahtia her face lit up. "Hey auntie Tia, K, and Joy." "Hey, love how are you settling in"? Joy asked. "Good I love it here; we got some new girls yesterday and they are nice." Mama T taking us skating tomorrow can y'all come." "We have school all day tomorrow, but we will do something this weekend with all of you." Karma spoke. "I want You to be a big girl and tell me who is Ezra." "Am I in trouble." Candice was about to cry. "No, sweetie you're not in trouble. I just know that something happened with you and this Ezra." Karma spoke softly and convincing. "I was being pimped out by a bisexual girl name Rochelle. I was forced to turn tricks with old men and Rochelle would get their check money. One of the old men told her boyfriend Ezra that my pussy was good, and he wanted me for himself. Ezra was already looking at me smiling and he would touch my butt sometimes when I walk by. One day he touched more than my butt and we started a heavy sexual relationship. Ezra started treating me nice and pleasuring me with his mouth. Ezra introduced me to the feel-good side of sex. I begin to like sex from him. I felt safe with Ezra. We cuddled and talked every day, he really loved me." "I felt a connection to Ezra. Ezra kept me from having sex with those old dirty toothless men. Ezra would pay his own money to Rochelle hiding me and keeping me to himself. He even stashed money in the sole of my boots that was supposed to go to Rochelle. One day Rochelle found out from old man Charlie that I have not been serving him. Ezra had told majority of the men not to come back, he had a few men thinking I was sold off and moved to another location. Rochelle came home early one day from uber driving. She caught Ezra and I in the 6-9 position. She totally flipped out. First, she beat me up. Then she let this gang of men rape and torture me while she took pictures and watched. Rochelle jammed a screwdriver and tv antenna inside my vagina. Ezra tried to help me, but she had the gang throw him outside. Rochelle then had me picked up by the man you all got me from." "So how old is Ezra"? Tia asked. "He's seventeen." "I like him a lot. I wrote his name so many times basically reminiscing about him and I." "Rochelle is the one I hate." Candice explained. Candice drew a knife going through Rochelle's name and had circled the name repeatedly. Candice confirmed that Ezra was her baby daddy. The girls all had the same look on their face when they walked out the room. Toyah notice their facial expression had changed. She had a gut feeling they were about to do something deep. "I heard everything that was said. y'all please leave it alone. That Rochelle bitch will get her Karma." Toyah said while speed walking trying to keep up with them. "Mama T you are right once again. Rochelle will get a taste of Karma fosho." Karma said giving Toyah a hug. Toyah knew deep down them girls were doing something heavy. Toyah walked back inside concerned but smiling at the same time. She knew who ever crossed her daughter got dealt with.

Joy remembered Hero telling her he was coming from Ohio when he was dealing with the pick-up of the girls. Joy did a statewide search for Rochelle and uber driver. Lady luck has struck again; Rochelle's information comes pouring in. Rochelle Bentley had a dirty laundry list of criminal charges. Rochelle is the leader of a female gang Bitches of Justice. "Plain and simple we pay ten stacks have Hero delivery her ass to the warehouse ASAP." Yahtia spoke angerly. Joy had a pleasant idea. "Let us go ahead and handle Urban while we got Hero in play. Kill two birds with one stone." "Sounds good fam. "Now we can speed up our much-needed baecation." I got a different approach for Mr. Urban Watts dusty ass. We not even going to have to put in work. Our enjoyment will come from watching." Karma said with a smile.

CHAPTER 23
THE LIST GOES ON

The ladies agreed they must find Ezra Login. He was going to support Candice and the baby, rather he like it or not. They had to figure out where his mind was at regarding Candice before they could decide a plan of action. Joy worked her magic and tracked him down. Joy managed to find a phone number, so she reached out via text. "Hello Ezra. I need you to contact me ASAP. This is regarding my niece Candice." Ezra replied, "Who dis?" Joy didn't give up any information but pressed her issue, "That is not important, just give me a call please. My name is Joy." Ezra did not respond after that. Even though he wanted to believe that someone was reaching out to him about Candice, he felt like it was Rochelle playing a sick game on him. Ezra made his way home, and Rochelle was there entertaining friends. "Rochelle let me holla at you for a minute" Ezra said, sounding irritated. "What's up boo?" Rochelle smiled, leaning in for a kiss. Ezra moved before she could land the kiss on him. "Why the fuck would you have someone text my phone about Candice?" Ezra snapped. Rochelle copped an attitude at the mention of Candice's name. "I wouldn't do no shit like that. Besides, that bitch is long gone. I know you not still caught up about that young bitch?" Rochelle questioned her boyfriend. Her jealousy was getting the best of her. "Matter of fact I am. You did not have to send her away. Especially not for your trifling ass insecurities" Ezra spat, staring Rochelle straight in the face. Ezra was so serious. "Nigga Fuck you." Rochelle snapped, walking away from him.

"Nah bitch fuck you and that dry pussy. That's why you can't keep a man or a damn woman. You just mad cause Candice pussy was fye and she stayed creaming on my face", Ezra yelled to her back. He did not stop there. Ezra cursed and shamed Rochelle in front of her friends, exposing all her secrets.

Rochelle was embarrassed, and her friends were embarrassed for her. Her friends got up to leave because it was getting awkward. Shortly after everyone was gone, Ezra stormed out of the house. He was still going off on Rochelle about her jealousy and underhanded bullshit. Ezra rode around for hours, smoking some gas and sipping on Hennessy. He had to clear his head and decide on his next move. Ezra wanted to reach out to Joy about Candice, but he did not know what to say. Taking a deep breathe, Ezra prepped himself to make the call. "It's now or never." Ezra said to himself as he dialed the number. Joy answered immediately. "Hello Ezra. It was nice of you to call." "So, what is this about? You know Candice?" Ezra questioned Joy. Ezra was hoping for the best but still skeptical. "I know that you know my niece, Candice. I also know that you are familiar with the fucked-up situation your dike girlfriend put her in." Joy paused for effect before continuing. "Candice is living in South Carolina and doing well." Before Joy could finish Ezra cut in. "Oh! My! God! Are you serious? I thought I would never see or hear from her again." Joy smiled as she listened to him go on about his love for Candice. It made her smile because this confirmed getting him to do right by Candice would be easy. "Well young man she is having your baby. My sisters and I are going to fly you down for a while so we can sort this out." Joy informed him. Ezra was beyond happy to hear this news. Ezra was in love with Candice and now they could be a family. "Go ahead and pack a bag, bring gifts, and be prepared to be a daddy. I will send you the travel details when it is time." Joy instructed before disconnecting the call. A text came through from Joy to Ezra as soon as their call was complete. "STAY THE FUCK AWAY FROM ROCHELLE. THAT BITCH ASS IS GRASS." Ezra sent back a thumbs up emoji. Ezra was already fantasizing about seeing Candice again.

Life for the crew was moving quickly. Joy was busy finishing classes and preparing to leave for the FBI. Karma and Tia were busy with school as well. The girls managed to have a permanent spot on the dean's list each semester. In between classes they helped Ivy and Toyah with the young girls. Yahtia made sure each of the girls were enrolled in school. She was like a proud parent when she found out they were acclimating well. Kimmie and Irma were on the Principal's Honor Roll list. The others were making the A's and B's as well. "The girls are doing great" Ivy gave Yahtia an update, showing her their notebooks and progress reports. "That is wonderful. I am simply happy that they have some form of normalcy now. They deserve all that the world has to offer." Yahtia beamed, sending the information to Karma. Yahtia knew her sister would want to know how they were doing. "You are doing a good thing here Tia. Make sure to take care of yourself while taking care of others" Ivy patted Yahtia on the back.

Joy sent Hero Rochelle's information along with payment. Rochelle was set to get a dose of her own medicine sooner rather than later. Rochelle made a situation for herself. Unfortunately for her, the tables had turned against her. The man she hired to take care of her problems, was now coming to back for her. Hero knew exactly were to get Rochelle, since they had done previous business together. "Piece of Cake." Hero thought to himself as he pulled up in front of Rochelle's house. Money was the root of all evil, and Hero knew money would get Rochelle's evil ass to come with him. Hero was dressed to impress, waiting in a drop top Jaguar. He looked like a foreign thug, with plenty of money. Rochelle walked up the steps heading to her home. "Rochelle!" Hero called her name smoothly, allowing his accent to come through. Rochelle was lost for a second. "What's up?" She asked questioningly and then realization hit her. "Pakistan! You got some more business in my neck of the woods huh." Rochelle was a little excited to see him. Seeing him always meant money. "While you here I can get you more of that black pussy you like." Rochelle offered. "That would be perfect but first I need you to take a ride with me. I have something you may be interested in." Hero used his businessperson voice so he would sound convincing. "Bet let me get my weed and cigars out the crib. Then we can ride." Rochelle disappeared into the house. Just like he thought, Rochelle came bouncing down her steps a few minutes later and got into his car.

Hero pulled off into traffic. Rochelle got comfortable and sparked her blunt. "Here open this" Hero handed her a bag. Rochelle pulled out a fifth of Hennessy. "Hell, yeah fam this just what a bitch needed after uber driving for the past ten hours." Rochelle poured her a big girl drink. Rochelle had taken two double shots to the head and was sipping the third. Rochelle sat back and enjoyed the effects of her drugs. "Yo! Why you are going…" Rochelle was about to ask why they were taking the highway exit, but she passed out. Hero laced the Hennessy. Hero continued to his destination without a care in the world. Hero knew Rochelle would be passed out for hours. Due to the substantial amounts of roofied Hennessy she drank. Hero had driven hours before Rochelle began to wake. She moved around slowly, feeling groggy with a banging headache. When she realized she was tied up, she spazzed out. "What the fuck Pakistan? I paid you all your money for every job. EVERYTIME!" Rochelle was frantic. "Shut the fuck up and calm the fuck down." Hero instructed her. He did not raise his voice but the tone he used made the hair on her neck stand up. Once she stopped talking, he explained to her that she was wanted. "Some people hired me to serve you up to them on a platter." Rochelle could not believe it. She did not know who would do such a thing. "What the fuck for? I never did anything to nobody. Come on man we better than this." Rochelle claimed her innocence.

Hero rolled his eyes at her ranting. "Hush. I don't want to silence you, but you know I will. So, for the last time Shut the fuck up and calm the fuck down. OR else." Hero stated firmly. Hero handed Rochelle the letter from Candice, like Karma asked him to do. Joy had faxed it to him at the start of his mission. Candice let Rochelle know how she really felt in the letter:

"I truly hate your dike ass. You put me through so much hell at my youthful age for no reason at all. All I ever wanted to do was go to school and become a prosecutor so I can put evil mutha fuckas like you away forever. You could have let me go several times, but you didn't. You kept me around for your own sick pleasure and monetary gain. I cried night after night, for three long years feeling sorry for myself. I wanted to just get up and leave but I knew that would have been an epic fail. Once I started fucking Ezra, I had a reason

to live. Because of him I fought through the pain, and we became a couple. I took pleasure knowing that you would kiss him right after he sucked my pussy, making me cum in his mouth. We laughed when you would suck my juices off his dick unknowingly. I would creep into your room while you and Ezra would have sex. Ezra had to see my face just to bust a nut. You did not even bounce or rotate on the dick. Ezra often said sex with you was like watching paint dry. So, a good pussy bitch like me fucked him hard and long. You cannot play with dick like that, you must be able to ride on command. While you were out in the world weighing your options trying to figure out if you were a man or a woman, I stole your man right from under you. Ezra made love to me every chance he Could; it was best in your bed, that dick slid right in on top of your satin sheets. Our nigga kept my legs across his shoulders laying pipe, telling me he loved me and only me. Your favorite nigga is my baby daddy ain't that some shit. You're not in control no more bitch. You are a pussy sucking dike that took advantage of me. I will find Ezra and we are going to raise our son together. When I see him imma jump in his lap and let him swim in this pussy just like he use to do. This is Candice if you have not guessed. My Auntie Karma can't wait to meet you she is so excited."

Rochelle had a look of pure fear on her face. She was ashamed of herself and the things she had done to Candice.

Rochelle did not know what she was about to go up against. She tried to figure out how in the hell did Hero end up helping Candice and come back for her. "Is there anything you can tell me Pakistan? I am totally confused" Rochelle asked with tears in her eyes. She was truly scared. "I never kiss and tell, you know that. Just chill" Hero said to her. Ignoring her tears. Rochelle cried in silence the rest of the way. Hero sent a text letting the crew know he was an hour out.

Yahtia and Karma had taken Candice on a shopping trip for some maternity clothes. "Hey Candi sweetie we gotta get going" Karma rushed Candice. "Yeah, baby doll we had something come up and we all need to get going" Yahtia cosigned. Candice waddled her way to the register with her final selections. Candice was carrying the cutest little bump already. Once they made their final purchased, they grabbed Joy and headed to the warehouse. Yahtia decided to let Candice tag along. Yahtia needed Rochelle to see that she had not broken Candice. The girls gave Candice a little make over, styling her perfectly. Candice had her hair in black and burgundy two-toned knotless braids, which hung down her back. Joy had Baby Mama do all the girls hair. Candice wore a jean skirt with a 'Poetic Justice' baby t-shirt with a matching jacket, showing off her slight bump. "Candice your job is to stand there and look beautiful ok." Yahtia instructed her. The idea was to let Rochelle see Candice as a boss bitch, making her much more jealous.

Candice was sitting at a table enjoying her pizza and wings, texting the other girls when Hero arrived with Rochelle. Hero brought her in and sat her at the table right in front of Candice. Candice had been around Yahtia, Karma and Joy long enough to know how to carry herself. "Hey Boo!" Candice put on her jubilant voice, "You want some wings?" Candice offered. Rochelle just gave her the side eye. "Nah. I'm good. What is this all about?" Rochelle asked as she turned up her nose in disgust. Candice stood up from the table, giving Rochelle a beautiful view of her entire body, baby bump included. Rochelle couldn't take her eyes off the exclusive Air Max 95' that Candice had on. While Rochelle was checking her out with envy, Candice stuck her hand in the wings marinating her hand with sauce. Candice smacked Rochelle across the face making sure to rub the sauce into her eyes, making them burn. The flaming spicy sauce from the wings was sure to do damage. Candice followed through by smashing the box forcefully into Rochelle's face. Rochelle was screaming in agony. Before Candice could thoroughly whip Rochelle's ass Yahtia stopped her. "Alright now baby gangster. I had to let you get your lick back, but we got it from here." Yahtia held up her hand to stop Candice from talking. "We need you to go sit in the car and talk to the girls like we are still out shopping. Can't have Mama T getting suspicious and kicking all of our asses." Yahtia said handing Candice some wipes.

Karma walked out and got the party started right away. "Hey bitch. I am Karma. These are my sisters Yahtia and Joy." Karma made introductions. "We have been trying to figure out why the fuck you felt like it was ok for you to man handle my niece the way you did." Rochelle tried her best to sound like a businesswoman and negotiate the matter at hand. Her eyes were still burning like hell. "That was not a new lifestyle for Candice. I bought her from an ex-girlfriend of mine, named Pooh." Rochelle responded. "That may be the case but Pooh didn't stick shit up her pussy and treat her like you did" Joy chimed in. "You're right. And I am sorry I wronged her I really am. Can we please manage this like adults?" Rochelle whined and begged, as she tried to stop the burning in her eyes. "Too late for all that, you came in with much attitude, keep that same energy." Yahtia said blowing the whistle loudly, right beside Rochelle's ear. The guys walked in one at a time, Kross first. He was carrying the largest pair of wire cutters ever seen. Craig followed, holding a medical kit. Ozias came in last with a bucket and an iron. "Hell yeah. Shit about to get real." Karma clapped her hands together.

Kross stuck Rochelle in the neck before she knew what was happening. It was a syringe full of anesthetic. Not waiting for the medication to work, Craig grabbed her right hand holding it above her head. "Remember guys, we can't do anything to her pussy. Hero needs her to make money." Joy reminded everyone. Craig nodded, holding Rochelle's hand still. In one clean cut Kross cut her fingers off, leaving only the thumb. Rochelle was in shock. Before she could scream the same thing was done to her left hand. Blood squirted everywhere. It looked like a massacre had taken place. Ozias was ready with the buckets of saline solution. Rochelle's hands were submerged in saline and then placed against a hot iron to seal the nubs. Both hands were wrapped quickly and efficiently so that an infection will not set in. "Hey you guys. I just got an emergency call. I have to get going." Hero walked back into the warehouse. Yahtia pushed Rochelle into Hero's arms. "She is all yours. Treat her right" Joy said full of sarcasm. Hero laughed and handed Joy Urban Watts location. "You guys can do this one on your own. You are just as professional as I am." Hero loaded Rochelle up in the car and started his engine. "Go get that mutha fuckar. Let me know if you need me." Hero said pulling off. Rochelle was passed out, from a combination of shock and anesthesia. When she wakes up, she will be in another country with no fingers, and possibly a dick in her mouth. Karma strikes again.

After putting all the tools away, the crew cleaned up a little bit and left. After dropping Candice off at the group home, they had a meeting. "Ok I just sent the travel itinerary to Ezra so he will be touching down soon." Joy announced to everyone. "And I have all the information on Urban." Karma wagged her eyebrows. "Say less, let's go get this bastard" Craig was hyped. Ezra received the text he had been waiting on. Ezra had a homeboy Memphis Bell, that he grew up with from a kid. The two were like brothers. "Hey bro I don't think it's a clever idea for you to travel all the way to South Carolina alone". Memphis decided he was tagging along, Memphis needed to have his brother's back same way Ezra would have his. "Shit just don't sound right strangers calling you about your secret girl who supposedly carrying your baby. Shit just sound made up to me bro." Memphis said while packing his bag. Ezra did not care it was a chance he had to take. He was so open for Candice, he had to see what was going on in person.

Kross, Craig, and Ozias were set to meet Ezra when he touched down. They were not going to put hands on him, but they were not going make it a walk in the park for him. The idea was to make a man out of him. Teach him to take accountability and responsibility for his actions.

Urban Watts was hanging out in an apartment complex on the outskirts of Columbia. This was a high crime and drug infested environment. Urban kept an entourage of criminals surrounding him. Whenever the crew made their move, it would have to be done, quickly and swiftly. Kross, Craig and Ozias let the ladies sit this one out. The three of them had been riding around casing the area. One of Urban's foot soldiers spotted them. They circled the block to get into position, but one of Urban's guys stepped in front of the jeep with a sawed-off shotgun. Thinking quickly on his feet, Kross let down the window and mased him. Ozias and Craig grabbed him and tossed him in the back. Urban stood one block over, unaware of what was about to happen. After hitting the guy with a few hard body shots and placing his tool in his mouth, he agreed to help. Craig coached him on what to say. "Hey fam. We got trouble in Bagdad," the guy Pete said, his eyes still running and burning from the mase. Pete was holding his ribs, making it look believable. "What the fuck! Why you not on foot patrol?

Why the fuck you crying and shit?" Urban rapidly asked the questions. "Just come the fuck on. We need to assist NOW!" Pete said tapping the side of the door. Urban walked up to the car about to get in, still skeptical.

Pete did exactly what he was told to do. Craig was lying in the back with a gun pointed directly at him. "Who the fuck is this ugly cornball mutha fucka driving? You moving funny as fuck Pete." Urban was weary and shook at this point, but he was moving towards the Jeep. He went to open the door and saw Craig. Urban took off running but not fast enough. Kross was on his ass. Kross forced him all the way into the van and Ozias pulled off. Urban's crew heard the commotion and came running but was too late. Ozias was in the wind by the time they got to the spot. "Y'all pussy boys will not live to talk about this." Urban cursed them. He continued fighting, cursing, and being extra annoying so Kross gave him a double dose of sleep meds. "Night Nigga." Kross said, impersonating Pinky from the movie "Next Friday". Ozias called Karma to update her on the mission. "Hey, love we got our favorite bad boy, he's on the way to you, we also have one of his buddies too." Ozias spoke in a lovey dovey tone. Kross and Craig made gaging noises just to be assholes. They teased each other often just like they were brothers for real. "Wow! Thanks for the bonus, babe. We are gonna need someone to tell his story." Karma blew her man a kiss through the phone and hung up. Joy sent the location and all the details to Craig's phone. Kross could not help but to see the text. He shook his head wondering where the ladies produced this list. "Please remind me never to cross any of our women. Sheesh" Kross said with a serious look on his face. "They definitely bout that life." Ozias cosigned.

Forsythe, Georgia. That is where they were taking Urban. Georgia was one of the most racist states in the south. Forsythe was like Klan capital of the world. The Klu Klux Klan and Neo-Nazis openly had rallies and marches. They performed discriminatory acts against all Blacks and Gays openly. The sheriff was a card toting member of the KKK so they never did anything, unless he helped. Tonight, they were scheduled to have their annual 'Save White America' rally. This was like the Super Bowl and Olympics for their kind. It was taking place on an old plantation, complete with white hooded hats, burning crosses, and white hooded sheets.

The guys pulled up to the rendezvoused point and the girls were waiting. Urban had to be woken up and pulled from the car. He was still groggy, but he focused on Karma. No one saw it coming. Urban spit in Karma's face. Ozias was on his ass instantly. Ozias beat Urban with the sawed off that Pete was carrying. "That's enough baby. Leave him to the hillbilly circus." Karma laughed. "Strip his ass down and if either of them makes the slightest move, light their ass up." Karma wiped her face. Before Karma walked off, she slapped blood from Urban's mouth. Karma fired up a pre-rolled to calm her nerves, while instructing her sisters on the next move, The ladies' gorilla glued a hot pink wig on Urban head." I want this bum nigga to shine bright like a diamond". Joy said to her sisters. "OK then I got a tube of lime green lip stick in my bag, hook him up sis Yahtia added". Urban began to speak against it, but Ozias placed the shot gun in his mouth then he participated with open arms. Urban was already the ugliest man that only a mother could love, but now he was Ms. Celia ugly. They dressed him in a *Black Lives Matter* shirt and a matching Black Lives Matter head band, Urban wore a pair of jean booty shorts that complimented his hairy legs. Urban was sure to get some attention with the over the knee socks that said Fuck Trump. Yahtia took pictures to capture the moment. When they were done everyone took selfies with Urban in the background. "It's GO TIME!" Karma called out through the walkie talkies. Everyone scrambled to get to the hill on the far side of the plantation. From there they would be able to see and record the entire show down.

On the way Craig and Ozias drove in close to the rally, firing shots into the air and screaming *"Black Lives Matter! Black Lives Matter!"* Those three words definitely raised a red flag shifting the attention on them. Urban was forced out of the Jeep and Craig and Ozias delivered a hard kick to his body causing urban to eat a mouth full of dirt and rocks. Karma and Yahtia had on ski masks and yelled out "Suck my dick you white faggots". That was the straw that broke the camel's back. Close to a thousand angry white men started running towards Urban. Urban was stuck on stupid for a few seconds, but he quickly got it together when he saw the mob of men running towards him. Urban turned to run, but between the 5-inch hot pink pumps that were duct taped tightly on his feet, and the ropes tied to his ankles he could not maneuver. The crew died laughing at the sight of Urban shuffle running and screaming like a bitch. "Looks like we got action boys", one of the KKK men said. "Take his ass to the field", another one cheered. The men were looking at Urban like the juiciest steak with all the fixings. "The Lord has provided us with a live nigger. And looks like he is one of them butt fuckers too." Members of the rally chattered and celebrated. The idea of torturing a black man made their tiny dicks hard. Moments later the crew could see Urban being dragged by the pink wig to the center of the field. "I think they are doing a racist praise dance or something." Joy said amused and confused. "Yeah, white people are so weird." Karma cosigned with her. They continued to watch Urban being violated, maimed, and tortured. This will be a great teaching story for the Klan to share with their young, I'm sure this episode will be marked as their most exciting kill.

CHAPTER 24
TEACHING INDEPENDENCE

After the rally, the guys dropped Pete back off in his hood. He was beyond traumatized. "Tell all the homies what happened, don't leave out shit be sure to tell how y'all was bullied by a rapist and an undercover punk. Y'all niggas better off without that pussy. We can give two fucks how y'all niggas run this block. Matter of fact you should take over now, the ball in your court take advantage. Our beef was with Urban. If you feel like you want to retaliate, my advice to you is, DON'T. You were only guilty by association, so leave quietly before we take you back to Trump world." Ozias threatened Pete. "You got it my man ion want no parts of nothing y'all got going on." Pete held his hands up in surrender. The boys laughed all the way back home. "That nigga breath stink or he shit out some horse turds." Kross said. "Oh, I know he did fam I couldn't wait to ditch his ass." Oh, Cousin Pete, Craig said laughing.

"Y'all know that lil nigga Ezra get here tomorrow." Ozias spoke to his brothers. "Yeah man, Yahtia been on my ass about that. Yahtia said we gotta make a man out of him." Kross said scratching his head. "Training day." Craig piped in. "That is what Joy called it." Kross laughed. Ozias laughed too. "So, which one of us is going to be Denzel?"

Ezra and Memphis landed in South Carolina, looking just like out of towners. They stuck out like a sore thumb. Since Memphis purchased his own ticket, the crew did not know he was coming. "Hey baby. Were we expecting someone with Ezra?" Craig called Joy to confirm. Craig was not trying to have his woman pissed off with him. Hell, he did not want his sisters pissed with him either. "Ummm no. But if he is not a threat, I do not see a problem with it. Just get me all his information as soon as you can so I can get his folder together." Joy instructed him. The guys met Ezra and Memphis at the baggage claim area. Once they were in sight Craig approached. "What's up man. I'm Craig and this is my big homie Kross." Craig extended his hand as a greeting. "What's good?" Ezra accepted Craig's hand, giving him a nice firm handshake. "This my brother Memphis he tagged along for support." They all shook hands like old friends. Ezra and Memphis grabbed their bags and began to walk outside. They assumed Kross and Craig were just showing them "Southern Hospitality" by introducing themselves. "Bro where the fuck is this Joy bitch. I told you it was a set up." Memphis said side eyeing everything. Unbeknownst to them, Craig and Kross were right behind them. "Please don't call her a bitch." Craig said firmly. Craig was willing to give Memphis a pass because shit does seem a bit suspect. Craig's voice scared Ezra and Memphis, causing them to jump and turn around. "Oh, my bad man. You know her or something?" Memphis asked. Memphis did not want any trouble, but he needed to make sure his boy was safe. "That's my ole lady. You were supposed to meet her, but I do not like her around strange men. You understand?" Craig used his no nonsense business voice. Memphis nodded in understanding. Kross had pulled the car around. "You guys are riding with us. Hop in." Craig instructed as he got into the front seat not waiting for either of them.

Memphis was still a little reluctant, but he followed Ezra, and got into the car. They rode in silence for a bit. Kross and Craig wanted to get a feel for the type of man Ezra was, so he observed him closely. After ten minutes or so, Ezra spoke. "When am I going to see Candice? Are you taking me to her now?" Ezra asked looking concerned. Ezra needed to know everything. Especially now that she was carrying his baby. "Slow your role Playboy, the boss ladies wanna meet you first. We must lay down some ground rules and create a game plan to benefit your newfound family. I can promise you it is all for your own good. Candice's too." Craig said explaining to Ezra.

Memphis sat in silence, observing as well. Ezra felt like they could trust Craig and Kross, but everything was so vague. Like always Kross had a bag of that Island Funk on him. Kross sparked up filling the air with mother earth's aroma. "Damn that shit smell good." Ezra and Memphis said to each other. Craig passed the blunt to the backseat. "Smokes even better bro." Craig added while choking on the thick smoke cloud. Memphis accepted the blunt only after he realized it was not laced with anything. "If we not going to meet Joy or Candice, then where are you taking us?" Memphis finally spoke up. Kross laughed. "We about to take you to get some grub and meet our big brother Ozias. "You can relax Memphis if we were going to do anything shady, we would have done it by now. Play your cards right and coming to South Carolina will be your biggest blessing." Kross said as he gave Memphis a boss man wink.

They went to '*Queen Beans Southern Kitchen*' for dinner. Ezra and Memphis had never had food that good. They went through three plates each and still got a to go box. "Man, that food taste like a bunch of black grandmas and big mamas in the kitchen." Memphis said rubbing his stomach. Craig laughed as he told them how the restaurant came to life. From his auntie Bean and cousin Boopie they are the best cooks in town, taught by my grandmother Net." Craig said. The men laughed over drinks and conversation. Memphis even loosened up a little. After dinner, the men made their way to the Extended Stay on Two Notch Road. Smoking double stuffed backwoods. "This is where you two gentlemen will call home for now." Ozias handed them their room key. "Say man, I need some of that smoke." Ezra made eye contact with Kross then pulled out a giant dope boy knot flipping through the money ready to pay. "Nah man your family until I find out otherwise." Kross said tossing Ezra a quarter sack. "Good looking fam." Ezra caught the bag in the air. "We will be back bright and early. Y'all about to meet Candice's aunties in the morning" Craig said shaking his head just thinking about how that was going to go.

The girls are out with Candice, picking her brain about Ezra. They want to know how she feels about being with him or raising a baby without him. Candice tells them she is prepared to do everything alone but does not want to. She misses Ezra and wishes that he could be a part of her pregnancy. Candice feels like if Ezra knew she was pregnant he would come for her. Craig sends Joy the info about Memphis and everything they found out about Ezra. Craig explains to Joy the profile he and the guys came up with about Ezra within the few hours of being around him.

"Ezra was not in love with Rochelle. Their relationship was all about money. Ezra is a dope boy and he and Rochelle collaborated on various illegal activities. Rochelle sold pussy and Ezra sold the dope. The two of them begin to fuck out of boredom. Rochelle would bring in her lesbian lovers and they would do freaky shit to Ezra. Him being a young street nigga of course he went for it. Candice was sold to Rochelle and shortly after that Ezra fell in love with Candice while Rochelle fell in love with him. Ezra wanted to save Candice, but he knew the consequences. Memphis is his long-time friend and he just want what is best for his boy, neither one of them is a threat. Once we train them and get them thinking like men, we may have room on the squad for them." Craig said as he ended his summery profile to Joy.

The next morning Kross, Craig and Ozias were at the room to pick up Ezra and Memphis at ten O'clock Sharp. The ladies were waiting at a nearby Starbucks. Yahtia rented out the conference room so they could conduct business freely. "You think you slick Tia you want to eat bagels and drink unlimited ice coffee that's the real reason we're here." Karma teased. "Yep." Yahtia responded. "I'm about to get me a caramel latte and two strawberry cream cheese bagels before the guys pull up." Joy said walking fast to the line. "Just fat." Said Yahtia. "Ask your brother about this thickness boo." Joy said laughing at Yahtia. The girls were wired up on ice coffee when the guys come in with Ezra and Memphis in tow. "Damn we were about to take a nap." said Karma. "I know bae we had to get their nerves right and let them puff puff before they came in, we know what their facing." Ozias said while having a seat at the table. "Hello Ezra, I am Joy, and these are my sisters Yahtia and Karma. "Hello ma'am nice to meet you." Ezra said with a shaky voice. "I am Memphis, Ezra is my best friend/ brother." "Glad to see you came all this way with your boy that show you are loyal." Karma said while shaking their hand. "Have a seat we have a lot of ground to cover." Yahtia spoke. I'm going to sound off first and then I will give you a chance to respond but hear me out completely." Yahtia said making the guys nervous.

"I have full custody over Candice as of now. Her wellbeing is my number one priority. Candice came from a sticky situation that I am not blaming you for. My sister's and I are very mad about the things she endured while with that bitch Rochelle. Candice has a lot of healing to do, and she is coming along smoothly with that. Candice is two months pregnant with your baby and she is positive it is yours. Candice will remain living here in South Carolina she will not be returning to Ohio. Candice will remain in my care until she is eighteen. Even then I will have a say so in how she moves. You must prove that you can take care of Candice and your kid. This will not be a fuck feast type of situation. You will not be allowed to lay up and twirls your thumbs and keep her on her back. Candice is only fifteen and her life will have boundaries and discipline even with a baby. You will be allowed to speak with Candice but not before you tell me your plan of taking care of her." Yahtia looked at Ezra with a mean mug waiting for a response.

"I respect all stipulations that are in place. Candice have experienced a rough life and I am glad she has begun to heal and see life from a different lens. I do know that I love Candice and whatever it takes she will be taking care of. I know the baby is mine I would interrupt the sessions with the old men, and it was over before it started. I made sure they had on a condom but most of them was only humping her leg they did not know the difference. I am only seventeen myself, but I been getting money in the streets since I was 12 years old. I am not proud of it but that is just how I was living. I have money stashed away back home to take care of Candice and supply all that she will need. I have two stacks right now for you to take her and buy her whatever she wants for her and the baby." Craig, Ozias and Kross were in a huddle. "I knew this nigga was getting money with a little guidance he will do numbers." Kross whispered.

The ladies all drilled Ezra but he fought back each time giving them the answers they wanted to hear. They could not find anything wrong with him. He was going to provide no matter what, Ezra stated that he would no longer sell dope now that he will be a new father. Bringing a kid in this world takes time and patience, so boy or girl he planned on giving his kid the best of him. The ladies would have kept going on, but the men had to stop them. "Leave it alone he is good, everybody ain't bad." Ozias said in Ezra's defense. Karma frowned up at Ozias knowing he was right. The ladies threw in the towel and left the rest up to the men.

CHAPTER 25
BAECATION WORLD

The guys put Ezra and Memphis to work, reconstructing the pizza warehouse. They were a tremendous help with the remodeling. Memphis surprised everyone with his knowledge and abilities about construction and electrical work. "Hey bro let me holla at you." Kross pulled Ezra away from the construction to speak with him privately. Kross had been watching Ezra closely and was thoroughly impressed with his work ethic. After talking with the guys, Kross decided that Ezra would make a good business partner. "How would you like to be a part of the big business? You know help line your pockets for you and your little family." Kross sparked up a pre-rolled blunt and passed it. "Damn bro that shit would be amazing. I would love to set up a dispensary in Ohio but shit not legal there yet." Ezra explained. Ezra was thinking of a way to get into business with Kross and the guys. Now was his chance, and he took it. "But I do know two major suppliers back home that would jump at the chance to get their hands on some of that Island shit. They both got train smoke money and do good business." Kross was intrigued so he asked a few more questions about the suppliers.

Ozias joined Kross and Ezra's meeting. "So, you telling me you can make one phone call and set up a major play?" Ozias was skeptical. "Yeah man. I know for a fact one of them in Georgia right now. It would be nothing for me to get shit cracking" Ezra boasted. "Go ahead then. Make the call" Kross instructed. Ezra pulled out his phone but hesitated. "This not a setup, is it? I told the girls I was done dealing and shit. I do not want no smoke with none of them. I'm trying to do the right thing for my family." Ezra was determined to gain everyone's approval, especially if that meant he could be with Candice. "Damn lil homie you really do love ya girl" Ozias nodded his head in approval. "But this is grown man business. To be kept between you and the men. Ya dig. Make the call. The women won't know nothing" Ozias told Ezra. Ezra did as he was told and less than fifteen minutes later, he had set up the play. "E, tell your people don't worry about nothing. I am driving up from Savannah right now. I will pick up for me and my brother. I got cash money too" Toy the buyer said to Ezra. Ever since Toy had been to Miami and experienced the Island Funk, he was obsessed with getting his hand on it. Now was his chance.

Ezra reiterated everything to the guys when he hung up with Toy. They ended up making $85,000 in profit from that deal. "If you can keep us plugged in, we will keep our mouths closed" Kross said handing Ezra twenty bands. "This is your cut. You'll see more in the future if y'all can keep the sales up." Ezra dapped Kross and split the money with Memphis on the spot. "Those two are definitely coming back. That, I am Sure of." Memphis spoke. Kross and Ozias nodded in approval. They loved the way Memphis and Ezra held each other down, with no questions asked. "That's what's up. We need someone to watch the dispensaries while we are out of town. Y'all down?" Ozias asked. Ozias knew that Ezra and Memphis would be able to manage the job, but he had to hear them say they would do it. "For sure bro" Memphis answered excitedly. "Great. Yahtia and I will be by later so you can facetime Candice" Kross spoke out as they started to go their separate ways. Ezra's face lit up, like a boy getting his first piece of pussy. Out of nowhere Ezra hugged Ozias, "Thank you man. Y'all don't know what this means to me" he said while still hugging Ozias. The hug caught Ozias off guard, and Ozias held his hands up in defense mode. This made everyone laugh, including Memphis. Once everyone got themselves together Craig shifted the embarrassment by dapping Ezra up. "Good looking out today fam. You really came through for us." Ezra gathered himself and dapped him back.

Yahtia did a pop-up visit to the group home. Ivy and Mama T were taking all the girls out for massages. "Hey Tia, you want to hang out with us today?" Mama T asked. "No not this time Ma. I'm here to take Candice to a teen parenting class." Tia responded while hugging her mother. "Wow. That is so impressive. Ivy and I have been getting her plenty of reading material to broaden her horizons. Candice needs to understand what is happening to her body." Mama T explained. Ivy interrupted the mother daughter duo before the conversation could continue. "Just drop her off at the massage parlor if you two get finished early." Ivy grabbed Toyah, and the girls followed them out the door leaving Candice with Yahtia. "Auntie Tia! I'm so glad I can hang out with you today" Candice wrapped her arms around Yahtia. "You look so pretty today. I have a shocking surprise for you" Yahtia hugged her back. "Oooooh! I love surprises. What you got me?" Candice said jumping up and down. Yahtia loved when Candice, or any of the girls acted like actual kids. "Calm down spoiled brat." Yahtia joked. "First you have to promise me a few things" Yahtia sat down beside Candice and waited for her to agree. "Of course. Anything" Candice said, but the excitement was replaced with uncertainty. "First, you cannot tell Mama T or Ivy. This cannot even go in your journal entries. Secondly, no matter what happens you must swear you will continue to do well in school and therapy. Stay focused no matter what." Yahtia was looking Candice in her eyes. This stare made Candice a little uncomfortable. It made her think she was going back to Rochelle or something. Candice nodded in agreement, but her anxiety was written all over her face. "Calm down lil mama. I swear it is a pleasant surprise" Yahtia reassured Candice, as she texted Kross.

Moments after the text was sent, the phone call came through. Yahtia made sure to have the camera facing Candice so that she could see Ezra's face. As soon as Candice realized who she was looking at, she cried hysterically. No coherent words were coming from her mouth. "Don't cry Candi girl. You might upset the baby" Ezra tried to calm Candice and keep his own emotions in check. "I want you to know that I am so proud of you for doing so good and being brave. I never stopped loving you." Ezra let his emotions come through his words. Ezra did not care who could see or hear him. He needed to let Candice know how he was feeling. "I am going to be here for you and our son. At least I hope it is a son. I will love a daughter too, but we need a boy first." This made Candice smile. She still had wet eyes, but she was not inconsolable anymore. "I am sorry I didn't protect you better. I swear to you I will protect you from this moment on from everything and anybody. Soon as your aunties say it is cool and they trust me with you I will be there every step of the way. Your only job is to make sure you deliver a strong healthy baby and take care of yourself. I will manage everything else baby." Ezra finally took a breath. He was so focused on telling Candice how much he loved her, he never gave her a chance to speak. Candice took his moment of silence as her que to speak.

Candice was talking so fast, trying to get everything out at one time, she began to studder. Yahtia was all smiles herself. Yahtia had never seen Candice this happy and bubbly. Yahtia touched Candice's arm with reassurance and walked away, giving her some privacy with Ezra. Yahtia recognized that glow anywhere. Those two were in love, the looks on their faces screamed it to the world. Yahtia made a mental note to talk with the crew. She knew that eventually she would have to let the two youngsters play out their love affair but for now it would be by phone only. Yahtia went into Ivy's office and read through some of the notebook entries while Candice caked on the phone with Ezra. After an hour Yahtia let Candice know, they had to say their goodbyes. "I love you Candi Girl and I will always be with you." Ezra kissed Candice through the phone. Candice blushed but returned the sentiment. "Oooh how sweet, Yahtia said then blew Kross a kiss before they ended the call." "Oh my god Thank You so much Auntie Tia!" Candice hugged Yahtia. Toyah interrupted their bonding moment. "What did Auntie Tia do to get this Kumbaya moment Mama T asked with a raised eyebrow?" Candice covered her mouth as if she were in trouble. Yahtia recovered quickly. "Hey Ma. It was nothing major. I just surprised Candice with some driving lessons. I figured she could start when we return from our vacation Yahtia said nervously." Toyah knew it was some shit in the mix. "Y'all training them early I see, Toyah said shaking her head with a motherly smirk on her face."

Yahtia talked to the other girls before she left. Yahtia did not want any of them to feel like Candice received special treatment just because she was pregnant. Yahtia wanted everyone to feel loved and supported, so she engaged with each of the girls. "Next time I will have to go with you girls to the massage therapist, especially if she is as good as y'all say she is" Yahtia joked with Kimmie.

Ozias spoke with Ezra and Memphis, giving them the instruction for the dispensaries. "It shouldn't be too hard fam. I am sure you can manage it." Ozias informed them while passing the blunt. "No doubt. But ummm. What about Candice. You think I can get her number or something. I do not want to wait three weeks to talk to her. What if something happens and she needs me while y'all gone." Ezra argued his point. Ezra really wanted Candice's phone number. "Fam that one ain't on me. You gotta get the ok from her aunties. But I will ask on your behalf." Ozias said sincerely. Ozias understood making sure Ezra was stable and able to take care of Candice, but he did not agree with keeping him away from his family. Ozias sent a text to the group asking the big question. "That is a hard NO boss. Karma said. Candice is in safe hands. If he misses her that much, he can write her a letter." Ozias relayed the message and gave Ezra the P.O. Box address to send letters and any gifts. "Damn bro. Why they so hard on a nigga?" Ezra said disheartened. "I don't even know fam. But you got this I know you do. Make the best of your situation and know that your family is in the best possible hands." Ozias patted Ezra's back for encouragement. Ezra nodded his head, deciding that he would write Candice a letter every day until he could talk to her again.

It was total chaos back on campus. "Y'all got six hours to pack. Our flight leaves at eight o'clock" Kross screamed out, notifying the crew of the time constraints. "I love it when you take charge baby, but you gonna have to stop yelling at me like that. It's doing something to me." Yahtia rolled her eyes. Kross did not notice the sarcasm. Kross had gotten used to her getting horny every time he bossed up and gave orders. Sometimes he would have to hold her off while he finished business calls, especially the ones from Trinidad. It was something about business and his accent that made his lady's pussy smile. Yahtia was slamming her room door she was frustrated as hell. Yahtia had no clue what to pack. "I am about to meet my future in laws, and I have to make a good impression." Yahtia fussed over her clothes while Karma and Joy passed a blunt and compared bikinis. "Girl you are stressing over nothing. I am sure Kross family will love you." Joy said handing Yahtia the blunt. "Yea sis chill out." Karma cosigned with Joy and pulled out a bag full of bathing suit cover ups. "I thought about you while I was online shopping." Karma showed off the beautiful wraps and robes. "Sexy and conservatives. You are meeting his grandma not dressing like a grandma" Karma laughed at the faces Yahtia made at her. Yahtia just wanted to make a good impression. Kross loved his family, especially his "First Lady." That is what he called his grandmother. "Y'all what if she doesn't approve of me? What if he leaves me because his grandma thinks I'm a slut?" Yahtia started to work herself up into a panic. Before anyone could do anything, she ran to the bathroom to vomit. Karma and Joy packed for Yahtia. "Girl get cleaned up and relax. We got you." They instructed Yahtia passing her a blunt.

Everyone was running around but managed to have everything ready ahead of time. Trinidad was the first stop of many, the girls could not wait to get the party started. The crew boarded the private jet with so much excitement. The flight crew became excited just watching them. Yahtia managed to calm her nerves enough to stop snapping at everyone. "OMG these seats are so soft." Joy raved as she rubbed the seats like she was performing foreplay. The flight attendant helped everyone get situated then she went over a safety video. "Now that the boring stuff is out of the way. TURN UP!" The young flight attendant yelled, sending champagne around to everyone. "Please stay in your seats until we take off." She added. Yahtia felt sick to her stomach during takeoff and ended up vomiting again. "Baby you not getting sick on me, are you?" A concerned Kross asked while wiping Yahtia with a cool towel. "I am fine love just my nerves." Yahtia gave him a weak smile. The girls figured out how to use the massage chairs and were in heaven. The flight was long, but smooth. They enjoyed a lobster dinner and more champagne. "This is better than any party bus I have ever been on." The young flight attendant laughed with the girls as they partied. Yahtia's nausea returned during landing. She vomits straight liquids like she was pissing out her mouth.

The crew stumbled from the plane. "Follow me. My Gammy sent a car for us." Kross said sounding like a kid. The guys started mocking him. "His Gammy." They said being dramatic. When everyone got to the front of the airport there was an extended stretch hummer limo waiting for them. All their luggage had been retrieved and was being loaded into the car. "Damn Kross your family got it like that." Craig said realizing that they were getting the celebrity treatment. "Bro I basically bagged me Island Royalty." Yahtia said rubbing on Kross. Kross just stood there looking silly from all the attention. The crew climbed into the limo and enjoyed the ride to the McDonald Estate. Kross remained quiet most the trip to his childhood home. Pulling up to the estate, the crew's reaction did not disappoint Kross. "Damn Kross. I knew you was rich, but not I grew up in the Scarface Mansion rich." Ozias said. Everyone was glued to the windows checking out the scenery. The only word to describe the house was a mansion, or a small castle. The outside was surrounded by waterfalls and large elephant ear plants. The landscaping was immaculate. It looked like the botanical gardens that people paid to see. There was a bridge crossing a pond leading to the front door. The pond had beautiful tropical fish and water lilies. "This is straight out of a fairytale book." Karma whispered. Joy and Yahtia were taking pictures like tourists.

Yahtia did a quick gargle and sprayed her clothing to make sure she did not smell like vomit. Yahtia was still so nervous, but it was now or never. Kross' grandmother met them at the door. "Is that my baby?" Kross' grandmother pulled him into a hug, and then hugged them all. "This is my first lady, my grandmother, Madeline McDonald." Kross introduced. Ozias and Craig bowed to her, causing Madeline to blush. "Ms. Madeline you are so beautiful." Joy and Karma gushed over her. "You must be the beautiful Yahtia!" Madeline acknowledged. "I am, your skin is so flawless you have a perfect glow." Yahtia complimented. "My recipe is fish guts and olive oil; it will keep you youthful and full of beauty." "Let me put that in my phone before I forget." Karma said being serious. Madeline grabbed Yahtia's hand and signaled for the others to follow her.

Madeline led the ladies into her sunroom, where her sister was waiting for them. There was a table with fruit, wine, and cheese. "Ladies this is my sister Diem." Madeline introduced everyone. "Welcome ladies. I hope you are ready for some island treats." Diem said as four of the sexiest masseuses came walking in from another door. They all stood by the massage tables. "Damn they fine." Karma let slip from her mouth. Diem smiled. "Yes, ma'am they are." Madeline removed her floral moo-moo and underneath was a two-piece black and diamond bikini. Diem removed her wrap and showed off her thong cutout one piece. The girls were shocked to see the sisters had bodies like Beyonce without a wrinkle in sight. "OK grandma Madeline you better work." Karma high fived Diem and grabbed her hand turning her around to show off her attire. Diem responded by blowing Karma a shot gun. Karma held up her hand signaling that she was good, but Diem kept blowing smoke her way. The girls instantly relaxed realizing that Madeline and Diem were going to be fun and easy to have a good relationship with. "First we get massages, then we party like rock stars." Madeline said laying on her bed. Everyone else followed suit. They laughed and joked as they received the best deep tissue massages. After 45 minutes the ladies were fast asleep and snoring. Madeline and Diem left them sleeping and went to find the boys.

Kross was in the garage showing off his car collection when Madeline and Diem found them. Madeline passed Craig a blunt. "Here, try this." Craig hesitated but reached for the blunt. Craig was unsure about having a smoke session with Kross' grandmother. "Gammy I thought I told you to behave" Kross pointed his finger like she use to do him when he was in trouble. "I can't always be good." Madeline said winking at him. "Besides this that shit I haven't let hit the states yet." Madeline pulled a baggie from her moo-moo letting Kross and the guys inspect the buds for themselves. "OMG! Grandma all the way live ain't she!" Ozias said. "Whoa!" Craig yelled as Diem smacked his ass. Diem was being fresh, trying to touch all over him. "TiTi Diem stop that. I told you about feeling on my friends." Kross yelled at her. "Go to the other side of the house and find Uncle Mack and let him give that thang a twirl." Kross aunt was like a dog in heat. Kross forgot to mention that his grandma and auntie were not like other women in their seventies. "My bad y'all these island ladies hit different than the grannies in the states." Kross said while laughing at Craig. "I'm about to go check on the girls. I need to make sure my auntie hasn't kidnapped them." Kross said jokingly. "No need baby. We left them sleeping." Madeline said to him. "Yep, we had full body massages, and smoked a bamboo blunt of that Blossom Fuzz and they were out like a light." Madeline laughed at the faces the guys made. "Grandma you had another man touching my woman. I know not." Kross was done with his wild grandma. Kross was ready to send her to her room too. Kross could not believe she was acting like a teenager on spring break. "Boy chill out. They are on vacation let them live a little. Besides, one of you handsome gentlemen have a bigger situation to deal with." Madeline said while smiling. "What are you talking about lil lady?" Kross asked. "Whenever someone cross over the pond and the fish swim schooling together that means someone is pregnant. Diem and I are not candidates. Our pussies are full of gray hairs and have spider webs and dust follicles." Madeline said being vague on purpose. "Someone is pregnant." Craig and Ozias said at the same time. "Wait so who ever steps over the pond with the swimming fish is pregnant." Ozias said needed clarity. "No fam she is saying one of the girls is knocked up." Whenever the fish begin schooling close together after a female cross over the pond that means a baby is lurking inside one of our ladies." Kross explained.

Madeline listened to the guys go back and forth about the possibilities. I am not for certain which one but it's one of them if not two." Madeline said sounding certain. Everyone looked at Kross for and explanation. Kross cursed in Trinidadian. "Gammy is never wrong we must keep a close eye on the ladies." Kross stated. Is this a Trinidadian myth or is this factual?" Craig asked. "Man listen this is real spill this pond has called out all my girl cousins and sisters." Kross said confirming. So, prepare for Mama T to kick somebody ass Kross added." OMG my mama is going to flip her wig fosho." Craig said feeling nervous. "Damn my pull-out game has gotten weak. Karma rides a nigga dick so good and them bullets be shooting all up in that pussy." Ozias said in a whisper hoping Madeline did not hear him. "I know what it's like when a woman got good pussy. I have fourteen kids I kept niggas lost in the sauce myself." Kross looked at Craig and Ozias and shook his head. "Damn, I need a blunt of that blossom fuzz shit grandma got." Ozias said wondering if Karma was the one holding.

Kross decided to give a tour of the estate. He drove a golf cart around the estate because walking would take forever. They were introduced to at least twenty-five cousins, fifteen aunts and uncles from both sides of the family. Two sisters and one brother. Diem was waiting for them when they arrived back at the main house. The boys sat on the patio with a bottle and a blunt, enjoying the meet and greet with family. "Kross help me out please." Ozias was a little frantic. Diem had set her sights on him now. Diem was trying to stick her hands in his pants and breathing heavy in his ear. "Auntie! My gal Karma is a bad bitch in the states, she is a problem we don't need." So, leave her man alone." Kross could not help but laugh as he watched his friends speed walk away from his auntie. "Diem is harmless I swear." She a real live cougar with a thing for American young black men, and you two fit the disruption perfectly." Kross said still laughing.

The next two days was filled with tours and island adventure. Everyone was amazed. Kross was so proud that he could show off his homeland to his new family. The ladies got a chance to shop at some of the boutiques, buying authentic island wear. "This jewelry is gorgeous." Joy said for the hundredth time. "It is all handmade, so no one piece is the same." Diem explained to Joy. While putting a bracelet on her arm. "That one suits you perfectly." Diem stated. After shopping and being pampered like queens. Madeline decided to schedule some fun of her own. "Ok girls, the men are about to kick it with Uncle Mack and the rest of the hoodlums. So, were about to have us a good ole time." Madeline said with her sneaky voice. Kross knew his grandmother and auntie were up to some bullshit by the way they were dressed. Diem had a bag full of singles and a whip around her neck. "Gammy please keep it PG. And please for the love of everything holy, keep auntie Diem in line." Kross begged. "Ahhh were all grown here; you talk too damn much. But for your sanity I will make sure we all come back in one piece." Madeline said and turned her attention to the girls. "It's sexy time. Ladies get dressed. I know you in love and shit but tonight Love don't mean a thing." Madeline winked causing Kross to slap himself.

The girls were getting dressed, under the guidance of Madeline and Diem. "What kind of fun we about to have grandma?" Yahtia asked. "I want y'all to see more of what the island has to offer. Some big muscle-bound oily island strippers." Madeline answered while stuffing a bamboo stick full of gas, "Oh No ma'am! I got my island man already. His name is Kross." Yahtia said. "She doesn't speak for all of us grandma. I'm in." Karma said pushing Yahtia out of the way. "Shit me too" Joy said following Karma. Everyone was looking at Yahtia now. "Honey I know my baby is everything and then some. But ain't nothing wrong with a lil peek a boo every now and then." Madeline high fived Diem, Karma and Joy. "Bitch we know you in love and shit, hell we all are. But you gotta take one for the team sis." Joy said with sarcasm. I have only seen one dick in my lifetime and I wanna see some more." Joy said doing a little grinding motion and air hump. "You, tell her Joy! I knew you were my favorite." Madeline joked. "Oh, hell NAH." I'm in grandma, but I got to be the favorite from now on." Yahtia laughed, but the jealousy was real. This was her grandma Yahtia was feeling salty. "All you sexy mamacita's are my favorite. Now let us go so we can see Both Hands make that thang jump." Madeline and Diem made their eyes jump seductively. "I'm about to put these pretty pink toes in a mutha fuckar mouth." Diem blurted out. "Ok Cardi B." Yahtia yelled out.

The guys were enjoying a chill evening with each other at the mansion. They were getting everything together for the next stop on the vacation and looking at financial investments. The girls were out with the McDonald sisters getting buck wild at 'The Strip Palace.' Joy had multiple lap dances and was looking to be the victim of a stage dance. Karma was tipping generously, and letting her hands roam freely. Yahtia tried to control herself but even she indulged a little bit. Madeline was having so much fun with the ladies. Since she and Diem were regulars, they were receiving the VIP treatment. All the dancers knew how and what to do to earn their money. Madeline was bent over one of the strippers getting her eagle on, her knees were flexing, and her booty was popping. Madeline could easily keep up with any twenty-year-old. Diem was riding one of the bigger strippers like her personal racehorse throughout the club. Diem was swinging her whip like she was Zorro. Everyone knew to move out of her way, and if they did not, they figured it out when she let the whip crack them.

Mr. Both Hands, Madeline, and Diem's favorite dancer was about to take the stage. He was paid in advance for Madeline and Diem's personal entertainment. "Oh My! I see why they call him Mr. Both Hands. I have never seen anything like that EVER." Yahtia said to Karma and Joy. Referring to his dick size. "Now that is a dick. It's like he got dick and back up dick." Karma said while thinking to herself if his dick would fit in her mouth. "I love the dick I got but I gotta touch and feel this ding-dong. Just gotta see if it is real." Joy said full of excitement. Joy then took off to the stage, followed by Karma and Yahtia. The ladies danced and twerked the night away. The islanders loved them. They ended up putting on a show for the strippers instead of the other way around. Diem caught all of it on camera. Around five in the morning the dancers finally tapped out. The owner Big Dudee turned the lights on. "Alright ladies, my people are tired so you gotta go." He said light heartedly, hugging Diem and Madeline. Big Dudee knew his dancers were compensated for their work. "Fine then. But we'll be back." Diem shouted, causing everyone to laugh.

The women came stumbling into the house around 6am sloppy drunk and full of marijuana, talking about monster dicks and sexy strippers. This did not go over well with the men. Madeline quicky went in defense mode for the ladies and got the men in line. "Stop bitching and complaining. They just had an enjoyable time. Y'all acting like they were tricking and dicking last night. If anything, say thank you because I know they got some new tricks up their sleeves." Madeline sassed Kross when he came to her with an attitude. "It's not that Gammy." Kross lied. "We are going to miss our flight because of this." Kross was pouting. "Boy hush. The pilot is on my payroll so y'all leave when y'all leave. You forgot we rich bitch." Madeline said laughing while smoking on a pre-roll. Ozias burst into laughter, until Kross gave him a mean mug. Despite being told to leave them alone, the men all tried to retrieve their women. They all got the same response. Nothing. "OH MY GOSH" y'all so damn worrisome. Leave them alone. If you wanna be mad, be mad with me. I am the reason they are in this situation." Madeline said. "Yeah, me too just chill." Diem cosigned with her sister. They gave the boys a serious' glare that punked them down. The boys decided they did not want any issues with Grandma Madeline or Diem. So, they shut the fuck up and sat their asses down.

A few hours later the girls woke up. Madeline had three cups of her hangover remedy waiting for them. "You all will be traveling comfortably in an island dress. The guys have been pissy all morning, so I had your things packed and sent to the plane." Madeline said to the recovering females. "Thank you, Grandma. They are still going to be mad though." Joy rolled her eyes. "Maybe. But I am sure you learned something that will put a smile on his face." Madeline gave Joy a knowing look and a wink. Diem handed them a flash drive. "This is the only copy of last night's adventure. I suggest you look at it and destroy it. No face, No case! Comprende." Diem smiled at them. Diem was a mess she reminded you of a Madea times ten. When the girls were finally dressed and ready to leave. Madeline and Diem escorted them to the men. They were impatiently waiting in the limo. "I had Pedro pack some of that blossom fuzz you guys like so much." Madeline addressed Kross, who was giving Yahtia the death stare. Kross hugged his grandma. "You are too much young lady, but I love you dearly." Kross whispered in her ear. "You better love me." Madeline kissed his cheek and then said her goodbyes to everyone else. Diem blew kisses to Ozias and Craig, gripping her breast and licking her nipples. They both stumbled over each other diving in the limo getting away from her. Karma and Joy laughed to their self. They had their men set up. They knew Diem would play the part. As soon as the limo door closed, they were off. "This baecation is officially underway. I hope you ladies still have some fun left in you." Craig said to them as they took off. They were headed to an unknown destination. Only the men knew where they were going, but the women were bound to love it.

CHAPTER 26
KILLING THE EVIL SPIRITS

The ladies slept for hours. The guys used this to their advantage and planned the next adventure. When the girls finally started to wake up, they all noticed the men acting sneaky. Yahtia began to rub Kross' shoulders, giving him a light massage. "Bae what's going on? You suck at the poker face." Yahtia was trying to pick Kross for information. He was not giving her anything though. "Nothing my sweet little buttercup." Kross said kissing Yahtia on the nose. Yahtia scrunched up her face and kissed him back. "Now I know something funky is in the air." Yahtia mumbled while still massaging him. Out of nowhere the pilot announced. "We are preparing to land. We have reached our destination. The Islamic Republic of Pakistan South Asia." The intercom went off with the signature static. All the men grimaced. The pilot had fucked up. He was supposed to announce when they were an hour from the destination so the guys could prepare the girls for what was about to happen. "Y'all niggas plan on selling us!?" Karma said, standing up from her seat. Karma had jumped to the worst possible conclusion and was prepared to fight. "We just have some unfinished business with Hero. This will be a short visit baby. I promise." Ozias grabbed Karma while he explained. Ozias saw how the idea of being violated in anyway affected her. "Baby, calm down you know I will go to war with the world over you." Ozias whispered in Karma's ear, while giving her a soft kiss on the cheek. "I am not comfortable being in this country. These sick fucks can flip at any time." Joy confessed. "Then BAM! We all are turning tricks and bussing it wide open." Joy added dramatically. "Joy don't talk so loud. We may be surrounded by listening devices and being watched". Yahtia said while looking around nervously.

The plane landed and the ladies were dragging their feet. Being in the one place they sent several of their enemies made them uneasy. When they finally made it off the plane Hero was waiting with three dozen of roses. He had one for each of the women. "Welcome to my country!" Hero said enthusiastically to the crew. Hero had really come to look at them as more than business partners. Hero now considered them family. "Ladies you break my heart. You are not happy to see me? No?" Hero's accent was thick. He held his hand over his heart, being dramatic. They could not shake the eerie feeling that came with being in Hero's homeland. "Don't worry about them Hero. They are just unpleasantly surprised." Craig said shaking Hero's hand. "Heavy on the unpleasant." Karma mumbled as she and the girls gathered watching the men. Hero bear hugged all the guys like they were long lost brothers. "I'm happy you all made it safely. You ready for the fun to begin." Hero wagged his eyebrows at Kross. Kross nodded, "Definitely Just tell me where to go. I got a vacation to get back to." Kross said eagerly. Hero broke down the specifics. He explained to the men. "This is going to go quickly and smoothly. Just follow me." Hero said as he led the way.

They were transported to a humongous fighting arena. Hero appointed two of his men to chaperone the ladies. "I need you two to stay with the ladies. DO NOT LET THEM OUT OF YOUR SIGHT!" Hero instructed two of his men. "Ladies these are two of my best men. They will make sure you have a good time." Hero smiled and motioned for the men to follow him. "Ummm? Where the hell you three going?" Karma asked, with much attitude. Karma was gearing up for a fight and Ozias saw it coming a mile away. "This will only take a few minutes. You will be with security the entire time. Trust me on this one." Ozias said begging Karma to chill out. Karma cut her eyes at him. Karma trusted him but not the situation. Kross kissed Yahtia sweetly and the men walked away without another word. "Ok we are going down fighting in this mutha fucka if anyone of these sheets wearing seasoned freaks come our way." Joy said pulling out a long metal strip. Joy had broken it off the plane and envisioned using it as a weapon if it came down to it. Karma and Yahtia busted out laughing. Joy joined them. "I am so serious." Joy swung the metal around in the air showing them how she was going to use it to hurt someone. At that moment they began to relax.

The guards led the ladies on a little tour of the facility. They were brought to a room that held several women. Some of them were working, and others were waiting to work. On the other side of the room, they spotted Molly. Molly was dressed in a maid's uniform serving drinks. When Molly returned to the bar she kneeled and began sucking a midget's dick. "Damn that bitch nasty." Joy said disgusted. Molly was certified and multitasked very well. Molly was sucking a dick and jacking one the same time. Karma stood there looking at her worthless ass mother, not feeling an ounce of regret. "Would one of you lovely men like to take a break an indulge in some of this sexual entertainment from the head doctor?" Karma said to the guards pointing at Molly. The guards looked confused. Yahtia did the dick sucking hand and mouth gesture to the men. Their faces lit up like a Christmas tree. "SUCKIE! SUCKIE!" the guards responded. "Not me" Yahtia said loudly, pointing at Molly. "Her." Karma walked over and stood over Molly. "These two gentlemen have a tab with the owner. So, make sure to give them whatever they want." Karma ordered. Molly looked up at Karma and she started to cry. Before she could shed any real tears. Molly had two more dicks stuffed in her mouth. "SUCKIE SUCKIE BITCH." Karma did an evil laugh as she walked off.

The girls walked out of the room the way they had come in. "We just let our bodyguards get their dicks sucked, now who the fuck is going to guard us?" Joy asked in a frantic. "Joy is right Karma. What if we get mistaken for one of the sex slaves?" Yahtia said, about to cry. "Calm down. I am uneasy too, but all the sex slaves have a serial number or bar code stamped across their shoulder. I remember hearing Hero mention that to Ozias." Karma explained. That seemed to put them all at ease just a bit and they continued the tour by themselves. They entered the next room and let their eyes take in the scene. People were engaged in some sort of sexual act everywhere. "If it wasn't incriminating, Hero could make so much money on porn hub with these freaks." Joy said watching a woman pussy pop on a handstand. Craig and Ozias came running up to them. "Why they hell are y'all not with the guards?" Ozias asked eyeballing Karma. Ozias knew she had something to do with it. All three of the ladies wore a dumb look, and none of them said a word. "Whatever y'all did keep it to yourselves. We got to get to our seats before the main event." Craig said grabbing Joy and Yahtia by the hand. Craig was damn near dragging them. Ozias grabbed Karma and did the same thing. "What the fuck bro? We refuse to watch these mutha fuckas fight one another, we're not at the Caesars Palace damn. And where the hell is Kross? I am trying to be a team player. I swear I am, but this place is not my cup of tea." Yahtia was totally frustrated she was giving her brother the business. "Yeah Craig. Whose damn idea was it to bring us here. This is downright ridiculous." Joy added. "Just relax man damn. It will all unfold in a few minutes and you ladies will be kissing us men and popping that pussy like y'all did at the strip palace." Craig said with a smirk on his face. The ladies rolled their eyes but followed Craig and Ozias to their seats.

As soon as they were seated a bell rang, and the announcer started to speak. "The Champion is back from vacation, and he is ready. Killer Karmelo will be facing an unknown contender." The announcer introduced Karmelo as the champion. They listened as the announcer announced. Karmelo had a record of 64-2. The crowd went wild at the mention of Karmelo's name. Apparently, Karmelo had survived the ultimate punishment and he was a crowd favorite. "What the fuck is this sick shit?" Karma stood up angrily. Ozias grabbed her to calm her down. "Baby just watch and listen please. I swear you are going to enjoy this shit." Ozias begged his woman. He did not anticipate it being this hard to keep the women calm. Karmelo stepped into the ring doing a little dance for the crowd. "His opponent the Trinidallion showstopper." The announcer introduced the unknown fighter. On que, the crew investigated the ring and there stood Kross, putting on his best Rocky Balboa stance. Kross was dressed in a black robe with Yahtia's picture on the back. His trunks were silk with Yahtia's face all over them. Kross was really representing for his lady. Ozias and Craig had a satisfied smirk on their faces. All three women were silent with shock. Everyone of their mouths were wide open. "Booooooooooo", the crowd started to boo Kross. "Oh, hell nah. Fuck y'all ugly dirt looking robe wearing mutha fuckas. Kick his ass bae." Yahtia jumped up yelling. "Bitch, sit yo ass down. We are in these people country and you wanna curse them out." Joy said pulling Yahtia back into her seat while giving her an icy glare. Yahtia gave Joy the finger. Before they could have their own showdown in their seats. The bell rang signaling the start of the fight.

Karmelo knew who Kross was and what he was there for the moment he laid eyes on him. It didn't matter to him though. Karmelo refused to go down without a fight. Karmelo had a strategy that had been working for him so far. Karmelo felt that if he came out gunz blazing and full speed in the beginning he would overwhelm the opponent making him the victor. Karmelo came out trying just that, swinging hard and fast. Wrong strategy this time. Kross dodged Karmelo's first few combos dancing around the ring. Karmelo swung with his right hand intending to knock Kross out. Kross side stepped the punch and landed a nasty upper cut to Karmelo's chin. Splitting it on contact. Making blood splatter everywhere. Kross didn't stop there. Kross followed up with a mighty left hook to the temple. Karmelo went down fast as lightening. The referee counted him out twice. Karmelo lay their motionless. The crowd was silent as the medics came to check Karmelo for any signs of life. Karmelo was dead before he hit the ground. "He is gone." The medic said as they lifted Karmelo's body from the ring. Karmelo Joel Boston was officially dead.

The crowd Was buzzing with mixed emotions. Karmelo had built a following and everyone wanted to know who the Trinidallion was. "Come on y'all. Let's get going." Ozias grabbed Karma's hand and lead them down a hallway. Craig and the other girls followed closely, so they wouldn't be separated. Yahtia broke out into a full sprint and jumped into Kross' arms. She wrapped her legs around his body and attacked his face with kisses. "Oh my God baby you really did that shit. You are so damn sexy." Yahtia said between kisses. The crew gathered around them and began congratulating Kross. "Move bitch damn. Let me hug my bro." Joy said while pushing Yahtia forcefully. Kross gave Joy a brotherly hug and went back to holding his woman. "Baby you never have to worry about that sick fuck ever again." Kross kissed and hugged Yahtia, then whispered into her ear. "You can sleep easy now baby. That scum bag is DOA. I will always protect you. I was made to love you. Forever." His deliverance of love and devotion made her weak in the knees. Yahtia was already head over heels in love with Kross, but this sealed the deal. Everyone was around them talking and celebrating the death of Karmelo. Kross and Yahtia were in their own world. "My friend that kiss looks scrumptious." Hero said, interrupting a sloppy sexy kiss being shared between the two lovers. Kross gave Hero a look. "I know I am a guest in your country, but I will go to war about this one here. I got a few rounds left in me." Kross said jokingly. Hero nodded in understanding. "NO! NO! My friend I don't want no parts of the Trinidallion Showstopper." Hero held his hands up in mock surrender.

Everyone shared a laugh as Hero dapped all the men up respectively. "These are yours." Hero handed each man a duffle bag, stuffed full of money. Kross gave Hero a puzzled look. "I'll take it fam, but that was free of charge. We all needed closure on that nigga." Kross stated. "I figured you would say something like that. This isn't payment for the fight. I took the liberty of placing a few bets on your behalf." Hero waved his hand indicating that he placed bets for everyone. "I made sure that everyone would be compensated for their time. You know for closure." Hero said using air quotes. "There is nothing wrong with beefing up our wallets my friends." Hero passed the last bag to Yahtia. "Damn Hero you fixed the fight?" Craig laughed. "I would never do something like that." Hero said with a straight face, causing everyone to laugh. "I simply took advantage of knowing the future. Why not make money off something you already had in the making?" Hero explained. "You damn sure ain't wrong." Kross grinned zipping up his duffle bag. They were all walking away with half a million dollars' worth of closure.

The crew loaded themselves and their new luggage into the jeep assigned to them. "My friends I know you are anxious to get back to your vacations. Before you go you can come watch while we burn the body, if you would like?" Hero asked the crew, but he made eye contact with

Kross and Yahtia. Yahtia shook her head no and Hero did not push the issue. "See you later my friends. And safe travels" Hero left to go burn the body. Hero left two guards that were there to escort the crew to their plane safely. "Hold up! Karma don't your dad have an insurance policy?" Joy asked. "Yeah. I am certain of it. Why wassup?" Karma questioned Joy. "Well get Molly to sign a piece of paper so we can have her signature. Then we can have Karmelo's body flown back to the states and dumped somewhere in South Carolina." Joy explained her plan to everyone. "Once the police receive an anonymous call about a dead body, you will get a call about your dead father. You show up, identify the body, and collect your grieving insurance pay. Feel me." Joy rubbed her hands together like birdman. "Your mind definitely works differently." Yahtia teased Joy. "First we gotta stop Hero from burning the body. Secondly, we have got to get Molly's signature before we leave. You will have to oversee all the funeral arrangements. Molly will be at home sick, with Covid." Joy said sounding devious. The crew looked at Joy in amazement. Joy was right of course but no one else had thought that far ahead. "Craig you better watch your back. Joy the type that can make a body disappear." Kross said with a serious look. Everyone laughed till it hurt. Kross' straight face made it that much funnier.

The crew had the bodyguards call Hero to come back to them. When he arrived, they gave him a quick run down of what they needed to take place. "No problem my friends. We do things your way." Hero stated and escorted them straight to Molly. During their walk the ladies spotted another familiar face. It was Hershey. She was being strapped in a swing by two sumo wrestlers. These two men were living out a fantasy. One was sucking her titties and the other one was fingering her pussy. Hershey was on the swing like a chocolate acrobat and these men were acting a damn fool over her. This was not her first rodeo. Hershey was enjoying the role she played. It was all fun and games for Hershey until one of the men pulled out a whip and grazed her with it like she was a slave. Hershey screamed and struggled against the restraints of the swing to get free. The wrestlers did not stop. They kept beating her with the whip until they had heard enough of her screams. Hershey's relief from being released from the swing was short lived. They roughly grabbed her and began to fuck her relentlessly. One in the front and the other in the back. The ladies almost felt sorry for her when the two wrestlers sandwiched Hershey in a sumo hug while forcefully fucking her.

Molly had finished her last client and was sitting in the corner on the floor. Molly smelt Karma walk up to her. She didn't have to look at her daughter to know she was present. "He is dead ain't he?" Molly asked knowingly. "Yep, he's in hell right now waiting on you." Karma snapped, pulling out a pen and paper. "Sign this paper so I can collect on his insurance policy." Karma rushed Molly. Molly did not put up a fight. Molly signed the paper with no resistance. "Just kill me too. That will be more money for you. You will never have to worry about me ever again. Just kill me please, I can't keep doing this. Please do me that favor, I am begging you." Molly's voice got louder and louder in between her begging pleas. Molly sounded very pitiful and was trying to be convincing. "Nah. Hell nah bitch. This is your home now. You should have made better choices as a mother." Karma snatched up the pen and paper and walked away. Karma refused to get caught up in Molly's pity party.

On the way-out Joy thought of something else. "Where is the no fingers girl?" Joy asked Hero. Hero explained that Rochelle had been bought by a lesbian couple. "To the best of my knowledge she is busy eating pussy all day every day." Hero laughed at the irony of the situation.

CHAPTER 27
COUPLES RETREAT

The crew shared a good laugh about Rochelle and her outcome. "Serves the bitch right" Karma laughed hard. Hero handed the girls a bottle of wine. "It has been aged for the better part of 100 years" he winked at them. "We love a good bottle of wine, actually I have been experimenting on making my own brand, but we love money too." Karma said to Hero. Yahtia and Joy poked their lips out at Hero. "Yeah, why the guys get money, and we get wine?" Yahtia asked. "The money is for all of you, I would not double cross my favorite American ladies." "This trip keeps getting better and better" Yahtia said walking up the steps to the plane. Yes, ma'am it is" Karma and Joy both co-signed. "Where to next?" The pilot asked. Kross handed Yahtia a glass bowl full of destination possibilities. "Pick one love." Kross kissed her cheek. "I will go anywhere in the world as long as I am with you." Yahtia said sweetly into his ear. Their moment was interrupted by Karma, who made childish throw-up noises. "Keep that up and Madeline's fish definitely going to be schooling." Craig mumbled earning him a look from Joy. "Santorini Greece, what you ladies think?" Yahtia asked. "Sounds like a plan." Said Karma, followed by a thumbs up from Joy. Yahtia handed the pilot the destination and everyone prepared for takeoff. "Well, at least we're not too far from our next stop." Joy said while everyone got comfortable for the flight to Greece.

Everyone was cuddled up and minding their own business as they anticipated their next adventure. While cuddled up next the Craig, Joy decided to question him about the fish and pond situation. Joy had overheard the guys talk about it more than once and the nosey part of her needed to know what was up. Unable to resist his woman. Craig told Joy Madeline's story about the pond of schooling fish. Joy acted like it was just regular information and kissed Craig to change the subject.

The men were extremely tired and were excited to see a limo waiting to take everyone to their hotel. All the guys fell asleep instantly. They needed to sleep off their jet lag. "Well, I am not sleepy so what we finna do?" Yahtia asked her sisters. The ladies decided they wouldn't have too much fun without the men. "Let's see what this jacuzzi action is like." Karma said as they put on one of the many bathing suits, they had brought with them. The trio got in the hot tub and relaxed instantly. They sipped wine and talked about everything, just like the old days. Joy decided that she needed to share what she had learned from Craig. "So y'all know my nosey ass had to ask Craig about the schooling fish comment, right?" Joy put it out there. "Girl I asked Ozias too and that negro ain't say shit." Karma rolled her eyes. "Well, I see I need to teach you some interrogation skills." Joy said suggestively causing Karma to splash her with water. "But no, seriously he told me all about the pond of schooling fish and what Madeline said." Joy went on to share everything with the girls that she had gotten from Craig. "I know older women are wise and all, but do you believe that it could be true?" Yahtia asked. "Ion know sis. But my grandmother would say things like Its going to rain, because she could feel pian in bones. And it never failed it rained every time." Joy shrugged at Yahtia. "I try to swallow all of Ozias' kids, but I have been playing a dangerous game for a long-time sis." Karma admitted. "First of all, that was an over share. Secondly. Me too. Craig and I never use protection and my period is late. But my cycle real funny acting so I'm not too worried." Joy said. It was awkwardly silent in the hot tub for a few seconds. "What why y'all nasty nut swallowing heffas looking at me?" Yahtia tried to play off the nervous look she had on her face. "Shiiiiittt! The one bitch that has been puking every damn where and eating off all our plates is very quiet right now." Karma and Joy said, grilling Yahtia.

Yahtia splashed both Joy and Karma. "Don't be trying to jinx me and my man because y'all wanna be free with y'all pussy!'" Yahtia laughed. "Right like you and Kross use protection." Joy laughed splashing her back. After the girls calmed down and stopped splashing the water. "Nah but for real. We all gonna take a damn test. We all guilty as sin and dick struck. So, after our excursion tomorrow we are going to ditch the guys and take a test." Yahtia laid out the plan for them. Joy and Karma nodded in agreement. "Good! Then we can see who around here got some titty milk." Yahtia pinched Joy and Karma's nipples and jumped out the hot tub. "You play too damn much. But ain't shit gonna be funny when Mama T find out how reckless we have been." Karma called behind Yahtia. "OOOOOH yeah Mama T already said she will beat our ass if either one of us slip up and do something foolish." Joy said getting out of the hot tub. Karma followed suit and they put on simple maxi dresses. "You right Joy. It doesn't matter who it actually is, we all finna get our ass kicked." Karma said. "It was worth it though." Yahtia said doing a wiggle with her body. "Hell yeah." they all laughed. For the next hour or so the girls ran around like little kids. Just having fun.

The next morning the ladies decided to be sweet and bring the men breakfast in bed. Ozias wanted pussy for breakfast, so he spent his morning trying to get a quickie. Karma wasn't having that and rushed him to get dressed. The crew had a full day ahead of them. Karma had scheduled a boat ride to the middle of the ocean, where there was a huge adult only water park. It was beautiful, and packed with slides, lazy floats, waterfalls, jet skis, and swim up bars. The water was glycerin like diamonds. The crew acted like kids at summer camp. When they were done at the water park, they boarded the boat and docked at a remote part of the ocean where the men were scheduled to have massages. Side eyeing the island girls, "y'all sure this is a clever idea. These hoes all cute and stuff." Yahtia said to her sisters. Yahtia was not really the jealous type but the idea of another beautiful women rubbing on her man wasn't setting well with her. "Girl bye. Them niggas know who they belong to. Craig knows he better not even lift his head up. PERIODT!!" Joy said using her best City Girl voice and adding in the neck slice. "Bitch when you right you right" Yahtia said. They all dapped each other up, letting the men enjoy their massages.

The boat ride back to the resort was silent. The crew was beyond tired and ready for a nap from the day party water adventure. Yahtia had to take slow steady breaths. She was getting sick to her stomach again. Yahtia didn't want to bring attention to herself, so she managed to hold it in. "Can you girls stay out of trouble while we go take power naps." Ozias asked smacking Karma on the butt. After the girls promised to behave the men left to go to their rooms. Before they left, "I am serious. Stay out of trouble and go shopping. On us. We are taking y'all on a date tonight and we need you to look model fine." Kross spoke for the guys. After the date plans were solidified, the men gave more than enough money to the girls for their shopping spree. "This is everything I ever thought it would be and we just getting started." Karma gushed. Once the men were out of ear shot. Yahtia and Joy headed towards the limo that would take them shopping. The men had thought about everything. The limo driver had been pre-paid to take them to the best shopping boutiques around.

While they were out shopping Yahtia managed to eat twice, even though they were scheduled for dinner in a few hours. "Y'all not hungry." Yahtia asked chewing her food loudly. "Damn sis. What the fuck, you must have a tapeworm." Karma said side eyeing Yahtia. "Must be. Whatever it is it has got to go. You know I had to go up a size on my dress. I'm not feeling that shit." Yahtia said, still eating. "Before we go back to the hotel lets stop by the pharmacy and grab three pregnancy tests." Joy said to her sisters. They all agreed and finished shopping. They found the perfect dresses with matching accessories. "Joy I tell you what. If your ass ain't pregnant you bound to get pregnant in that dress." Karma whistled at her sister as she modeled a gold bandage dress. "Hell, yea she is." Yahtia hyped it up. On the way back the girls made a stop. "Fat ass grab the pregnancy tests and come on. Don't you get not one more snack." Karma yelled at Yahtia. When they got back to the resort the guys decided that they too needed proper clothes for date night. "Good idea. Y'all should go do that right now." The ladies rushed them out of the room. They were trying to hide their anxiety, but it didn't work. "I'm not stupid, they are up to something." Kross said. "Hell yea bro. I been noticing a change in Joy and Yahtia too." Craig sounded off. "It must be the new soil and the breathing of another country's air." Ozias said trying to put his brothers' minds at ease.

The ladies gathered around the bag as Karma handed out the pregnancy tests. They were all nervous. After reading the instructions the ladies took turns in the bathroom peeing on the stick. The ladies all placed their test on the countertop not paying attention to the order. After waiting the three minutes they stepped in the bathroom together. "I'm so damn nervous y'all" Yahtia said with a shaky hand. Joy was biting her fingernails and Karma closed her eyes. "Ok y'all ready? Said Joy. Like the big kids they are, the girls held hands. "On the count of three we look. 1- 2- 3!" Karma counted off. Two of the tests had one line, meaning they were negative. The third one had two bright pink lines, indicating it was positive. "OMG whose test is this?" Karma picked up the stick. "Which one of you hoes is pregnant?" Karma scolded her sisters, like she wasn't in the same predicament. "You mean which one of us hoes are pregnant?" Joy corrected her. "Well, who is it? Who tested positive? I don't remember which one is mine" Karma said. Joy and Yahtia just shrugged their shoulders. "I just tossed my test hoping for the best, I have no idea where it landed" Yahtia said. "Yeah, sis I wasn't even paying attention" Joy admitted. They had placed their test on the counter side by side, they were moving with nervous energy no one knew which test was theirs.

Karma took a big breath. "Ok so we are going to have to retest. This time we will do it separately so there is no mix up" Yahtia said nervously. Yahtia was feeling nauseous again but didn't want the vomit in front of everyone. After the girls agreed to the retest. Yahtia put them out. "Ok love y'all but get out I need a nap for tonight" Yahtia rushed them out. As soon as the door closed, Yahtia darted to the toilet and emptied her stomach contents. While she was finishing up her business, Yahtia heard Kross come in the room. "Hey babe. You ok. It sounds like you are vomiting again?" Kross asked concerned. Frantic, Yahtia tossed all three of the tests in the drawer. "Yeah, I'm fine as wine love. Just can't wait for date night" Yahtia lied. She was indeed ready For date night, but everything was not fine. "What the fuck is wrong with me?" Yahtia whispered to her reflection as she turned the shower on. Kross made dinner reservations for everyone at 'The Sky Lounge'. Kross peeped it on Yahtia's vision board, she presented in one of her classes. It was a fancy restaurant built on the roof top of the tallest hotel. It had a glass floor that extended beyond the building itself.

So, it appeared like you were floating on the clouds. Breathtaking was not even a good enough word to describe the view.

The crew was ready, and everyone was on their grown and sexy shit. All the men were extra sexy looking like GQ models and Rico Suave doubles. "Mandatory shots" Kross said, pouring everyone a shot. Kross accidentally wasted Hennessey on his all-white retro J's. "Damn it. Y'all head on out. I gotta fix this." Kross ran to the bathroom to wipe off his shoes. Kross began rambling through the drawers looking for a clean white rag, and he stumbled across the pregnancy tests. Kross was frozen in time. His eyes had focused on the positive test. BOOM! BOOM! BOOM! "Man, what the fuck. You taking a shit or something? The ladies have already headed to the limo!" Ozias said through the door, rushing Kross. "Where is Craig?" Kross asked walking into the room. "He in the hallway waiting on your pretty boy swag ass" Ozias teased. Kross smacked his teeth and held up the pregnancy tests. Ozias opened the door and snatched Craig inside the room. This was an emergency to say the least. "What the fuck y'all niggas in here doing?" Craig pulled away from Ozias, and eyeballed Kross. "I tell you what I will not be getting cursed out by none of the ladies if we are late, I am gonna snitch on y'all two" Craig crossed his arms. Kross held the tests in Craigs face, just like he had done to Ozias. Realizations set in. "Which one of them is it?" Craig asked a dumb question. "They don't have no damn names on them bro" Kross said sarcastically. "Soooo, I guess this means that the fish are swimming, and the chickens are clucking" Ozias laughed. Kross and Craig stared at him, not finding shit funny. Madeline's fish premonition came flooding back into their minds. "Madeline was on point with her predictions". Craig said. They stood there stunned for a few more minutes. "Damn bro! one of us really about to be a daddy" Ozias whispered, daydreaming about Karma carrying his seed. The guys decided to play it cool until the time was right. "Well at least we know why they been acting so damn weird" Craig said trying to make light of the situation. "Right. Now let's go before the girls come back to kill us for being late" Kross said walking out of the door. Each of the men hoped that the girls would come clean and put an end to their suspicions.

They arrived at the restaurant in style. They were taken to their table and a waitress helped them strap in. Everyone was excited and nervous, about several things. The table was lifted, and they were in awe as they began the thirty-story ride to 'The Sky Lounge'. "Baby are you feeling ok" Kross asked Yahtia, when he noticed she looked a little pale. Yahtia nodded her head, but everyone could tell she was lying. Yahtia had a queasy feeling in her stomach. She opened her mouth to tell her friends she didn't feel good but instead she threw up everywhere and all over everyone. Her dress was ruined, as well as Kross' suit. The smell was starting to make the others gag as well. Kross hit the emergency button so the staff could lower the table. The staff helped get everyone unbuckled and safely off the platform, before they cleaned up the mess. "Ok we are going to the hospital right now. You're showing signs of covid" Kross demanded. "No. I just need to lay down. I'll be fine I promise." Yahtia defended weakly. "Hell no. I ain't going for it. What the hell are y'all three hiding. I found these in the bathroom drawer" Kross pulled out the three pregnancy tests from his pocket. The ladies looked like they just got caught with their hands in the cookie jar. "Well, somebody answer the man. This is important news and one of you need to fess up", Ozias said giving Karma a side eye.

Rolling her eyes, "Don't look at me. I didn't do nothing at least not by myself I didn't. And anyway, we can't tell y'all nothing because the tests got mixed up, so we don't know who the positive test belongs too" Karma explained. Karma hated feeling like a kid being chastised. "We about to fix this shit right now" Kross said grabbing Yahtia's hand and headed back to the limo. Everyone piled in silently and waited for what happened next. Kross rubbed Yahtia's back all the way to their next stop. The pharmacy. "This time we won't get them mixed up", Kross said with finality. They all headed back to the resort. Kross passed each test to his brothers and told them to watch closely. The ladies were in their room with their men taking test number two.

The next three minutes felt like three days. They felt like kids waiting on Christmas. Craig and Joy were negative. They sent a text to the group telling them the news. Karma and Ozias did the same, "Ain't us. We negative." When Yahtia and Kross didn't respond or reply with their results everyone knew. Yahtia was officially preggo. Kross stared at the positive test. "So, it was you. You are the pregnant one?" Kross asked, more as an affirmation than a question. "Yeah, I guess so" Yahtia started to let the tears fall. Kross and Yahtia decided to just stay in their room and share the moment together. Karma and Joy were ready to be with their sister, but they understood that the couple needed this time alone. Craig and Joy joined Karma and Ozias for dinner inside the restaurant at the hotel. This was a bittersweet moment for the crew. It was no doubt that this was going to change a lot of things, but no one knew how, and that was the scary part.

After dinner everyone went their separate ways and waited. The next morning Joy and Karma were up bright and early, waiting outside of Yahtia's room. They were waiting for her or Kross to come out so they could go in. Apparently Kross had turned Yahtia's phone off because it was going straight to voicemail. When Craig and Ozias woke up to an empty bed, they went looking for the women. The two opened their room door, only to see Karma and Joy snuggled up against Kross and Yahtia's room door. Craig took and picture and sent it to Kross. "Bro they not going nowhere, so let them see Tia. Karma about to spaz and Joy not giving up no pussy until she talks to my sister so open up" Craig texted Kross. Thirty minutes later Kross opened the door, startling Joy and Karma. "Where is Tia? Is she ok?" Karma asked about to cry. "She good fam. She's in the shower right now. I googled an OB doctor for her. We gotta get her some vitamins and something for her nausea. Y'all are more than welcome to come with us." Kross explained. He knew the girls were worried, so he decided to share this with them. Karma and Joy raced to their rooms so they could get dressed.

It was a family affair because everyone in the crew went. In the limo the girls had a million and one questions for Yahtia. They engaged in their sister girl talk like the guys were not even there. The guys didn't have as much to say but they were taking it all in. "Craig, I hope you're not salty with me bro" Kross stated genuinely concerned about his relationship with Craig, who he considered a brother. "Never" Craig waved him off. "I knew you were a good man from the gate. You will go to war for my sister, and she loves you, that is all that matters" Craig replied. "I was sweating bullets waiting on them results, I am so relieved that it is not Joy" Craig added.

"Nigga what. I pissed eight times waiting on them three minutes to be up" Ozias chimed in. "Y'all niggas about to have a niece or a nephew", Kross smiled for the first time. "One thing for certain, two things for sure, we better make the best of this trip because when we return to the states, we all about to catch it from Toyah Beeks AKA Mama T". Craig sounded off. Kross heart dropped a little at the thought of having to tell Mama T. Craig had a memory of what his dad Juan told him about what he would do to the man that makes his daughter pregnant.

After the OB visit, the crew decided to stay in Greece for the rest of the vacation. A lot of plans had to be cancelled for Yahtia, but nobody cared. They were all putting her health and the health of the baby first. Besides Kross was not having none of that extra shit anyway. It was like instant lock down. Kross would not let Yahtia do anything that he felt wasn't good for the baby. When they went to the amusement park Yahtia could only walk around and eat, while watching Joy and Karma have the time of their lives. "Look baby a Faris wheel" Yahtia wagged her eyebrows at Kross, remembering their first time. "One day I will have to buy out another park and see if you still got it" he flirted back. Kross kept Yahtia company that day and every other while they were in Greece. Even though it wasn't what she had planned for the vacation, Yahtia wouldn't trade any of these memories for the world. They ended their vacation in Greece with a horse and carriage ride through the town. There were three carriages, one for each couple. The ladies felt like true queens as they were paraded around. Cutting the trip short, the next morning everyone had breakfast together and headed back to the states. They were too anxious to have any real fun. Everyone wanted to make sure Yahtia, and the baby were perfect, so they were getting Yahtia a full physical and ultrasound as soon as possible.

CHAPTER 28
THE MAN WITH THE PLAN

Craig slid the pilot instructions for when they arrived in the states. The crew landed at Boggs airport and immediately loaded into the waiting limo. They were in Denver Colorado, where Craig was about to lay down his future with Joy. "We don't need our luggage. This is just a short stay. And Surprise" Craig explained glancing around at everyone. "More surprises, you guys are just lovely" Joy said with a bright smile. "Oh no sir. Don't look over here. We are all surprised out. This surprise is all for you" Kross said rubbing Yahtia's flat belly. Everyone shared a laugh. "So, if this is for Joy then that means I am next on the surprise list" Karma said giving Ozias a hard look. Their conversation was cut short when the limo came to a stop in front of a large two-story house with a two-car garage. Everything was nice, including the neighborhood. Everyone was stunned, just walking around and admiring everything. When they got to the front porch, Craig reached under the mat for the keys and opened their door. "Ok, now this is strange. Why the hell are we in an Airbnb? Joy asked. Craig laughed, kissing Joy on the cheek. "It's not an Airbnb babe it's our home" Craig grabbed Joy's hand and led her inside.

Joy's jaw dropped as she processed what was happening. "I refuse to let you come all the way to Colorado without me. So, I bought us this home so we can start our life together, while you start your career." Craig explained. Joy started to bounce up and down like a kid. "Are you serious bae? I love it! I love you!" Joy responded kissing Craig quickly and sloppily, before she took off running through the house. The house was fully furnished and decorated, thanks to the interior designers Craig hired. The girls followed behind her, equally as giddy, admiring everything. When Joy made it to the living room she laid down in the floor and began making a snow angel in the plush carpet. "Damn bro, you did your grown man shit with this one." Yahtia said giving her brother a hug. "Yeah, nigga why we didn't know about this?" Karma asked with attitude, reaching for a congratulatory hug. "Because then it wouldn't have been a surprise." Ozias answered. "Hell yeah. Y'all can't hold water if you were paid to do it." Kross chimed in. Joy inspected the house for another ten minutes or so before she came downstairs running. "OMG baby that tub is everything I can't wait to use it" Joy was rambling about the master bathroom until she noticed Craig on one knee at the bottom of the stairs with a black velvet box in his hand. Before Joy could say a word Craig spoke up. "It's a must that you be mine, I know we haven't been together long, and we don't have to get married next week. I just want you to commit to me and be my wife when we both see fit. Joy White will you MARRY ME?!" Craig finished his speech. "Hell, yeah she will." Karma spoke up for Joy. Ozias gave her an elbow to shut her up. Fighting tears, "Yes Craig, I will marry you!" Joy exclaimed, helping him from the floor and into a kiss. They forgot there was people in the room as they shared a passionate steamy kiss to seal the deal. Their kisses lead to touches, and it was about to get hot and heavy until the crew began to make some noises. "UUUM we are in the room bro." Yahtia said loudly.

Craig and Joy separated reluctantly, "I have one more surprise and then we can head back to South Carolina" Craig addressed the crew as he led them back to the limo. Craig showed the crew his weed dispensary that his designers went over the top creating the perfect image. Craig made sure to create a convenient atmosphere and offer the perfect amenities. "While you busy at work fighting crime ill be here working getting the crime started." Craig said jokingly. "Bro I am so proud of you. You have really set the bar high for the rest of us. Let me find out you are truly the big brother out of the bunch". Ozias gave his I am proud of you speech to Craig. Ozias needed his brother to know he meant everything he was saying. "Yeah

Craig. I am thoroughly impressed. I have to step my game up" Kross chimed in. "Kross, I owe you the most my nigga. You gave my homie O and I a chance to join forces with you and get some real money. That's love bro." Craig expressed his gratitude and hugged Kross. Craig was teary eyed, but they were tears of joy. Craig was honestly the happiest he has ever been in life. "Alright. Enough of that sensitive stuff" Craig joked wiping his face. "Let's go home" he said, once again leading everyone to the limo. The crew was all together, and so happy. They loaded up for the ride back to South Carolina, but not before Yahtia's reup on more snacks.

Ezra and Memphis proved themselves to be young bosses. They not only kept the business running smoothly, but they exceeded the profit goals set for them. The two young men proved their hustle skills. It was known they were street hustlers, but the last few weeks proved that they were go getters as well. Their work did not go unnoticed. Kross had peeped game long before now. Kross felt as though Ezra and Memphis had the same thing in them that Craig and Ozias have. Kross knew he was going to make them permanent members of the team.

While the crew was away, Candice made herself a Facebook page. Her profile picture was a stuffed cat with her initials, CW. Ezra knew it was her as soon as she sent him a friend request, because she loves cats. Ezra was nervous and excited to hear from her. The two talked, texted, and facetimed each other every chance they could. They had a real teenage love affair going on, and it was noticeable to anyone who looked. Ezra felt bad for sneaking around with Candice, but he was willing to accept the consequences. Ezra would deal with anything and go up against anybody for his Candi girl.

Troy was living in hell. He was beaten and bullied daily. The guards turned a blind eye to what was going on between Troy and D-Ray's crew. Troy managed to get a hold of his public defender and requested a meeting. "You gotta do something about this shit. I can't keep being violated like this" Troy cried to his attorney. Troy sat in that visitation box and told his lawyer everything he was going through and how the officers did nothing to help him. When Troy left that meeting, he knew he was going home.

The public defender filed a complaint with the court, against the county jail and all the correctional officers for gross negligence. To avoid any unnecessary trouble the director granted Troy an early release, with time served. Troy was excited and when he was called for ATW to be released, he provoked all the guys, especially D-Ray. "Fuck all y'all crab ass niggas!" Troy grabbed his dick and shook it as he screamed out the insults. Once the gate was closed behind him Troy really got bold and started calling everyone names and flipping them off. It was his time to shine. Troy would not have to wake up doing laundry or sucking dick anymore. "Fucking Punk ass faggots" Troy spat over his shoulder. D-Ray remained calm, somehow, he knew Troy would be back.

Back on campus Adreama was having issues with two seniors, Yuri and Anastasia. They were furious because Joy was not around to do their work, and they were taking it out on Adreama. They needed Joy to do their thesis paper and she was no where to be found. "Y'all need to really chill the fuck out. Joy ain't even on that shit no more. Where the fuck y'all been at. Joy a whole new bitch and she got much back up. Y'all might want to just leave before shit get bad" Adreama clapped. Adreama was really trying to save these two former friends of hers. "Bitch what you mean? That hoe been doing our work forever, what's changed? You have always provided us with work by Joy." Yuri questioned with attitude. "Yeah, I bet you got your paper done." Anastasia backed her friend up. "As a matter of fact, I do, and I completed it myself. Because like I said before Joy ain't on that shit no more so y'all gonna have to figure out another way to graduate." Adreama said, defending Joy and letting these two know they really needed to kick rocks. It was obvious that without Joy, or someone else help they would not be graduating. That fact alone caused them to jump Adreama. Adreama held her own against the two girls, but they got the best of her. Yuri and Anastasia didn't play fair. They fucked up Adreama's face badly. Adreama was fighting back but the two against one had a big advantage. "Hand me the scissors!" Yuri instructed Anastasia as she held Adreama down. Yuri then cut Adreama's pony tail off. Tell joy she's next if she doesn't get in touch with us. Purple Pinky helped Adreama clean herself up. "Them tricks barking up the wrong tree Adreama vented to Purple Pinky.

CHAPTER 29
REVEALING MORE TRUTH

The crew returned to South Carolina safely, but they were worn out. They had a bad case of jet lag. "No rest for the weary", Kross said kissing Yahtia on the cheek. "You have a doctor appointment in 45 minutes" he announced and placed her bags in her room. Kross managed to secure Yahtia an appointment with the best OB/GYN doctor in the city. Rolling her eyes, Yahtia groaned audibly. "You about be aggy this whole pregnancy huh?" Yahtia asked him, grabbing her purse. Kross just smiled then said, "just like you are going to stay nagging". "No nigga I'm going to stay gagging, something I should have been doing then I wouldn't be pregnant". "Ok show me them gag reflexes tonight then". Kross said with a hard dick. The expecting couple enjoyed a laugh then were off to see about their little nugget. Everyone was extremely tired and wanted to rest badly, but there was much work to be done. Joy and Karma took a quick shower and then jumped into the emails they had received over the past two weeks. Final exam week was approaching and all three of the girls had several assignments due. Joy also agreed to help Yahtia and Karma graduate early.

While the two girls were working diligently, Craig and Ozias were moving in slow motion getting all the luggage to the dorm room. They were barely making it. "Come on use your muscles! HERCULES HERCULES!" Joy clapped doing her best impression of the grandma from

The Klumps. "Girl please. You have overdosed me on that good pussy for two weeks. I have nothing left. Especially no big dick energy." Craig said totally drained. "Looks like you will be using that rose for a while" he teased. Joy did a little air hump dance, "Don't sleep on the rose playboy. It definitely gets the job done" Joy responded. After taking note of Craig's tired face Joy decided she would help with the bags. The four of them ended up sitting in the living room being lazy. Jet lag was getting the best of them. "Y'all hungry?" Karma asked rubbing her growling stomach. Karma had gotten so used to room service and fine dining she didn't want to cook. "Let me see what we have to eat in here" Karma opened the refrigerator. "Girl ain't shit in there. I already checked. I just ordered Instacart so you will have some essentials shortly" Ozias kissed the top of Karma's head and then went to lay down.

Adreama had noticed that the girls had returned but she was trying to let them get settled. Adreama just watched and waited for the right time to let them know what Yuri and Anastasia were up to. Karma decided to clean out the fridge since food was being delivered. They had left a pack of shrimp in the refrigerator, and it was beyond spoiled, so Karma disposed of it outside. "Hey Karma, hope you enjoyed your trip" Adreama greeted Karma, genuinely happy to see her. "Hell yeah. Girl we had some awesome adventures and made plenty memories. Come up to the room and we can fill you in on all the excitement" Karma invited Adreama. Adreama gladly accepted the invitation. "Ok bet I will be right up" Adreama made it up seconds after Karma walks through the door. "What's been going on at Grady Dreama? You been holding the fort down, right?" Joy greeted Adreama as soon as she walked into the room. "Hell yeah. You know me" Adreama quipped. "Wait! What the fuck happened to your face." Joy asked loudly. "That is what I wanted to tell y'all." Adreama gave them the factual's of what happened. "Yuri and Anastasia came by looking for you to do their thesis paper." Adreama removed her hat, showing them what was left of her hair. "I want pay back on them hoes, now I must get my hair cut in a style and may have permanent scaring. Adreama said fuming.

Joy understood the assignment, as usual. Joy gathered all the information on the two ladies within the hour. Yuri and Anastasia had made a name for themselves as Suga Mamas. They often paid for a lay. The two was not easy on the eye, they paid niggas like they paid for food. Some niggas took it all the way and fucked them, but most niggas just led the women on for money. Joy found out that Yuri and Anastasia both have been arrested for prostitution in the past and she used that to formulate a plan. Using her newfound FBI buddies, placing them on a mission. Joy got two of the youngest, finest FBI agents in her online group. Joy had them set up a sting operation. "When those humpback sluts lay eyes on these muscle bond hunks, they will be sure to empty their bank account." Joy was thinking out loud as she set up the play. "Since this is not their first time, they will get prostitution and solicitation third offense, two years in jail and a six thousand dollar fine. Second degree lynching will be added on after they finish their sentence, sending them right back to prison for more time. That'll give these bitches time to think" Joy laughed, finalizing the plans. "Take this pic sis" Joy had Karma take a picture of her and Adreama. They were holding up a perfectly typed thesis paper. "What is this for?" Adreama questioned. "Them bitches going to do them two years looking at this picture on the wall." Joy said smoothly. "Y'all some bad bitches, I tried to warn them hoes." Adreama said smiling with a bruised face and missing hair.

Joy looked around and realized she needed to tie up some loose ends. "Aye sis. While the guys are asleep, I got one more person I need to knock off my list. Then I will be done and dedicated to my job. I got to bury my past so I can focus on my future, ya feel me." Joy said with finality. "What is the code for this one?" Karma asked, lighting an L and passing it to her sister. "This mission is a code purple. Hoodies and gloves are all we need for this one" Joy responded, passing the blunt back to Karma. "So, who is the mark?" Karma asked keeping the weed in rotation. "Mumba Shavez" Joy answered but didn't offer any information right away. Karma and Joy loaded up into the uber and that is when Joy began to fill Karma in on Mumba Shavez, and why she had to get got. Mumba was an African swim coach who would torture Joy because she was an excellent swimmer and excelled above her expectations. Joy was a natural in the water. Mumba also would teach her own kids while teaching Joy. When Joy was out swimming her kids, Mumba would hold Joy's head down under water causing her to nearly drown several times. Joy became accustomed to the cruelty, and she learned to hold her breath under water and when Mumba held Joys head down it didn't phase her much. During swimming competitions Mumba would tell Joy she had to lose to her kids and Joy would win each time because Joy wanted to make her big sister Yolanda proud. After practice Joy had walked into the boys' side of the locker room looking for fresh towels, Joy walked in on Mumba sucking one of the boys penis. Mumba could not recover from that and was embarrassed that her secret was out, Mumba had plans to get rid of joy since that day.

One day during practice Joy was all alone with Mumba in the swimming pool working on back strokes. Mumba decided to place arm and leg weights on joy, and they were on extra tight making it impossible for Joy to get them off. Mumba then pushed Joy in twelve feet and walked out of the swim building. Joy went straight to the bottom. Joy had placed a blade in her swim top earlier that morning because she was planning to cut Mumba if she placed her head under water. Joy somehow maneuvered the blade with her mouth and freed her hands making it to the top in just enough time.

Joy started training at another YMCA on the opposite side of town. Joy became a coach herself teaching small kids to swim. Joy would train herself and she continued to outshine Mumba and her kids. Mumba still tried to defeat Joy. Mumba sabotage the water twice at the pool Joy was working and training at. The shit never stopped so Joy gave up her one dream and relaxing therapy because Mumba would not let her be great.

Joy and Karma stood outside of the YMCA where Mumba worked. They were waiting for the parents to pick up their kids. Once the kids were gone Joy and Karma planned to give Mumba a big surprise. When the last kid was picked up Mumba decided to swim a few laps. Karma eased the front door closed and locked it. Karma closed all the blinds and Joy striped down to her panties and bra. Joy entered the pool undetected and approached Mumba. On que, Joy began splashing water around making a whole scene so that Mumba would notice her. "Sorry, this is a private pool no public swimming." Mumba said sounding like a true African.

"You don't own this pool you tongue tied bitch; I can swim if I want too." Joy said while laughing. "Now wait a damn minute." Mumba said moving towards Joy. Once she got closer Mumba realized it was Joy. "Hey coach, don't look so black, have you been drowning any kids lately?" Joy said sarcastically. Mumba was exiting the pool, using the pool step ladder. Karma gave her a kick to the face causing her to fall backwards into the pool. Joy grabbed Mumba by her neck and man handled her under the water for several minutes. When Joy finally released her, Mumba was breathing hard, huffing and puffing for air. "You can do better than that. You're a damn swim coach." Joy said maliciously, pushing Mumba's head back under water for a second round of treatment. Joy held her head under the water a little longer That time around. "Please. Please, stop" Mumba begged Joy breathlessly, when Mumba was finally let out of the water. Joy dumped her under the water again and again. On the final dunk, Joy held Mumba's mouth open while she was under water. That caused her to swallow and inhale lots of water. When Mumba was dragged out of the water, she was breathless and coughing up water.

Joy slapped her around for a few and Karma played along for the fun of it. "What now ma'am?" Karma asked, ready for whatever. Joy just smiled and said, "Watch me work sis, keep pounding on that bitch until I'm done." "Copy dat said Karma. Joy used the office to type a letter of confession:

"I am Mumba Shavez and I have been committing horrible violent acts against kids that I coach. I have been abusing kids for years, making them hold their breath under water and nearly drowning them. I would whip them across their backs with a metal rod if they did not meet my requirements for the pool laps. I have been molesting a group of boys that are enrolled in my weekend class, from the ages of 8-12. I purposely touched and fondled their penis and performed oral sex on them, they were forced to do the same to me. Without shame I tied ankle and arm wights to a child and threw her into the twelve feet, leaving her alone to drown. This has been wearing me down and I am tired of holding this secret. I need to be punished, have no mercy on me for all the harm I have caused these innocent kids."

Joy and Karma forced Mumba to sign the letter and notarize it. Joy had Adreama contact her brother Adam at Channel 7 news, telling him there was a breaking news story and he would have the exclusive. Adam had a camera crew on the scene within thirty minutes flat. Adam went live with the story and by the end of the news footage, the police were there to arrest Mumba. The news camera man made sure to get a close up of her being handcuffed and placed in the back of the patrol car. "Mumba will be charged with multiple counts of child endangerment, child neglect, and intent to harm a child, and several counts of child molestation. The exact number will remain unknown until all the children have had a chance to come forward." That was the final word of the news segment.

Joy and Karma were already on their way back to campus. "Sis you sure that was the only name you needed to get crossed off your list, because I'm ready for war, I feel like smacking a few bitches, what's up?" Karma asked Joy loudly and crunk. "Calm your ass down, yes sis I'm hanging it up, but I'm sure you and Tia gone keep me busy covering y'all tracks." Joy said giving Karma a serious look. "Yes, ma'am sister FED, well I got a long line of bitches to smack then imma change. Karma said winking her eye at Joy.

Craig and Ozias woke up from their nap to several missed calls from Ezra and Memphis. "What up lil homie?" Ozias called Ezra back. "Just wanted to go over these numbers Memphis and I put up over the last few weeks. I also wanna see Candice" Ezra explained. "Ok bet. Meet us at the warehouse in fifteen minutes" Ozias replied and hung up. Craig reached for a brotherly hug as soon as they got out of the car. Before any words about business could be exchanged Ezra confessed. "I have a confession", his voice was soft. "Tell it lil nigga" Ozias said. "Candice found me on Facebook, and we've been talking the entire time y'all were gone. We exchanged numbers and she sent me her address. I remembered that I wasn't supposed to be with her like that, so I just drove by. Candice was in the yard looking beautiful. She gave me a Miss America wave and blew me a kiss" Ezra recalled his time with Candice. Ray Charles could see this fool was head over heels in love with Candice. "I circled the block like a pervert just to keep getting a look at her. I didn't want to blow up our spot, so I forced myself to leave. But I need my woman man." Ezra came clean about everything. "I appreciate your honesty lil bro. I can see you are a man in love, and I am not going to hold that against you. But this is another one of our secrets. You got to play by Karma and Yahtia's rules or shit will get rough for you" Ozias explained. Ezra nodded in understanding. "Alright then. Let's see how bad you ran my business into the ground" Craig teased changing the subject. Memphis handed the books over to Craig without another word. Craig and Ozias texted Kross with an update. They were thoroughly impressed with the work done in their absence.

Kross felt so much better after he and Yahtia left the doctor's office. Yahtia and the baby both had a clean bill of health. Yahtia was eight weeks pregnant. Her constant nausea was caused by the first trimester morning sickness, and the greenery she had been smoking didn't help. "Baby I think we need to tell Toyah and Juan. I want everything out in the open, so I don't have to stress or hide anything" sneaking around is never good Kross said looking at Tia for approval. Yahtia had flowers delivered to her mom and Ivy showing thanks to them for all their hard work and dedication to the group home. Toyah calls Yahtia. "Thanks for the beautiful flower arrangement, I love them." "Your welcome mommy, Kross and I will be stopping by after dinner to speak with you and dad." "Oh, so is that why I got flowers, you have some bad news, you better not be pregnant Tia." Toyah said screaming through the phone. "Ma what made you say that." "I know my child bring your ass now, fuck waiting after dinner. you done made me a grandma before my time DANMIT TIA." Kross looked at Yahtia with a nervous look. "Don't get scared now Mr. lets tell her now and get it out the way." Yahtia said. "How the hell did she figure that out within the first nighty seconds of conversation?" Kross asked. "Just like Grandma Madeline, the old heads know some shit." Yahtia said while grabbing Kross hand.

CHAPTER 30
OPENING DOORS & CLOSING DEALS

Kross and Yahtia made their way to her parents' house. They both walk in and Yahtia had her thumb in her mouth. That was something she did when she was nervous. Toyah and Juan were sitting on the couch facing the door. Looking for immediate reactions. "Hey mom and dad", Yahtia then bent down to hug them. Kross extended his hand and spoke as well. After a few second of awkward staring Toyah speaks first. "So, am I right are you pregnant Yahtia?" "Yes ma'am." Yahtia said with her head down. "No need to be ashamed about it, you just have to deal with it at this point. I am not totally mad, but I am disappointed. You could have easily gone to that clinic and gotten on birth control. There's a store all over town that carries condoms. But woulda, coulda, shoulda, ain't going to help us with this. Toyah said in her motherly voice. "I said to myself when this day came that I would kill the man who violated my daughter pureness. The thought of my baby girl doing grown woman activities do not set well with me. "Juan spoke slow and clear. Craig had called ahead and put in a good word for Kross. Toyah and Juan listened to their son bold and confidence statements about Kross being the perfect man for Yahtia. Craig begged them not to ask questions but craig swore on his life Yahtia was safe. When Craig delivered information to his parents that Kross eliminated some of Yahtia's demons and fears. Toyah knew then she could fully except Kross and not be so hard on them. Toyah eased Juan over as well, because Juan was about to rock that orange jump suit with pride.

"I am standing before you two taking full responsibility of this situation. I don't like to brag to often but I'm fighting for my life here. I am very well off with my finances, and Yahtia and our baby will be taken care of properly. Yahtia will have the best doctors and I will be active with her pregnancy and take away any unwanted stress. I don't hit woman, and I love you daughter with all of me." Kross laid it on thick. He even got on his knees begging for them to except him and forgive him and Yahtia for being reckless. It was almost ten minutes of silence in the room. Kross and Yahtia wore a dumb look on their face, the silence had them paranoid. Out of nowhere Juan grabs Kross into a bear hug squeezing him tight, Kross didn't know if it was an attack or a hug until Juan said welcome to the family. Kross let out a huge release of air from his chest. For once in his life Kross felt like a lil bitch.

Nekendra had welcomed Troy back in her life. Troy was up to no good as usual. Troy had begun to sniff coke and his drinking was out of control. Troy started fighting Nekendra friends, he even punched her pregnant niece fighting her like a man. This nigga was a true woman beater, Troy did not come close to fighting them niggas in the county or any other nigga at that. Troy continues to run over females like Deebo Samuel on the 49ers home field. Everybody Nekendra associated with hated Troy, cousins, friends, mom, kids sister, brother, aunts and uncles. Nekendra's group of loved ones had multiple intervention with her regarding her abuse. The family was never successful with a breakthrough that would last. Nekendra was indecisive about leaving Troy. She played the back-and-forth game giving Troy the upper hand. Nekendra was defiantly a victim of domestic violence.

Uvoka's stay in the hospital was longer than expected. Her case manager found her a bed in the salvation army woman's shelter program. Uvoka was going through hell, she could have easily gone back home to her family in Charleston South Carolina, but her pride was not going to let her do that. Uvoka's family had high expectation of her, and she did not want to disappoint them. Uvoka was placed on psychiatric medications. Uvoka was showing symptoms of a break down and she was now labeled unstable. Uvoka needed round the clock supervision. Uvoka was told that if she leaves the Salvation Army her next of kin would be notified. Uvoka was aware that she could not be alone she was now property of the state's medical mental institution.

Molly tried to kill herself twice. Karma made it plain and clear to Hero that she was to live and suffer the consequences. Karma would understand if Molly crossed the line and became a threat. Then she would be collecting on another insurance policy. Until then payback wasn't enough for Karma. Karma received half a million dollars from Karmelo's policy. After his body was found and Identified, Karma had a check in her hand days later.

Karma, Yahtia and Joy finally sympathized with Ezra about seeing Candice. Ezra had a long list of stipulations, but more than willing to comply. Ezra was down for whatever and he was super excited and appreciative of the opportunity to show his fatherly role. He was able to attend the next visit for the ultrasound and could not stop talking about it. Ezra proved his self by staying in South Carolina working with the guys and buying gifts every chance he could. Candice doctor's appointment went well, her vaginal scaring is healing tremendously. Candice cried when the doctor announced she was having a girl. Ezra was there to hold her close and enjoy the moment. Candice had already given her baby girl the name Patience. Candice explained to Ezra the meaning behind the name, and he loved it. Patience was something that she mastered well, so she wanted her baby to remind of her that.

Memphis found him a young lady that he became deeply attracted to. He was considering relocating to South Carolina. Memphis loved the money flow, his track record was nothing but failure and disappointment back in Ohio. Memphis even talked with his family back home to join him. The family were all willing to give it a try, they needed a new start as well.

Kross was impressed by Ezra and Memphis work ethic and dedication. So, he took the liberty in getting them a five-bedroom two story home, they would fight over the top or bottom amongst themselves. After the two young bucks received that news, it was official, they were now residents of South Carolina.

Months on in and the ladies had been putting in overtime to pass their classes and take extra courses so they could graduate early. Joy was becoming uptight about her moving situation that was coming up within the next week. "Sis no need for you to be pussyfooting around, you already know it is go time." Karma said to Joy because she continued to drag around not wanting to pack. "I know sis, I am going to miss the fuck out of y'all. I finally have a sister hood with the most wonderful girls I know, and nothing is worth that to me." "Girl we going to visit you all the time once you and Craig get settled." Yahtia said shifting the momentum. Yahtia and Karma helped Joy start packing and they had a pillow fight and ordered takeout like always. Joy had a knot in her stomach because Nekendra was not answering her calls. Joy knew it was because of Troy so she could only hope for the best, she refused to get off track with her career.

CHAPTER 31
MOVING DAY

All the way up until moving day the ladies were joined at the hip. The guys were holding it tight as well. Kross and Craig finished putting the last load in the U-Haul truck. Ozias begins to look sad as reality kicked into gear that Craig was really leaving. Ozias was going to miss his boy; they had been down like four flats since they were puppies. "After Joy leave for her first assignment, ill be back home to kick it with you fellows". Craig said to Ozias and Kross while giving them a brotherly hug. The guys tried to eliminate their emotions and stick to the man code by having tough skin, but they were just as bad as the ladies.

Yahtia, Joy, and Karma were having a *Color Purple* moment hand clapping to Ms. Celie and Nettie famous song:

"Me and you, us never part. Makidada. Me and you, us have one heart. Makidada. Ain't no ocean, ain't no sea. Makidada. Keep my sista away from me."

They clapped so hard until their hands were red. They did a thirty-minute hug and finally said a final good-bye. Joy had two days to settle in then it was straight to the money. Joy called Nekendra several more times during the ride. Craig knew Joy was feeling some type of way by Nekendra not answering. Craig grabbed Joy's hand. "She will call back babe." Craig said in a low tone. Ezra was young but he was on his grown man shit for once.

Ezra and Memphis were now homeowners and having a brain fart over how to decorate the house. Memphis knew his time with Ezra was limited. His boy was trying to be a family man. "I think imma just let Candi girl decorate this shit. Especially our room and the nursery." Ezra said still undecided on what couch to put in his man cave. Money wasn't an issue. The two friends had generated enough money to buy any and everything their hearts desired. "Yeah man imma keep my lil area until I find me a house. I ain't trying to be no live in Manny" Memphis joked, seriously. "No hard feelings bro I understand." Ezra responded. Ezra wasn't going to rest until he had his family under one roof. Ezra and Candice were having chaperone dates. Candice figured out how to sneak out just like the average teen, but Ezra was playing by the rules and would force her to return. Ezra was not trying to fuck shit up with the crew by betraying their trust. Ezra refused to have sex with Candice until she was completely healed, inside and out. "Candi girl of course I love you and will always want you. But we can't. I want everything to be perfect for us" Ezra had to explain to a crying Candice. Candice snuck out again but this time she showed up in a sexy short set, with a round baby bump ready to be with her man. A man could only resist so much, Ezra made her feel good and ate her pussy until she could not stand. Ezra let a load off in his boxers unexpectedly, he had been sexually frustrated for a while. Him hearing Candice get off made the thunder roar in his direction.

Karma had been secretly taking classes and educating herself in the winery business. Karma learned how to grow the sweetest grapes and enlarge them with out harmful fertilizer or steroids. After becoming a wine chemist and making some of the best concoctions the wine industry has ever tasted. Karma decided to invest her money in buying her own wine vineyard. Yahtia was unable to drink so she had Adreama and Purple Pinky riding the wave with her. They were wine tasters, plus Karma put them in position to help her get established. The three ladies were putting in the work, countless hours making their mark and keeping a buzz at the same time. The ladies were calling it a night and headed back to the dorm. Trying to declutter their mess they were cleaning up wine bottles and glasses. Pouring wine together ready to dispose it down the drain. Karma was struck in the nose by a sweet smell from one of the glasses she raised the glass to examine the smell then the taste. Karma passed it along to Adreama and Purple Pinky to do the same. "Sis this shit is awesome what is it?" Adreama asked "I have no idea but let's figure out what all we mixed and poured out. Six bottles of wine and eight hours later the ladies had a winner. They came up with the sweetest tasting wine that had a smooth buzz effect. Karma decided on the name Cupcake Paradise. "Hell yeah, that got a mean catch phrase and the wine remind you of a cupcake taste." Purple Pinky hyped up the name. Karma waited a week before she presented her newfound dessert wine to the heavy hittas of the industry. Karma tweaked the taste and made sure her recipe was to perfection. Karma worked her way all the way to the top being offered top dollar for her recipe. Karma was no fool. Karma decided to speed up the finalization process of the vineyard. Karma was about to market her own wine. Karma accomplished in weeks what it took most people months and years to do. Determined to become successful and heavy on the cash flow, Karma was setting herself up so she could enjoy and relax the rest of her life peacefully. Karma endured enough at an early age to last a lifetime. Money, love, and happiness was all she wanted.

Ozias had been on edge because Karma had stayed out all night twice. Ozias seen Karma and Adreama hanging closely and that was a red flag for him. Ozias could not figure that part out he always known Adreama to be a thot and a coke head. Ozias went to vent to Kross about Karma's sudden disappearing acts. "I think she's cheating bro." said Ozias "Hell no not Karma, you over thinking it fam." Kross responded "Karma didn't come home two nights back-to-back, and she has been getting up early and coming in late for weeks now. Not to mention she's hanging tight with Adreama lately, when the fuck have you known her to leave Tia side. Ozias continued to plead his case. "Damn bro, shit is a bit thick now that you put it that way". Kross spoke.

Days later Ozias followed Karma to the wine vineyard. Karma was meeting with another wine vineyard owner by the name of Conner O'hare. Conner was a well-groomed white man dressed in a suit and carried a briefcase. When the man reached to hug Karma, Ozias came out of thin air. "Excuse me if you know what's good for you bro you will step the fuck back". Ozias said with attitude he was so tempted to slap the white boy like Will Smith did Chris Rock at the Oscars. "Ozias what are you doing here?" Karma asked by screaming with a shocked look. "I should be asking you that, who the fuck is this white boy?" Ozias said with a mean mug and his chest poked out. "Conner my apologies this is my jealous fiancée Ozias, please excuse us for a moment." Karma said being embarrassed by Ozias's behavior and surprised appearance. Conner was green to the situation, he stood there at attention ready to salute. Conner was totally frightened from Ozias bad boy look. "This is not what you think, I'm here about business. Just behave yourself and follow me so I can redeem myself and close this very important deal. If shit go left because of your insecurities, you will have blue balls for life." Karma said as she rolled her eyes at Ozias and then snatched his hand and walked back to Conner's presence to finish what she started. Karma explained to Conner what had just happened. Conner was actually tickled by it, but Ozias did not find shit funny. The two managed to get all the paperwork completed and everything was now in the oversight of Karma when it comes to Scrumptious Twist vineyard. Ozias grabbed Karma and flooded her with apologies. "You were staying out at night and hanging with Adreama. I thought she turned you out, and you were giving my kitty to that white boy". Ozias said as he looked dumb trying to get out of the doghouse. Karma laughed because she knew she would have done the same shit. Karma continued to fill him in on her new wine she was about to market. They popped a bottle and enjoyed a walk through the vineyard fields feeling the cool breeze. "Every property needs a proper baptism, so let's bless the grounds with some sweat and a whole lot of cum Ozias said while taking off his shirt". Karma picked a grape from the vine bush beside them and placed it in her mouth she then started kissing her man and stripping the rest of his clothes off. That was the first of many sexcapades in the vineyard.

CHAPTER 32
BABY MAMA

Troy would not let Nekendra be great. He begins to publicly embarrass her by sending videos to random people on Facebook messenger of their sexual activities together. Troy would hide her car keys keeping her from doctors' appointments and work. He sabotaged her clothes and personal belongings. The neighbors filmed him destroying her car for the second time. Troy was pure evil, and he aimed to keep Nekendra miserable. No one could understand why, because she was good as gold to him. Troy had a never-ending ego and was pure pussy for continuously swelling up at females. Troy turned a blind eye to any nigga that was bout that life and would chin check his ass. Nekendra's family was so tired of Troy's fuckery, so they hid her out for awhile to try to open her eyes up about this retard. Nekendra sister Za'Drea was at her wits end with Troy, she has had countless run-ins with the bastard. Za'Drea was ready to gut him like a fish and hire a hit man to take Troy out. Troy was looking for Nekendra night and day, she was his drug he had to have her. This was OBSESSION at its best. Troy's day would not flow well if he did not do something hurtful to Nekendra. Her being away from him hurt his soul, Troy did not have control and he wasn't able to adjust that. Nekendra took a Lyft to work, happy as can be as always. Troy was waiting outside of her job hiding in a bush next to her building. When Nekendra was in arms reach of him he came out of hiding and grabbed her by the arm. "HELP, HELP." Nekendra screamed out while whaling on Troy trying to break his grip. A co-worker came to the rescue pounding away on Troy's head with a stapler she quickly grabbed from the desk. Another co-worker called the police. Troy let go of Nekendra's arm then walked fast to his car, upset his plan failed. Troy had a gallon of vodka and a few beers awaiting in his car he consumed big swigs throughout his ride. Troy ended up in front of Nekendra's mom house. Troy called Nekendra's job several times making threats to her about harming her mom and son if she did not come home and leave with him. Nekendra said everything she could to ease shit over and talk Troy down. She felt the seriousness in his voice and knew Troy would make good on his threats if she did not hurry. As Nekendra was leaving her job the police were pulling up asking questions about a man attacking an employee. Nekendra gave the police a bogus story and they left. Nekendra arrived at her moms' house in a Lyft. Troy was sitting outside on the hood of his car drinking a 24-once Bud-ice beer. Nekendra went straight in the house to make sure her mom and son were ok. Her mom was furious about Troy's behavior and begged Nekendra to call the police. "Don't worry mom he's just woofing, if I ride with him, he will leave us alone and go on about his business". "Besides I am leaving him for good I promise this time. My new friend Cade will be here tonight, so I must clear the air and stand my ground once and for all". "Ok that sounds good but, Troy is drunk Nekendra you do not need to ride with him". Nekendra's mom Tammie said with tears seeping from her eyes. Nekendra went upstairs to talk with her son Tevin. Minutes later Troy was acting out blowing the horn, screaming at Tammie how he was going to kill Nekendra. Tammie was standing in the door shaking her head calling Troy an idiot. Tammie's blood pressure was through the roof, she wanted this nigga to leave her daughter alone. Tammie texted Za'Drea to see if she could stop Nekendra from leaving with Troy. Za'Drea immediately rounded up her girls and rushed to try and stop Nekendra. Before Nekendra went out the door she went to the kitchen and placed a folder on the kitchen table.

Nekendra got in the car and Troy sped off. The two argued at each other screaming back and forth. Nekendra pleaded that she have had enough, she told Troy it was over, and he was going to have to accept her decision. Troy was increasing in speed by the second, still turning up his vodka and screaming at Nekendra. "Fuck you bitch, you can't leave me". Troy was driving like a maniac acting like a deranged dare devil. Nekendra was begging him to slow down, she begins to cry and call her mom and son on the phone. Tammie and Tevin heard the loud commotion and Nekendra screaming begging and pleading for Troy to let her out. Troy snatched the phone from Nekendra and threw it out the window. Troy was rocking back and forth pressing hard on the accelerator acting as if he was on a rollercoaster ride. As Troy was hanging a curve on a back road his speed increased and the car went off the road flipping over crashing into several trees. Nekendra died on the scene from the crash. She suffered multiple blunt forced injuries. Troy only had facial and leg injuries, the paramedics did all they could to breathe life back into Nekendra. Troy was cut out the vehicle and taken to the hospital where he will be arrested when he's released. Troy will be charged with dui involving death, driven under suspension habitual offender, and open container. His alcohol level was 0.13%, Nekendra's family will not stop until Troy is put away for life and held accountable for killing her. This was no accident he deliberately caused her death.

Tammie was awakened by the police at her door. Before the officer could get it all out, Tammie broke down and fell to her knees. "LORD NO, NOT MY BABY. NOOOOOO, NOOOOOO. The screams grew louder and louder. The police held her up and stayed by her side until family arrived. Tevin begin to cry and was so sad. Before the night was over the news had begin to surface. Tammie's apartment complex begins to fill with loved ones and friends showing love for Baby Mama. She brought the city out. So many people were in a up-roar and sadden by the news. Late that night Tammie was sitting around at the kitchen table with her sisters having coffee. They all notice a folder on the table, inside the folder was Nekendra's life insurance policy. No one knew what to say the room was totally silent. The family had a thousand questions about this coincidence, but the one person who knew the answer was no longer here.

Back at the dorm, Yahtia and Kross were up late eating ice cream and donuts when they notice a news flash. No names were mentioned but for some reason Yahtia felt a chill come over her body and knew it was

Nekendra. After logging into Facebook, multiple people were live Infront of Tammie's apartment. People were posting RIP Baby Mama, so Yahtia knew shit was real. Her and Kross got dressed and went to see what they could find out, the whole time Yahtia was focused on Joy. Kross texted Ozias the info, so he and Karma were meeting them at the apartments.

"Omg who the fuck going to tell Joy about this madness." Karma said after she gave Yahtia a hug. Ozias calls Craig. "What's up bro, everything ok?" Craig answered the phone in a paranoid state of mind, by the time being 3am. "Nah fam, the unthinkable just happen to Baby Mama." Ozias then explained all that he knew. Craig raised up out of bed and had a look of fear all on his face. "FUCK, Joy left last night to go on assignment, I want hear from her for two weeks. Craig explained to Ozias who had him on speaker. "What the fuck?" Karma and Yahtia yelled out. "I'm on the next flight out fam, y'all keep my sister calm". Said Craig.

People gathered around Nekendra's purple car with balloons and teddy bears. A candlelight vigil was held, friends and family spoke great things about Nekendra. A domestic violence advocate addressed the crowd about helping some one who may be struggling with abuse and being mistreated by a boyfriend or husband. The situation can't be taken lightly, hopefully this will be a wake-up call for the next female or females that is afraid to seek help. Nekendra was a hair stylist and worked as a CNA assistant, she was loved by many and was the life of the party. The world knew her as BABY MAMA and rocking Converse Chuck Taylors, and wearing purple and Mickey Mouse clothing every chance she could.

The next few days the family gathered around trying to make since of losing their Nekendra. Shit was hard and awkward as hell everyone was on ten. Za'Drea was a complete mess, she could not stop crying. The local news was airing the car wreck around the clock. Seeing the car put fire cramps inside of your stomach and made you want revenge in the worst way. Visualizing Nekendra spending her last minutes and seconds of life trying to break free and get out of that car puts a gut-wrenching pain inside your soul. Praying for the family is a must at the current time, they need a spiritual healing and strength that only the all-mighty God can give them.

Troy was finally released from the hospital and taken to the county jail where hopefully he will rot. The sick bastard had the audacity to have an attitude with the family at the bond hearing. Acting like they did something wrong and not supposed to want justice for Nekendra. The Judge was in an outrage by his belligerent behavior and held him in contempt of court.

D-Ray had gotten word of what went down, he clenched his lips together causing him to frown when his homie said Nekendra died. D-Ray instantly started thinking about his favorite aunt Nikki. D-Ray knew this time, he had Troy for the long haul. D-Ray was waiting on Troy to enter the floor so he could resume his Nightmare. "You can't seem to stay away from this place HUUH NIGGA, you had your superman cape on when you were last here". D-Ray said right before spitting in Troy's face. Troy opens his mouth to mumble out something but, D-Ray and his goons started beating his ass and this time they were heavy on the licks. This was going to be a repeat for Troy's entire stay at the county.

CHAPTER 33
WRAPPING IT UP FOR NEW BEGINNINGS

Joy was home from her first two weeks of working with the FBI. She was exhausted from the training she had to endure in between regular assignments. Joy notice Craig was acting stand offish but blocked it out because she was dying for a bath. Joy was running a hot bubble bath when the doorbell rang. The girls along with Ozias and Kross flew out to give Joy the information in person. Joy being the geek queen she is, she read right through the girls. Yahtia emotions were unstable, and she cried bloody murder soon as she hugged Joy. Karma and Craig both held Joy's hand. "Just say it already, its Baby Mama, isn't it?" She's back in the hospital, damn that, Troy?" Joy blurted out. Yahtia runs out the room crying hysterically at this point Joy was now shaking, Joy raised up from the couch and held her chest. "Please don't tell me", Joy repeated a serious of times. Karma delivered the news to Joy speaking low with her cracking voice. Joy went straight to her suite case and grabbed a picture of her and Nekendra and held it to her heart. Joy is naturally distraught by the news. Because she has another assignment in two days. Joy couldn't take bereavement time like a normal job. Her boss Yurzele gave her 24 hours to send her condolences and get back. Joy decided to stay in Colorado and use the 24 hours to grieve and be with Yahtia and Karma. Craig, Ozias, and Kross let the ladies do their own thing. The ladies spent the day talking about all the good and fun times Joy and Nekendra had. Joy had already set up trust funds and bank accounts for the kids. "Hey sis, how you wanna handle this hoe ass bitch ass nigga" a swollen Yahtia asked. Yahtia was still trying to be a rider knowing damn well Kross wouldn't let her go to the bathroom alone. "Girl what you gonna do throw up on him?" Karma joked. D-Ray and his goons already going ham on that hoe nigga". Karma added. "That's good for now but imma let karma get his ass" Joy laughed mincingly. Joy explained to them that with her position she had certain privileges. "This bum will never see the sun EVER again. Imma make him wish he was dead" Joy said typing away. Joy emailed a letter to the judge giving Nekendra's account of years of abuse. Joy was using all her intelligent resources to do everything she could to make that nigga pay. Joy kissed her sisters and wiped her tears. "I will eventually fight back and be strong, you two are all I got. Thank y'all so much for picking me as a sister, I love y'all." Joy said as she reached out for Karma and Yahtia's hand. "Girl we love you more, you stuck with us "MISS" FBI". Yahtia said while still crying. "Girl shut your crybaby ass up". Karma teased. "We will be ok and believe me when I say, that bitch nigga ain't never coming home." Joy said with an evil smile.

MOVING FORWARD-FIVE MONTHS LATER

Karma and Mama T and all the girls along with Ivy planned a baby shower for Candice and Yahtia. Craig and Ozias and Memphis did their own shenanigans for Ezra and Kross. Juan decided to follow the men on this one, he was getting side eyed by Mama T. The doorbell ranged and Juan answered it to avoid Toyah's stare. The delivery man Handed over a gold wrapped box. It was an unlimited black card for the Babies R Us super store from Hero to Kross and Yahtia. Hero had more love and loyalty to Kross and the Crew than members of his own organization. Hero labeled himself their honorary God Father. With that being said mutha fuckars better tread lightly against the crew, or they can end up joining Molly.

Yahtia and Karma finally decided to let Candice and Ezra have unsupervised dates. Once the baby is born, they could do family outings but there was no living together until Candice graduated high school and registered in college. They also had to see a family therapist and check in twice a week with any member of the crew. The young couple accepted the terms and conditions.

While everyone decorated the nursery and enjoyed the shower, Ivy tapped Karma. "Let me talk to you" Ivy told Kimmie to tell Karma what she shared in therapy. Kimmie went into detail about the abuse she dealt with and how it was starting to affect her dreams. Karma instantly thought of Yahtia and how Karmelo had scared her for life. "Baby do you trust me?" Karma asked the little girl Kimmie who nodded yes. "I don't need to know anything else. I trust you will handle this?" Ivy spoke addressing Karma before leaving the room. Karma nodded yes and closed the door. Kimmie went in giving full details on how she wants to kill a few people that wronged her. "I want people to eat their karma, I want revenge in the worst way, can you teach me how to be a bad bitch auntie Karma? I want to wear skirts like you and auntie Tia and Joy. Irma and Shavon do to". After meeting with Kimmie it was more than right Karma speak with Shavon and Irma. They too added fuel to the fire, a lot of shit resurfaced and woke up the angry KARMA MUNSTER. Karma rejoined the shower and out of habit sent the girls a text message.

"IT DOESN'T STOP WITH US THE LIST GOES ON
"A NEW GENERATION UNVEILS"
"A BITCH IN A SKIRT IN TRAINING"

DOMESTIC VIOLENCE IS A SERIOUS ISSUE 95% OF THE TIME, IT›S TOWARDS WOMEN, BUT WE DO HAVE SOME MEN THAT FALL VICTIM IN THIS CATEGORY. NO MATTER HOW IT PLAYS OUT, DOMESTIC VIOLENCE IS A CRIME, AND IT IS WRONG. I LOST MY SISTER DUE TO A COWARD TAKING HER LIFE. MY SISTER WAS A VICTIM OF DOMESTIC VIOLENCE. A MAN STRIPPED AWAY HER SELF-WORTH AND CONSTANTLY PHYSICALLY AND VERBALLY ABUSED HER; HE HARMED HER IN OTHER WAYS CAUSING DISFUNCTION AND CONFUSION IN HER LIFE. IT WAS NOT MY SISTER'S FAULT THAT SHE TRUSTED A MAN AND GAVE HIM CONTINUOUS LOVE. I WANT MY SISTER'S STORY TO SAVE AND OPEN DOORS FOR VICTIMS. PAY ATTENTION TO THE WARNING SIGNS, THE YELLING, THE NAME-CALLING, THE PHYSICAL ABUSE, VERBAL ABUSE, THE STALKING, AND JEALOUSY. IF YOU FEEL UNCOMFORTABLE IN A RELATIONSHIP, GET OUT. DON'T GIVE UP YOUR CHANCE TO BE HAPPY. EVERY WOMAN DESERVES A HAPPY AND HEALTHY RELATIONSHIP/ MARRIAGE. A MAN HAS NO RIGHT TO HIT A WOMAN; A SLAP TO THE FACE IS WRONG. A PUSH, EVEN A PINCH, SHOULD NOT BE OVERLOOKED BECAUSE IT WILL LEAD TO MUCH WORSE. MY SISTER WAS A LOVING PERSON LOVED BY EVERYONE; HER LIFE ENDED SO TRAGICALLY, ALL BEHIND THE HANDS OF A MAN. PLEASE CONTACT YOUR LOCAL POLICE IF YOU ARE SOMEONE YOU KNOW IS A VICTIM OF ABUSE OR DOMESTIC VIOLENCE.

VICTIM CONTACT RESOURCE CENTER BY PHONE OR TEXT

1-855-484-2846

DOMESTIC VIOLENCE AND INTIMATE PARTNER VIOLENCE

NATIONAL DOMESTIC VIOLENCE HOTLINE

HOTLINE: 1(800) 799-7233

AVAILABLE 24 HOURS A DAY, 7 DAYS A WEEK VIA TEXT AND ONLINE CHAT.

It doesn't matter who did what, what is happening within you, your experience of your life is entirely your making- this is your Karma

KARMA
HAPPENS

KARMA IS GONNA HIT SOME OF Y'ALL REAL HARD FOR BREAKING PEOPLE WHO HAD NOTHING BUT GOOD INTENTIONS FOR YOU.

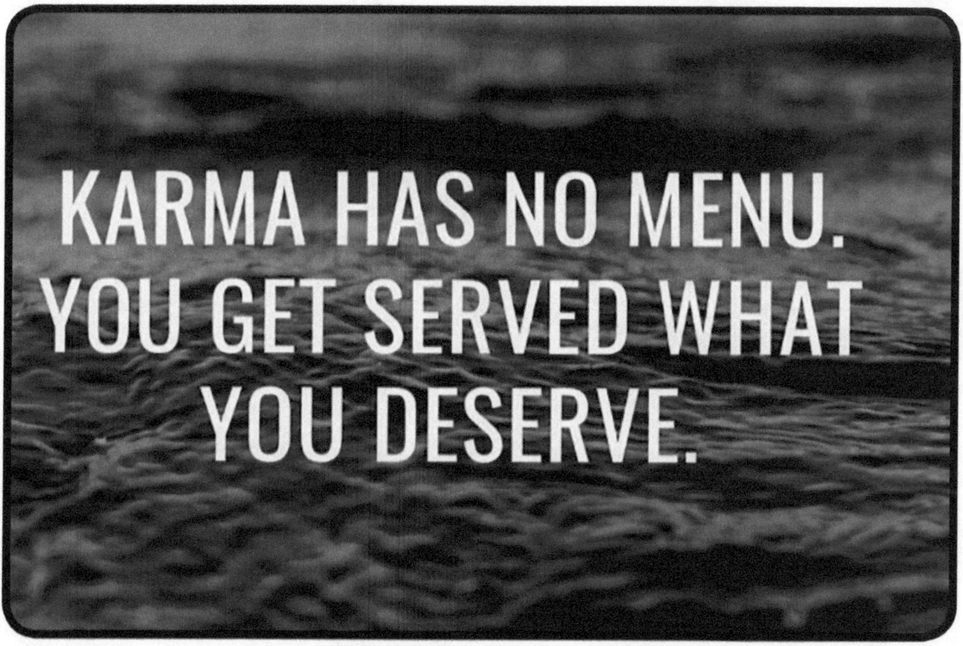

KARMA HAS NO MENU.
YOU GET SERVED WHAT
YOU DESERVE.

Karma Says
If you focus on hurt,
you will continue to suffer.

If you focus on the lesson,
you will continue to grow.

Don't waste your time on
REVENGE

Those that hurt you will
eventually face their own
KARMA

DEAR KARMA I HAVE A LIST OF PEOPLE THAT YOU MISSED.

LAW OF KARMA:

"Never try to play with people around you, for you may never know that they play better than YOU."

KARMA
No need for revenge.
Just sit back & wait.
Those who hurt you
will eventually screw up
themselves
& if you're lucky,
God will let you watch.

Zaneta Cannon Robinson

KARMA
NO NEED FOR REVENGE. JUST SIT BACK AND WAIT. THOSE WHO HURT YOU EVENTUALLY SCREW UP THEMSELVES AND IF YOU ARE LUCKY, GOD WILL LET YOU WATCH

"This is your karma. You do not understand now, but you will understand later."